AIDS, Culture, and Gay Men

UNIVERSITY PRESS OF FLORIDA

Florida A&M University, Tallahassee
Florida Atlantic University, Boca Raton
Florida Gulf Coast University, Ft. Myers
Florida International University, Miami
Florida State University, Tallahassee
New College of Florida, Sarasota
University of Central Florida, Orlando
University of Florida, Gainesville
University of North Florida, Jacksonville
University of South Florida, Tampa
University of West Florida, Pensacola

AIDS, Culture, and Gay Men

Edited by

Douglas A. Feldman

University Press of Florida
Gainesville/Tallahassee/Tampa/Boca Raton
Pensacola/Orlando/Miami/Jacksonville/Ft. Myers/Sarasota

15   14   13   12   11   10   6   5   4   3   2   1

A record of cataloging-in-publication data is available from the Library
of Congress.
ISBN 978-0-8130-3431-7

The University Press of Florida is the scholarly publishing agency
for the State University System of Florida, comprising Florida A&M
University, Florida Atlantic University, Florida Gulf Coast University,
Florida International University, Florida State University, New College of Florida, University of Central Florida, University of Florida,
University of North Florida, University of South Florida, and University
of West Florida.

University Press of Florida
15 Northwest 15th Street
Gainesville, FL 32611-2079
http://www.upf.com

In memory of my good friend Steve Patterson (1940–2003)

Contents

Acknowledgments

I would like to thank John Byram, Gillian Hillis, Michele Fiyak-Burkley, and Nevil Parker of the University Press of Florida for their very helpful publishing assistance; Robert Burchfield of Doghouse Editing and Research Services for his excellent editorial assistance; and Jackie Deats of the College at Brockport, State University of New York, for her superb secretarial assistance.

AIDS, Culture, and Gay Men: An Introduction

DOUGLAS A. FELDMAN

It is unclear if Cole Porter, the composer of numerous Broadway musicals, purposely used these lyrics as a double entendre in referring to "the top" as the male partner who engages in insertive anal sex, and "the bottom" as the male partner who engages in receptive anal sex. Certainly, as a gay man he knew the values, attitudes, beliefs, and language of the gay male culture in the United States during the first half of the twentieth century.

In conducting HIV/AIDS social/behavioral research among men who have sex with men (MSM) today, during the first half of the twenty-first century, it is important to know about the sexual behavior of MSM. For example, many MSM are exclusive "tops," many are exclusive "bottoms," but also many are "versatile" (engaging in either receptive or insertive anal sex, sometimes during the same occasion), and many others do not engage in anal sex at all.

But it is unquestionably as important to understand the underlying culture of gay men. In the developed world, and increasingly among the wealthy and middle class of the developing/less-developed world, for example, being a "bottom" does not necessarily equate to being effeminate, while being a "top" does not necessarily equate to being masculine. More significantly, gay male culture in most of the developed world, and increasingly in much of the developing/less-developed world as well, is structurally different from straight male culture. It is not just a matter of what one does in bed. Gay male culture functions as if it were an ethnic group. Indeed, in the United States it is likely that most gay male members of ethnic groups think of themselves as gay first and, for instance, African American, Irish American, Italian American, or Mexican American, second.

It needs to be pointed out, however, that there is—in reality—no singular gay male culture. While it might be argued that there is a unified gay "sensibility" of which all self-defined gay men in the Western world are aware, though not necessarily share, the cultural heterogeneity of same-sex desire is quite vast. Forsythe (1994) has demonstrated, for example, that in San Francisco alone there are thirty-four different gay subcultures, ranging from "leather" to "goth." Along this line, Peacock and colleagues (2001) analyze five MSM subgroups in San Francisco (leather, men of color, activists, men who go to clubs, and younger). While the gay community is often conceived of as monolithic, it clearly is not. The authors suggest an alternate "multi-constitutive model" of community to account for this cultural heterogeneity.

In this volume, we use the phrase "the gay community," even though we fully recognize that there is not a singular gay community, in order to distinguish between the cultural world of gay/bisexual men and the behavioral world of MSM—which often would include the same-sex behaviors of not only gay and bisexual men but also men who define themselves as heterosexual and who live outside the gay world, do not see themselves as part of it, and yet are equally driven by same-sex desire.

The emphasis in HIV/AIDS research on MSM has been on sexual behavior and psychological issues. Yet to better understand the social and cultural dimensions of MSM, it is essential to recognize and understand the cultures of gay men, bisexual men, transgendered men, and straight MSM. Cultural anthropologists, unquestionably, are in a unique position to achieve this understanding.

This chapter offers an overview of some of the research that has been carried out by anthropologists since the 1980s. It looks at anthropological research on MSM, HIV, and substance abuse; anthropological research on HIV risk, sexual behavior, and HIV prevention among MSM; anthropological research on the culture of MSM; and other anthropological research on HIV and MSM. It concludes with an overview of the volume's chapters. This volume gives the reader a sampling of some of the ongoing research by leading anthropologists in this field through original, not previously published, commissioned chapters.

While there is no accurate census of gay and bisexual men, it is perhaps reasonable (using a 6 percent rate) to estimate at least 7 million adult gay and bisexual men in the United States, and at least 169 million adult gay and bisexual men globally. Since 1981, when gay men were first made aware of what is now known as HIV/AIDS, the gay male community has been severely affected by this growing health crisis.

Anthropological Research on Gay Men, HIV, and Substance Use

The largest body of anthropological research on gay men and HIV has been in the area of substance use. Numerous studies have focused upon the increased risk for HIV among gay men who use drugs and/or alcohol (Celentano et al. 2006; Clatts and Sotheran 2000; Clatts et al. 2001; Clatts et al. 2003; Clatts et al. 2005a, 2005b; Gorman 2003; Gorman et al. 2004; Slavin 2004a; Stall 1987; Stall and Wiley 1988). In an early prospective study of gay men in San Francisco, Stall and colleagues (1986) learned that there is a strong relationship between drug and alcohol use during sex and non-compliance with safer sex techniques to prevent the spread of HIV. Bolton and colleagues (1992), however, take issue with Stall and colleagues' findings. Their research of a cohort of gay men in Belgium shows that, among this population, there is no relationship between alcohol use and sexual risk taking (for updated findings on gay men in Belgium, see chapter 14 in this volume).

Gorman (1996) discusses the link between HIV disease and the use of speed among gay men. Gorman and colleagues (1997), using an ethnographic approach, indicate that HIV research on MSM who use drugs had not received, until the mid-1990s, the same attention as had similar research on heterosexual drug users. In a study using focus groups and individual structured interviews of ninety-eight MSM in six American cities who smoked crack or injected drugs, Rhodes and colleagues (1999) learned that only 42 percent identified publicly as gay or "homosexual," that 51 percent had one or more female sex partners in the past year, and that their drug use, rather than their sexual orientation, formed the core of their personal identity.

Among the conclusions reached in an experimental study at a substance use disorder treatment agency designed to serve gay men, Stall and colleagues (1999) found that substantial HIV risk reductions can occur after initiation of treatment. Clatts's (1999) ethnographic study of drug-addicted MSM portrays a rather bleak picture of a startling dysfunctional gay world focused on street hustlers, backroom sex, crack, and alcohol abuse in the mean and uncaring streets of gay New York.

In a cross-sectional survey of 2,174 MSM in four major American cities, Stall, Paul, and colleagues (2001) learned that both recreational drug and alcohol use were highly prevalent, while current levels of multiple drug use, three or more alcohol-related problems, frequent drug use, and heavy-frequent alcohol use were not uncommon. Deren and colleagues (2001) determined that drug-using MSM are clearly a heterogeneous group and that prevention messages addressing this diversity are needed. Lankenau and Clatts (2002) conclude, in a small study in New York City, that ketamine injectors represent an emerging, though often hidden, population of injection drug users, particularly among high-risk, street-involved youth.

In a study of 3,492 young MSM conducted in seven American cities, 66 percent reported use of illicit drugs, 28 percent reported use of three or more drugs, 29 percent reported frequent drug use, and 4 percent reported injection drug use. These practices were more common among participants who were white, self-identified as bisexual or "heterosexual," had run away, or had experienced forced sex (Thiede et al. 2003).

Lankenau and colleagues (2004), using an "ethno-epidemiological" approach, found that crack injection may be an important factor in the current HIV epidemic. In an ethnographic study of a gay nightclub in Sydney, Australia, Slavin (2004b: 265) discovered that "drug experiences are a significant element in the production of vital affective sociality that also includes a range of other activities such as dancing, socializing and sex" (some of these issues are further discussed in chapter 12 of this volume). In a long-term ethnographic study (Gilley and Co-Cké 2005) among gay American Indian men, many reported feeling alienated from their tribal communities because of homophobia and heterosexism. Often they turn to gay bars and clubs for social support within the gay community, exposing themselves to alcohol and substance abuse.

Clatts and colleagues (2005c) found that those young MSM who use club drugs on a chronic basis were more likely to have tried to commit suicide and were more likely to have depressive symptoms. A study of 569 young MSM in New York City revealed that a prior experience of homelessness and currently being homeless are both strongly associated with higher levels of lifetime exposure to drug and sexual risk, as well as higher levels of current drug and sexual risk (Clatts et al. 2005). Clatts and colleagues (2007) report that in a study of seventy-nine male sex workers in Hanoi, Vietnam, nearly three-quarters of those who had receptive anal sex with a male client did not use a condom. Drug use, particularly marijuana, Ecstasy, amphetamines, cocaine, and smoked heroin, was common.

The Anthropology of HIV Risk, Sexual Behavior, and HIV Prevention among MSM

Another large area of HIV/AIDS research concerns among medical and applied anthropologists has been the question of risk taking among MSM, the sexual behaviors that put MSM at increased risk, and what prevention interventions can be successfully implemented that would reduce the risk for HIV (Auerwald and Eyre 2002; Feldman 1994; Feldman and Miller 1998; Gwadz et al. 2004; Gwadz et al. 2006; Kotarba and Lang 1986; Lang 1990a; MacKellar et al. 2007; Silenzio 2003; Slavin et al. 2007; Stall et al. 1988; Stall et al. 2008; Vincke and Bolton 1995; Welle and Clatts 2007). In a recent editorial in a gay monthly magazine, the editor writes:

> For the last quarter century, the gay community has fought to shed the stigma of AIDS as being a gay disease. For the most part, we have been successful in that fight. But somewhere along the way, it seems, we have managed to convince *ourselves* that it is no longer a gay disease. So much so, that it is now commonplace to find gay men of all ages engaging in highly risky bareback sex.
>
> It is way past time to click our heels and return to reality, people.
> . . .
> The writing is on the wall. We are bound to see another AIDS epidemic sweep through our community that will once again cast gay men in a dirty and disease-ridden light. Unlike the first wave of infection that stole so many wonderful people from us, we know better this time. (Booth 2008: 5)

Feldman (1985, 1986a) conducted a very early study in 1982–1983 looking at behavioral change and awareness of the then new epidemic of HIV/AIDS in New York City among gay and bisexual men. One of the key findings was that MSM had begun decreasing their number of sexual partners—from 6.8 to 3.6 per month—long before there was any discussion of condoms or the discovery of HIV as the cause of AIDS. Less-educated gay and bisexual men were more likely to have more sexual partners than better educated gay and bisexual men, while better educated men showed steeper declines in their number of partners after learning about AIDS (Feldman 1986b). Feldman (1989) also examined the considerable adversity experienced by gay male teenagers through their coming-out process due to the AIDS epidemic during the late 1980s. They needed to decide whether to be tested for HIV, whether to postpone sexual activity, how to select a partner, and which kinds of sexual practices to engage in. It was recommended that school and community-based health education programs be developed to teach gay and bisexual youth about safer sex.

Stall (1990) and Stall and colleagues (1990b) presented data from a five-year prospective study showing that most gay men in San Francisco, at that time, were practicing safer sex, although relapse from effective prevention was a growing problem. Parker and colleagues (1991) argued that in the early 1990s, one of the key impediments to effective HIV prevention was the lack of sex research on a global level, since it was difficult to respond to AIDS by drawing on a preexisting body of knowledge.

Carrier and Magaña (1991), in a study of Latino men in Southern California, pointed out that anthropologists can help control the spread of HIV/AIDS by providing program directors with accurate ethnographic data on the range of sexual behaviors of targeted populations. The authors also indicate that less acculturated Mexicans living in California are likely to engage in either insertive or receptive anal sex, but not both, while U.S.-born middle-class Mexican Americans are more likely to follow the Anglo pattern of engaging in both insertive and receptive anal sex.

Stall and colleagues (1992) found that for young gay men, reporting a lower attributed risk for HIV infection to unprotected anal sex, a higher concern about becoming HIV infected, and living in San Francisco for a shorter length of time are positively correlated with higher risk-taking behavior. In a discussion of HIV prevention approaches and multipartnering behavior, Bolton (1992) argued against the partner-reduction strategy. Instead of contributing to a reduction in HIV transmission, it has exacerbated the problem by undermining the sex-positive approaches to risk reduction that have proven effective.

Schiller and colleagues (1994) pointed out that people with AIDS are portrayed either as minority street people abandoned by friends and family or as white gay men who live within a gay community. In either case, they are seen as socially deviant. The construction of HIV has facilitated distancing and denial of personal risk by those outside "high-risk groups," impeding prevention efforts. In methodological papers, MacKellar and colleagues (1996) and MacKellar, Valleroy, Behel, and colleagues (2006) discussed how young MSM are recruited into the Centers for Disease Control and Prevention's (CDC's) Young Men's Survey at such venues as dance clubs, bars, and street locations. Behaviors and psychosocial factors associated with HIV infection can be used to design culturally relevant and age-specific prevention activities for young MSM.

In a study supporting the general effectiveness of HIV prevention efforts in Belgium, Vincke and colleagues (1997) discovered that younger gay men like using a condom with both insertive and receptive anal sex more than do older gay men. They also found that younger men with a steady partner report more gratification from insertive anal sex with a condom than do older partnered men.

In the Young Men's Study conducted by Valleroy and colleagues (2000) in seven American cities, the prevalence of HIV infection among young (eighteen-to-twenty years old) MSM was high (7.2 percent), increased with age (9.7 percent among twenty-two-year-olds), and was higher for blacks (odds ratio: 6:3). Only 18 percent of the HIV-positive men knew they were infected before they were tested for this study, few (8 percent) were receiving anti-retroviral therapy (ART), and the prevalence of unprotected anal sex during the previous six months was high (41 percent).

In a study conducted among HIV-positive MSM in Australia, Kippax and colleagues (2003) asked how the men believed they became infected. Within partnered relationships, breakdown of negotiated safety (usually an agreement to always use condoms outside the relationship, but not within the relationship), love and intimacy, and fatalism were among the explanations given. Within casual sexual encounters, pleasure, lack of control, and particular sexual settings were cited. It was also learned that many MSM believed that HIV infection was inevitable or unavoidable in some circumstances (Slavin et al. 2004).

In the continuing Young Men's Study, MacKellar and colleagues (2005) showed that of the 439 young MSM with unrecognized HIV infection, 51 percent had unprotected anal sex in the previous six months, 59 percent perceived that they were at low risk for being infected, and 55 percent had not been tested in the previous year. In a related study, it was found that many new sex partners may be unintentionally exposed to HIV from young MSM, particularly those who are black and who disclose being HIV negative based on an earlier test.

Anthropological Research on HIV and Gay Men's Culture

Throughout the 1990s and the early 2000s, there has been an explosion in research about MSM by anthropologists, particularly focusing upon socio-cultural dimensions. Interestingly, however, most of this research has little or nothing to do with HIV/AIDS. While the absence of HIV/AIDS in anthropological "queer studies" is reminiscent of ignoring the proverbial "800 pound gorilla in the room," there is certainly legitimacy to studying gay and bisexual men without always focusing on health concerns. However, the absence of HIV/AIDS research in "queer studies" is remarkable, if not problematic.

During the 1990s and the 2000s, we began to see some research on gay men that focuses on cultural factors and HIV/AIDS by several anthropologists (e.g., Bateson and Goldsby 1988; Bloom 2001; Carrier 1990, 1995; Daniel and Parker 1993; Feldman 1990; Feldman and Johnson 1986; Lang 1990b; Leap 1995; Lorway 2008; Parker 1991; Parker and Caceres 1999). Gorman (1991) adroitly argues that it is essential to understand the culture experienced by gay men in order to comprehend the salience of the AIDS crisis. He cites, for example, one informant who said: "AIDS is like a war. You never know who is going to go next. Who can you depend on? Which friend is going to leave? Will I be one of the survivors?"

Melody (1994) discusses political activism within the American gay community as a response to the inaction of the Reagan administration to AIDS. He reviews the growth of ACT UP (AIDS Coalition to Unleash Power) and concludes that this group had an extraordinary influence in changing policy at the Food and Drug Administration and at the National Institutes of Health, and in fostering the Ryan White Program.

Using ethnographic research conducted in Porto Alegre, Brazil, Klein (1999) discusses the emergence of gay communities (for example, *travestís*, *bofes*, *bichas*, *gays*, *homens*, and *passivos*) in contemporary Brazil during the 1990s, and how both gay rights groups and AIDS service organizations play a central role in the dynamics of gay cultural development. Using a telephone survey of 2,881 MSM in four major American cities, Mills and colleagues (2001) found that MSM who resided in "gay ghettos" (predominantly gay and lesbian neighborhoods) were more likely than MSM not living in "gay ghettos" to be involved in the gay and lesbian community, to identify as gay, and to have been tested for HIV, and less likely to have only male sexual partners.

Lorway (2006) questions the view that characterizes AIDS in Africa as an unambiguous heterosexual epidemic. Based upon twenty months of ethnographic research in Katutura, Namibia, he discusses the cultural setting of young MSM in the community as they deal with state-sponsored antigay rhetoric and social stigma within the community. Padilla (2007) discusses his ethnographic research among two categories of male sex workers in the Dominican Republic who cater to gay male tourists. While the relationship is essentially economic, both the sex workers and their clients are motivated to camouflage this in their construction of a more fulfilling emotional relationship.

Eyre and colleagues (2007) describe the dynamics of romantic relationships among African American gay and bisexual male adolescents in Oakland, California. Among the more interesting findings is that they do not initiate sex with the partner; instead, it usually occurs days or weeks after the couple first meet. However, usually the couple eventually experiences conflicts over infidelity and breaks up, often resulting in low self-esteem, trying to get back with the partner, and revenge sex.

Other Research by Anthropologists on HIV/AIDS and MSM

There are several studies by anthropologists that do not fit neatly into the above topics. Parker and Carballo (1990) point to both the importance and the paucity, especially around 1990, of qualitative sexual behavior research by anthropologists on MSM and HIV/AIDS. The long-standing neglect of research in this area has been problematic without a preexisting global database on MSM sexual behavior. Bolton (1994) similarly argues that social and behavioral scientists need to give higher priority to research on controversial subjects, including those related to sexual orientation.

Stall and colleagues (1996) found, in a study of 2,593 gay and bisexual men in two American cities, that one-third of them did not know their current HIV status, and of those who knew that they were HIV positive, three-quarters followed medical recommendations for the treatment of HIV infection available. They conclude, in a follow-up paper, that additional efforts are needed for MSM characterized by relative youth and lower social support (Stall, Pollack, et al. 2001). Kammerer and colleagues (1999) describe the difficulties that transgendered people encounter in obtaining health and social services, including targeted HIV prevention.

Carrier (1999) discusses some of the ethical concerns he has encountered in field research on Mexican MSM since 1968. He points out: "When knowledge from an ethnographer's private sex life is used to inform field research on human sexual behaviours, a careful and continuous review must be made with respect to the ethicality of its effects on the research design" (1999: 207). (Related issues of ethical concerns are discussed by Penha and colleagues in chapter 9.)

MacKellar and colleagues (2002) compared first-time HIV testers with repeat testers in a study of 3,430 young MSM in seven U.S. cities. Compared with first-time testers, repeat testers were more likely to report recent risk behaviors and to acquire HIV (7 versus 4 percent). Many young MSM soon acquire HIV after repeated use of HIV counseling and testing services, and it is recommended that these services be improved with enhanced behavioral interventions. More recently, MacKellar, Valleroy, Anderson, and colleagues (2006) learned that nearly half of young MSM participants had not undergone testing in the past year. Of those who had been tested recently, many MSM, especially those who are black, had already acquired HIV. It is recommended that to reduce HIV transmission and facilitate early diagnosis and entry into care, increased HIV testing among young at-risk MSM in the United States is needed.

Parker and colleagues (2004) applaud what they see as a shift in sexuality research to an examination of sexual health and sexual rights, reviewing the literature on same-sex marriage and sexual oppression and discrimination. Parker (2007) looks at sexual rights, including the right of people to good sexual health, access to sexual and reproductive health services, and the right of women to choose to have an abortion or not. Lesbian, gay, bisexual, transgender, and "queer" scholarship and activism, including HIV/AIDS activism, have played a central role in calling attention to sexual diversity.

Outline of the Book

After reaching a four-decade-long low in 1999 among MSM in the United States, syphilis cases began increasing again—a direct measure of increased unprotected sex among MSM, especially among urban gay-identified men. Accordingly, we turn first in this volume to an examination of the relationship between increasing syphilis rates as a marker of unprotected sex and growing HIV infection among MSM. Bloom and colleagues (chapter 2) examine how social stress within the American gay community has elevated both syphilis and HIV rates. Some of the social responses have been flight, isolation, blame (or scapegoating), and ostracism. Drug use often puts some gay men at increased risk for HIV infection and syphilis. The authors look at responses that decrease the biological impact of social stress.

The next chapter continues with an exploration of the psychological impact of having HIV/AIDS. Stanley (chapter 3) examines why many HIV-positive gay men do not adhere fully, or at all, in taking their prescribed medications. Based upon her research using in-depth interviews, she learns that many gay men are reluctant to give up their personal autonomy. They often equate the authoritarianism of the medical establishment with the homophobia they have experienced in their own lives. By employing holistic forms of healing, they can assert their personal autonomy.

Leap and Colón (chapter 4) focus on the relationship between language and AIDS among HIV-positive gay men. Language has been used to cast gay men as the stigmatized "other." But by looking closely at how gay men use language, we can learn how to better develop effective programs that serve the gay community.

Collins and Harshbarger (chapter 5) review the efficacy of several group-level and community-level intervention programs targeting MSM primarily in the United States. They conclude that four HIV interventions meet the criteria for inclusion in the CDC's Diffusion of Effective Behavioral Interventions (DEBI) project, designed to diffuse HIV/STD prevention interventions to community-based organizations (CBOs) and health departments in the United States. One of the key difficulties has been "translating" prevention research into effective real-world programs given by CBOs for MSM.

Feldman (chapter 6) autobiographically describes the experience of developing an AIDS community-based organization during the 1980s in New York City that primarily served HIV-positive gay men. The AIDS center developed strong, and sometimes violent, opposition from the politically conservative community. This chapter details how political alliances were formed either supporting or opposing the location of the AIDS center. The AIDS Center of Queens County today thrives, serving the HIV-positive community in New York City's borough of Queens.

Gay men in the United States are at an elevated risk for methamphetamine addiction, and often use the drug for sexual arousal in frequently unsafe sexual encounters. Lyons (chapter 7) looks at a sample of MSM who attended Crystal Meth Anonymous (CMA) meetings, which functioned in the general tradition of Alcoholics Anonymous meetings, using the twelve-step program. Lyons examines the program components of honesty, facing reality, taking one's "inventory" (or personal assessment), taking it "one day at a time," group fellowship, and spirituality to focus on changes in sobriety and sexual behavior. It appears that attendance in CMA meetings does lead to changed behavior among program participants.

The next three chapters look at Latino gay men in Connecticut and New York City. Clair and Singer (chapter 8) focus on Latino and non-Latino MSM in Connecticut. In a comprehensive statewide study (N = 331), they report that AIDS stigma and "structural violence" play central roles in the lives of Latino MSM in the state. They further note that, compared with white, non-Latino MSM and African American MSM, Latino MSM are more likely to self-identify as bisexual. They are also more likely to have significantly lower incomes and sell sex for money or drugs, and less likely to report using condoms and to report communicating with their sexual partners about HIV. The authors have developed, as a consequence of this study, an antihomophobia social-marketing program for the Latino community of Hartford, Connecticut.

Penha and colleagues (chapter 9) discuss the ethical concerns of conducting sexual research and ethnographic fieldwork among Latino MSM in the New York City area. They compare the different ethical guidelines developed by the two leading psychological and anthropological organizations, observing greater ethical flexibility among anthropologists. In the end, the research team developed a set of guidelines that prohibited sex and drinking between researchers and their informants.

Muñoz-Laboy and Parker (chapter 10) look at the "erotic landscapes" of bisexually active Latino men in New York City. A case study of the sexual life of one informant is presented from his first sexual encounter at the age of fifteen into his twenties. His sexual relationships included both men and women, as well as both protected and unprotected sex. The case study examines the dynamics of his relationships from "one-night stands" in public venues to love affairs. The implications for HIV/STI prevention programs are examined. These programs need to be carefully tailored so that the content of messages and interventions would be culturally specific for the Latino bisexual population. A salient point is that public venues for sexual activity do not necessarily increase HIV risk.

Neumann and colleagues (chapter 11) compare HIV prevention interventions for MSM conducted in the United States with Australia. The two countries have often used different approaches to understanding and changing HIV risk among MSM. The authors look at intervention, formative, and survey studies in both countries. They recommend routine data collection in the following areas: attitudes, HIV testing, correlates of risk behaviors, risk reduction strategies, sexual risk behaviors, connectedness to the gay community, the range of sex practices, exposure to and use of medical and behavioral prevention services, and treatment of HIV-infected MSM.

Continuing the focus on Australia, Slavin and Ellard (chapter 12) look at why some gay men continue to have unprotected anal sex, even though they are fully aware of the consequences and risk of HIV infection. Using data from interviews with gay men in three Australian cities, they examine cultural meanings of condomless anal sex in relation to dominant ideals of romantic love and unity, using David Schneider's analysis of Western kinship and his concept of "substance," family, and love to understand the nature of HIV risk among gay men. Gay male couples often see condoms as an impediment to personal intimacy.

The final two chapters take us to two European countries: Greece and Belgium. Riedel (chapter 13) examines the historical development of AIDS in Greece as it relates to gay men and the changing politics of that nation. Traditionally in Greece, as is true in many other areas of the world, sexual identity was not defined by same-sex desire, but rather by the passive position one assumed. In Greece, AIDS during the 1980s was seen as something both foreign and not significantly related to same-sex sexuality. Indeed, in the early years people were learning about AIDS even before the first cases in the country were confirmed—what Riedel terms an "epidemic of information." As the actual epidemic of HIV/AIDS grew, there was a general reluctance to see it as a problem affecting the Greek gay community.

Vincke and colleagues (chapter 14) turn their attention toward gay life in Belgium. While attitudes toward gay men and lesbians in Belgium are very tolerant, gay youth there have exceptionally high rates of suicide. In a study conducted by the authors in Belgium, older gay men are more convinced than younger gay men that engaging in sex currently is less safe when compared with the past. Those with a lower educational level were more likely to be optimistic about new HIV treatments. Overall, it was learned that about three out of five gay men were generally practicing safer sex.

Gay men have been at the center of the AIDS epidemic since the very beginning. This volume takes the reader into a deeper understanding of the cultural dimensions of gay male behavior and thought as they relate to this epidemic.

Acknowledgments

I would like to thank all of the many anthropologists who sent me their publications, abstracts, and bibliographies in preparation for this chapter.

While many of the peer-reviewed published papers and book chapters written by (mostly American) anthropologists (as first or second author) about gay men and HIV/AIDS are mentioned or cited in this chapter, clearly many others are not, and I would like to apologize for their exclusion. I would also like to thank Tabetha Wilson for her research assistance in the preparation of this chapter.

References

Auerwald C. L., and S. L. Eyre. 2002. Youth homelessness in San Francisco: A life cycle approach. *Social Science and Medicine* 54(10): 1496–511.

Bateson, M. C., and R. Goldsby. 1988. *Thinking AIDS: The Social Response to the Biological Threat*. Reading, Mass.: Addison-Wesley.

Bloom, F. R. 2001. "New beginnings": A case study in gay men's changing perceptions of quality of life during the course of HIV infection. *Medical Anthropology Quarterly* 15(1): 38–57.

Bolton, R. 1992. AIDS and promiscuity: Muddles in the models of HIV prevention. *Medical Anthropology* 14(2–4): 145–223.

———. 1994. Sex, science, and social responsibility: Cross-cultural research on same-sex eroticism and sexual intolerance. *Cross-Cultural Research* 28(2): 134–90.

Bolton, R., J. Vincke, R. Mak, and E. Dennehy. 1992. Alcohol and risky sex: In search of an elusive connection. *Medical Anthropology* 14(2–4): 323–63.

Booth, D. 2008. Editor's view: Don't shed all layers. *About Gay Life Magazine* (Buffalo, N.Y.), May, 5.

Carrier, J. M. 1990. Update on AIDS in Mexico. In *Current Directions in Anthropological Research on AIDS*, ed. D. A. Feldman, 7–9. Special Publication No. 1. Miami, Fla.: AIDS and Anthropology Research Group.

———. 1995. *De Los Otros: Intimacy and Homosexuality among Mexican Men*. New York: Columbia University Press.

———. 1999. Reflections on ethical problems encountered in field research on Mexican male homosexuality: 1968 to present. *Culture, Health and Sexuality* 1(3): 207–21.

Carrier, J. M., and J. R. Magaña. 1991. Use of ethnosexual data on men of Mexican origin for HIV/AIDS prevention programs. *Journal of Sex Research* 28(2): 189–203.

Celentano, D. D., L. A. Valleroy, F. Sifakis, D. A. Mackellar, J. Hylton, H. Thiede, W. McFardland, D. A. Shehan, S. R. Stoyanoff, M. Lalota, B. A. Koblin, M. H. Katz, and L. V. Torian. 2006. Associations between substance use and sexual risk among very young men who have sex with men. *Sexually Transmitted Diseases* 33(4): 265–71.

Clatts, M. C. 1999. Ethnographic observations of men who have sex with men in public: Toward an ecology of sexual action. In *Public Sex/Gay Space*, ed. W. L. Leap, 141–55. New York: Columbia University Press.

Clatts, M. C., M. Giang Ie, L. A. Goldsamt, and H. Yi. 2007. Male sex work and HIV risk among young heroin users in Hanoi, Vietnam. *Sexual Health* 4(4): 261–67.

Clatts, M. C., L. Goldsamt, and M. V. Gwadz. 2005. Homelessness and drug abuse among young men who have sex with men in New York City: A preliminary epidemiological trajectory. *Journal of Adolescence* 28(2): 201–14.

Clatts, M. C., L. Goldsamt, A. Neaigus, and D. L. Welle. 2003. The social course of drug injection and sexual activity among YMSM and other high-risk youth: An agenda for future research. *Journal of Urban Health* 80 (4 Suppl. 3): 26–39.

Clatts, M. C., L. A. Goldsamt, and H. Yi. 2005a. Club drug use among young men who have sex with men in New York City: A preliminary epidemiological profile. *Substance Use and Misuse* 40(9–10): 1317–330.

———. 2005b. Drug and sexual risk in four men who have sex with men populations: Evidence for a sustained HIV epidemic in New York City. *Journal of Urban Health* 82(1 Suppl. 1): 9–17.

———. 2005c. An emerging HIV environment: A preliminary epidemiological profile of an MSM POZ party in New York City. *Sexually Transmitted Infections* 81(5): 373–76.

Clatts, M. C., and J. L. Sotheran. 2000. Challenges in research on drug and sexual risk practices of men who have sex with men: Applications of ethnography in HIV epidemiology and prevention. *AIDS and Behavior* 4(2): 169–79.

Clatts, M. C., D. L. Welle, and L. A. Goldsamt. 2001. Reconceptualizing the interaction of drug and sexual risk among MSM speed users: Notes toward an ethno-epidemiology. *AIDS and Behavior* 5(2): 115–30.

Daniel, H., and R. Parker. 1993. *Sexuality, Politics, and AIDS in Brazil: In Another World?* Bristol, Pa.: Falmer Press.

Deren, S., M. Stark, F. Rhodes, H. Siegal, L. Cottler, M. Wood, L. Kochems, R. Carlson, R. Falck, K. Rourke, R. Trotter, B. Weir, M. F. Goldstein, and L. Wright-De Aguero. 2001. Drug-using men who have sex with men: Sexual behaviours and sexual identities. *Culture, Health and Sexuality* 3(3): 329–38.

Eyre, S. L., C. Milbrath, and B. Peacock. 2007. Romantic relationships trajectories of African American gay/bisexual adolescents. *Journal of Adolescent Research* 22(2): 107–31.

Feldman, D. A. 1985. AIDS and social change. *Human Organization* 44(4): 343–47.

———. 1986a. AIDS health promotion and clinically applied anthropology. In *The Social Dimensions of AIDS: Method and Theory*, ed. D. A. Feldman and T. M. Johnson, 145–59. New York: Praeger.

———. 1986b. "Totally safe sex" or AIDS. *American Journal of Public Health* 76(5): 588.

———. 1989. Gay youth and AIDS. *Journal of Homosexuality* 17(1–2): 185–93.

———. 1990. Introduction: Culture and AIDS. In *Culture and AIDS*, ed. D. A. Feldman, 1–7. New York: Praeger.

———. 1994. Introduction. In *Global AIDS Policy*, ed. D. A. Feldman, 1–6. Westport, Conn.: Bergin and Garvey.

Feldman, D. A., and T. M. Johnson. 1986. Introduction. In *The Social Dimensions of AIDS: Method and Theory*, ed. D. A. Feldman and T. M. Johnson, 1–12. New York: Praeger.

Feldman, D. A., and J. W. Miller. 1998. *The AIDS Crisis: A Documentary History*. Westport, Conn: Greenwood Press.

Forsythe, J. A. 1994. Personal communication.

Gilley, B. J., and J. H. Co-Cké. 2005. Cultural investment: Providing opportunities to reduce risky behavior among gay American Indian males. *Journal of Psychoactive Drugs* 37(3): 293–98.

Gorman, E. M. 1991. Anthropological reflections on the HIV epidemic among gay men. *Journal of Sex Research* 28(2): 263–74.

———. 1996. Speed use and HIV transmission. *Focus* 11(7): 4–6.

———. 2003. Research with gay drug users and the interface with HIV: Current methodological issues for social work research. *Journal of Gay and Lesbian Social Services* 15(1–2): 79–94.

Gorman, E. M., B. D. Barr, A. Hansen, B. Robertson, and C. Green. 1997. Speed, sex, gay men, and HIV: Ecological and community perspectives. *Medical Anthropology Quarterly* 11(4): 505–15.

Gorman, E. M., K. R. Nelson, T. Applegate, and A. Scrol. 2004. Club drug and poly-substance abuse and HIV among gay/bisexual men: Lessons gleaned from a community study. *Journal of Gay and Lesbian Social Services* 16(2): 1–17.

Gwadz, M. V., M. C. Clatts, N. R. Leonard, and L. Goldsamt. 2004. Attachment style, childhood adversity, and behavioral risk among young men who have sex with men. *Journal of Adolescent Health* 34(5): 402–13.

Gwadz, M. V., M. C. Clatts, H. Yi, N. R. Leonard, L. Goldsamt, and S. Lankenau. 2006. Resilience among young men who have sex with men in New York City. *Sexual Research and Social Policy* 3(1): 13–21.

Kammerer, N., T. Mason, and M. Connors. 1999. Transgender health and social service needs in the context of HIV risk. *International Journal of Transgenderism* 3(1–2): 1.

Kippax, S., S. Slavin, J. Ellard, O. Hendry, J. Richters, A. Grulich, and J. Kaldor. 2003. Seroconversion in context. *AIDS Care* 15(6): 839–52.

Klein, C. 1999. "The ghetto is over, darling": Emerging gay communities and gender and sexual politics in contemporary Brazil. *Culture, Health and Sexuality* 1(3): 239–60.

Kotarba, J. A., and N. A. Lang. 1986. Gay lifestyle change and AIDS: Preventive health care. In *The Social Dimensions of AIDS: Method and Theory*, ed. D. A. Feldman and T. M. Johnson, 127–44. New York: Praeger.

Lang, N. G. 1990a. AIDS and the gay community in Texas: New developments. In *Current Directions in Anthropological Research on AIDS*, ed. D. A. Feldman, 9–11, Special Publication No. 1. Miami, Fla.: AIDS and Anthropology Research Group.

———. 1990b. Sex, politics, and guilt: A study of homophobia and the AIDS phenomenon. In *Culture and AIDS*, ed. D. A. Feldman, 169–82. New York: Praeger.

Lankenau, S. E., and M. C. Clatts. 2002. Ketamine injection among high risk youth: Preliminary findings from New York City. *Journal of Drug Issues* 32(3): 893–905.

Lankenau, S. E., M. C. Clatts, L. A. Goldsamt, and D. L. Welle. 2004. Crack cocaine injection practices and HIV risk: Findings from New York and Bridgeport. *Journal of Drug Issues* 34(2): 319–32.

Leap, W. L. 1995. Talking about AIDS: Linguistic perspectives on non-neutral discourse. In *Culture and Sexual Risk: Anthropological Perspectives on AIDS*, ed. H. ten Brummelhuis and G. Herdt, 227–38. Luxembourg: Gordon and Breach.

Lorway, R. 2006. Dispelling "heterosexual African AIDS" in Namibia: Same-sex sexuality in the township of Katutura. *Culture, Health and Sexuality* 8(5): 435–49.

———. 2008. "Where can I be deported?" Thinking through the "foreigner fetish" in Namibia. *Medical Anthropology* 27(1): 70–97.

MacKellar, D. A., L. A. Valleroy, J. E. Anderson, S. Behel, G. M. Secura, T. Bingham, D. D. Celentano, B. A. Koblin, M. LaLota, D. Shehan, H. Thiede, L. V. Torian, and R. S. Janssen. 2006. Recent HIV testing among young men who have sex with men: Correlates, contexts, and HIV seroconversion. *Sexually Transmitted Diseases* 33(3): 183–92.

MacKellar, D. A., L. A. Valleroy, S. Behel, G. M. Secura, T. Bingham, D. D. Celentano, B. A. Koblin, M. LaLota, D. Shehan, H. Thiede, and L. V. Torian. 2006. Unintentional HIV exposures from young men who have sex with men who disclose being HIV-negative. *AIDS* 20(12): 1637–644.

MacKellar, D., L. Valleroy, J. Karon, G. Lemp, and R. Janssen. 1996. The Young Men's Survey: Methods for estimating HIV seroprevalence and risk factors among young men who have sex with men. *Public Health Reports* 111 (Suppl. 1): 138–44.

MacKellar, D. A., L. A. Valleroy, G. M. Secura, B. N. Bartholow, W. McFarland, D. Shehan, W. Ford, M. LaLota, D. D. Celentano, B. A. Koblin, L. V. Torian, T. E. Perdue, R. S. Janssen, and Young Men's Survey Study Group. 2002. Repeat HIV testing, risk behaviors, and HIV seroconversion among young men who have sex with men: A call to monitor and improve the practice of prevention. *Journal of the Acquired Immune Deficiency Syndrome* 29(1): 76–85.

MacKellar, D. A., L. A. Valleroy, G. M. Secura, S. Behel, T. Bingham, D. D. Celentano, B. A. Koblin, M. LaLota, W. McFarland, D. Shehan, H. Thiede, L. V. Torian, R. S. Janssen, and Young Men's Survey Study Group. 2005. Unrecognized HIV infection, risk behaviors, and perceptions of risk among young men who have sex with men: Opportunities for advancing HIV prevention in the third decade of HIV/AIDS. *Journal of the Acquired Immune Deficiency Syndrome* 38(5): 603–14.

MacKellar, D. A., L. A. Valleroy, G. M. Secura, S. Behel, T. Bingham, D. D. Celentano, B. A. Koblin, M. LaLota, D. Shehan, H. Thiede, L. V. Torian, and Young Men's Survey Study Group. 2007. Perceptions of lifetime risk and actual risk for acquiring HIV among young men who have sex with men. *AIDS Behavior* 11(2): 263–70.

Magaña, J. R., and J. M. Carrier. 1991. Mexican and Mexican-American male sexual behavior and spread of AIDS in California. *Journal of Sex Research* 28(3): 425–41.

Melody, M. E. 1994. Acting up academically: AIDS and the politics of disempowerment. In *Global AIDS Policy*, ed. D. A. Feldman, 160–84. Westport, Conn.: Bergin and Garvey.

Mills, T. C., R. Stall, L. Pollack, J. P. Paul, D. Binson, J. Canchola, and J. A. Catania. 2001. Health-related characteristics of men who have sex with men: A comparison of those living in "gay ghettos" with those living elsewhere. *American Journal of Public Health* 91(6): 980–83.

Padilla, M. B. 2007. "Western Union daddies" and their quest for authenticity: An ethnographic study of the Dominican gay sex tourism industry. *Journal of Homosexuality* 53(1–2): 241–75.

Parker, R. G. 1991. *Bodies, Pleasures, and Passions: Sexual Culture in Contemporary Brazil.* Boston: Beacon Press.

———. 2007. Sexuality, health, and human rights. *American Journal of Public Health* 97(6): 972–73.

Parker, R. G., and C. Caceres. 1999. Alternative sexualities and changing sexual cultures among Latin American men. *Culture, Health, and Sexuality* 1(3): 201–6.

Parker, R. G., and M. Carballo. 1990. Qualitative research on homosexual and bisexual behavior relevant to HIV/AIDS. *Journal of Sex Research* 27(4): 497–525.

Parker, R., D. di Mauro, B. Filiano, J. Garcia, M. Muñoz-Laboy, and R. Sember. 2004. Global transformations and intimate relations in the 21st century: Social science research on sexuality and the emergence of sexual health and sexual rights frameworks. *Annual Review of Sex Research* 15: 362–98.

Parker, R. G., G. Herdt, and M. Carballo. 1991. Sexual culture, HIV transmission, and AIDS research. *Journal of Sex Research* 28(1): 77–99.

Peacock, B., S. L. Eyre, S. C. Quinn, and S. Kegeles. 2001. Delineating differences: Subcommunities in the San Francisco gay community. *Culture, Health and Sexuality* 3(2): 183–201.

Rhodes, F., S. Deren, M. M. Wood, M. G. Shedlin, R. G. Carlson, E. Y. Lambert, L. M. Kochems, M. J. Stark, R. S. Falck, L. Wright-Deaguero, B. Weir, L. Cottler, K. M. Rourke, and R. T. Trotter II. 1999. Understanding HIV risks of chronic drug-using men who have sex with men. *AIDS Care* 11(6): 629–48.

Schiller, H. G., S. Crystal, and D. Lewellen. 1994. Risky business: The cultural construction of AIDS risk groups. *Social Science and Medicine* 38(10): 1337–346.

Silenzio, V. M. 2003. Anthropological assessment for culturally appropriate interventions targeting men who have sex with men. *American Journal of Public Health* 93(6): 867–71.

Slavin, S. 2004a. Crystal methamphetamine use among gay men in Sydney. *Contemporary Drug Problems* 31(3): 425–65.

———. 2004b. Drugs, space, and sociality in a gay nightclub in Sydney. *Journal of Contemporary Ethnography* 33(3): 265–95.

Slavin, S., C. Batrouney, and D. Murphy. 2007. Fear appeals and treatment side-effects: An effective combination for HIV prevention? *AIDS Care* 19(1): 130–37.

Slavin, S., J. Richters, and S. Kippax. 2004. Understandings of risk among HIV seroconverters in Sydney. *Health, Risk and Society* 6(1): 39–52.

Stall, R. 1987. The prevention of HIV injection associated with drug and alcohol use during sexual activity. *Advances in Alcohol and Substance Abuse* 7(2): 73–88.

———. 1990. Relapse from safer sex: The AIDS Behavioral Research Project. In *Current Directions in Anthropological Research on AIDS*, ed. D. A. Feldman, 11–13. Special Publication No. 1. Miami, Fla.: AIDS and Anthropology Research Group.

Stall, R., D. Barrentt, L. Bye, J. Catania, C. Frutchey, J. Henne, G. Lemp, and J. Paul. 1992. A comparison of younger and older gay men's HIV risk-taking behaviors: The Communication Technologies 1989 Cross-Sectional Survey. *Journal of the Acquired Immune Deficiency Syndrome* 5(7): 682–87.

Stall, R., T. J. Coates, and C. Hoff. 1988. Behavioral risk reduction for HIV infection among gay and bisexual men: A review of results from the United States. *American Psychologist* 43(11): 878–85.

Stall, R., M. Ekstrand, L. Pollack, L. McKusick, and T. J. Coates. 1990. Relapse from safer sex: The next challenge for AIDS prevention efforts. *Journal of the Acquired Immune Deficiency Syndrome* 3(12): 1181–187.

Stall, R., M. Friedman, M. Marshal, and S. Wisniewski. 2008. What's driving the U.S. epidemic in men who have sex with men. Abstract 53. In *Program and Abstracts of the 15th Conference on Retroviruses and Opportunistic Infections*, February 3–6, Boston.

Stall, R., C. Hoff, T. J. Coates, J. Paul, K. A. Phillips, M. Ekstrand, S. Kegeles, J. Catania, D. Daigle, and R. Diaz. 1996. Decisions to get HIV tested and to accept antiretroviral therapies among gay/bisexual men: Implications for secondary prevention efforts. *Journal of Acquired Immune Deficiency Syndromes and Human Retrovirology* 11(2): 151–60.

Stall, R., L. McKusick, J. Wiley, T. J. Coates, and D. G. Ostrow. 1986. Alcohol and drug use during sexual activity and compliance with safe sex guidelines for AIDS: The AIDS Behavioral Research Project. *Health Education Quarterly* 13(4): 359–71.

Stall, R. D., J. P. Paul, D. C. Barrett, G. M. Crosby, and E. Bein. 1999. An outcome evaluation to measure changes in sexual risk-taking among gay men undergoing substance use disorder treatment. *Journal of Studies on Alcohol and Drugs* 60(6): 837–45.

Stall, R., J. P. Paul, G. Greenwood, L. M. Pollack, E. Bein, G. M. Crosby, T. C. Mills, D. Binson, T. J. Coates, J. A. Catania. 2001. Alcohol use, drug use and alcohol-related problems among men who have sex with men: The Urban Men's Health Study. *Addiction* 96(11): 1589–601.

Stall, R., L. Pollack, T. C. Mills, J. N. Martin, D. Osmond, J. Paul, D. Binson, T. J. Coates, and J. A. Catania. 2001. Use of antiretroviral therapies among HIV-infected men who have sex with men: A household-based sample of four major American cities. *American Journal of Public Health* 91(5): 767–73.

Stall, R., and J. Wiley. 1988. A comparison of alcohol and drug use patterns of homosexual and heterosexual men: The San Francisco Men's Health Study. *Drug Alcohol Dependence* 22(1–2): 63–73.

Thiede, H., L. A. Valleroy, D. A. MacKellar, D. D. Celantano, W. L. Ford, H. Hagan, B. A. Koblin, M. LaLota, W. McFarland, D. A. Shehan, and L. V. Torian. 2003. Regional patterns and correlates of substance use among young men who have sex with men in 7 U.S. urban areas. *American Journal of Public Health* 93(11): 1915–921.

Valleroy, L. A., D. A. MacKellar, J. M. Karon, D. H. Rosen, W. McFarland, D. A. Shehan, S. R. Stoyanoff, M. LaLota, D. D. Celantano, B. A. Koblin, H. Thiede, M. H. Katz, L. V. Torian, and R. S. Janssen. 2000. HIV prevalence and associated risks in young men who have sex with men: Young Men's Survey Study Group. *Journal of the American Medical Association* 284(2): 198–204.

Vincke, J., and R. Bolton. 1995. Social stress and risky sex among gay men: An additional explanation for the persistence of unsafe sex. In *Culture and Sexual Risk: Anthropological Perspectives on AIDS*, ed. H. ten Brummelhuis and G. Herdt, 183–204. Luxembourg: Gordon and Breach.

Vincke, J., R. Bolton, and M. Miller. 1997. Younger versus older gay men: Risks, pleasures and dangers of anal sex. *AIDS Care* 9(2): 217–26.

Welle, D. L., and M. C. Clatts. 2007. Scaffolded interviewing with lesbian, gay, bisexual, transgender, queer, and questioning youth: A developmental approach to HIV education and prevention. *Journal of the Association of Nurses in AIDS Care* 18(2): 5–14.

2

Gay Men, Syphilis, and HIV

The Biological Impact of Social Stress

FREDERICK R. BLOOM, JAMI S. LEICHLITER, DAVID K. WHITTIER, AND JANET W. MCGRATH

Responses to sexually transmitted disease (STD) epidemics have included considerable efforts by governments, communities, individuals, health-care advocates, and public health systems. In the past twenty years, this included the notable example of HIV prevention, but it also includes prevention of herpes simplex virus—type 2 (HSV2), syphilis, gonorrhea, chlamydia, and others. Following the initial onslaught of HIV among gay men in the United States, gay men, as individuals or members of communities, have taken steps to reduce sexual risk by changing their behaviors and often expecting those changes to be adopted by others. This resulted in a normative change that set a moral imperative extolling those who were "safer," while exerting social control on others who were not (Odets 1995). As we discuss, some of these changes may be undergoing a reversal (Chen et al. 2002).

Syphilis Increases in Gay Men

After reaching the lowest rate in more than forty years in 1999, primary and secondary syphilis cases in the United States increased in 2001 and 2002. Primary and secondary syphilis rates increased 12.4 percent in 2002, up to 6,862 from 6,103 in 2001 (CDC 2003). Increasing rates are attributed to men who have sex with men (MSM) because the increases have occurred largely among men. Several large U.S. cities have reported outbreaks of syphilis among MSM (CDC 2000, 2001, 2002; Chen et al. 2002; Ciesielski and Beidinger 2000; Kahn et al. 2002). Importantly, current increases in syphilis are noted most often among urban gay-identified men rather than other categories of MSM (for example, closeted men). Gay-identified men reside more frequently in urban centers (Laumann et al. 1994). Many of these new syphilis cases were diagnosed in men who were already infected

with, and receiving medical care for, HIV (CDC 1999, 2000, 2001, 2002; Ciesielski and Beidinger 2000; Kahn et al. 2002). For the most part, increases
in syphilis have followed a reduction in gay men's safer sex practices (Chen
et al. 2002).

Social Responses to the HIV Pandemic and Syphilis in Gay Men

The following hypothesis will provide a possible explanation of driving forces
for a behavior change toward riskier sex practices, and the resulting increase
in syphilis affecting gay men: it is hypothesized that a complex interaction
of behavioral changes based on gay men's understanding of preventing HIV
transmission, system-level changes implemented in response to the HIV
pandemic, and effects of the HIV pandemic on gay men's social environments have resulted in unintended increased syphilis infections among gay
men. There have been numerous responses to the HIV pandemic. Some are
based on individual behavior change (for example, reduction of partners,
use of condoms, and so forth). Others have been at a systems level (for example, development of improved chemotherapeutics for HIV,[1] categorical
HIV clinics,[2] and other interventions). These changes have been largely a
direct response to the HIV epidemic and have resulted in a reduction of
HIV transmission and improved health outcomes overall for persons living
with HIV infection. However, the driving forces for more recent responses
(for example, increased sexual risk behaviors including, but not limited to,
"barebacking,"[3] increasing drug use, and Internet use) may not be so easily
identified. Following McGrath (1991), we propose that these changes in behavior are also social responses to the ongoing HIV/AIDS pandemic. Data
collected from people living in or working with communities undergoing
increases in syphilis affecting gay men will be presented to support this
hypothesis.

Rapid Ethnographic Assessment of Syphilis in Gay Men

Rapid ethnographic assessment, based on the HIV/AIDS rapid assessment
procedures (RAP) (Scrimshaw et al. 1991), has been used by the Centers for
Disease Control and Prevention's (CDC's) Division of Sexually Transmitted Disease Prevention (DSTDP) to assist local health departments in the
development of disease prevention strategies, particularly when addressing
increases in syphilis among gay men. As of the end of 2003, assessments of
increases in syphilis for gay men were conducted in Broward County (Fort

Lauderdale, Florida), Los Angeles, Multnomah County (Portland, Oregon), Philadelphia, and Seattle.

Planning, data collection, data analysis, and report development of the RAPs were undertaken as a collaborative effort among federal, state, and local public health programs. Ethnographic assessments were performed by CDC staff who had experience conducting ethnographic fieldwork. Assistance from local health departments and community agency staff was sought whenever feasible.

Data Collection and Sampling

RAP data collection in all sites experiencing increases in syphilis for gay men began with the task of defining access points to the target population: gay-identified men. Some sites included a specific focus on HIV-positive gay men.[4] In all cases, a list of community organizations offering services (for example, health, entertainment, or other services) to gay men was provided by representatives of the state or local health department. Additional information on social venues and social service and health agencies, as well as other community information, was obtained from local print media, from Internet searches, and ultimately from contacts interviewed during the ethnographic assessments.

The ethnographers conducted all observations and interviews in geographic areas with a visible gay presence, including gay neighborhoods, gay entertainment districts, social service agencies, and health clinics, or at the local health department if more convenient for the interviewee. Observation and recruitment of respondents also took place in these target areas.

Respondents were approached at public venues or interviewed by appointment at agencies providing health or community services to gay men. Assessments were conducted during daytime and evening hours over four to seven days at each of the geographic sites. Respondents were asked for referrals, thus expanding the sample through snowball sampling (Bernard 1988). This technique is useful in following social networks and in reaching individuals in groups who are normally considered hard to reach. In addition, sampling was purposive to facilitate sampling individuals with a broad range of demographic characteristics, such as ethnicity and age (Bernard 1988).

Interviews and conversations were organized around topics relating to STD transmission, particularly syphilis. Though only a fraction of the interviews elicited attitudes and opinions about HIV/AIDS, the interviews yielded a rich variety of information about gay men's social responses to HIV/AIDS and the impact of those responses on sexual risk behavior for STDs.

Social Responses to HIV/AIDS

Flight and Isolation

Flight and isolation are responses to social stress and have been identified as social responses to epidemics (McGrath 1991). Individuals experiencing depression from widespread loss of relationships (such as HIV-related deaths of friends) may further isolate themselves from others and their normative influences. Flight from everyday pressures and responsibilities may look like an attractive alternative. Substance use can assist such an escape and alter sexual decision making. Some gay men who experienced wholesale devastation from AIDS had been socialized into a sociosexual world with extreme recreational and leisure characteristics. Some of these aspects may be fallen back upon or even reasserted as a response to this stress. Bathhouses, massive drug bacchanalia in the form of circuit parties, sex parties and clubs, and gay resort attendance have all begun to reemerge in the aftermath of acute AIDS mortality.

Fort Lauderdale, Florida, which has experienced significant rates of increase in syphilis among gay men, may serve as a geographic and aggregate example of this flight response. One theme used by respondents to describe Fort Lauderdale in particular is that it is "a fantasyland." That is, it is a place where people can be outside of the regular world. As one HIV-positive thirty-year-old gay man suggested, "In this community a lot of people just don't want to be themselves. They want to be something or somebody else." Another respondent calls it the resort mentality:

> People come here to escape—and to escape HIV. This includes the positive men as well as the negative who come here on vacation. The positive men to [get away from] the winters, to have a good time, go to the gym, and live on Social Security. It's the flight fantasy. They want to go away from HIV even though they have it. (HIV-positive forty-year-old gay man)

Sex itself can provide a "time out" or escape from stress and worry. Not surprisingly, one recent study found sexual risk taking by gay men while on vacation may be significantly elevated over that at home (Whittier et al.

2005). An epidemiologic alert was recently issued by the state of California about travel to Palm Springs, a popular gay resort area, based on concern that travel to that destination may play a role in syphilis transmission among MSM in the United States. Findings indicate that a vacation from stress may take the form of exemption from imposed standards.

Isolation may play a role in promulgating sexual risk taking. Those who flee may actually isolate themselves both as a group and as an individual in the process of taking flight. The congregation of HIV-positive gay men popularizing areas like Fort Lauderdale and Palm Springs (and the emergence of HIV in these areas' existing gay populations) may have helped normalize HIV seropositivity in a way that also reduces AIDS consciousness and concerns. Men who were socialized in gay communities prior to AIDS may seek these "leisure spaces" looking for activities and relief from AIDS-related social stress. Younger gay men, or those who are just coming out, may enter these spaces with an assumption that this social space is normative.

Assignment of Blame

The assignment of blame is another common response to epidemics and is well documented for HIV (Farmer 1992; Gagnon and Nardi 1997; Gorman 1992; Herdt and Boxer 1992; McGrath 1991, 1992). In the assessments conducted in response to increases in syphilis among gay men, we found a rich discourse on blame, with two primary themes: blaming those at risk for STD transmission, (partners, HIV-positive gay men, and others), and "blaming systems" (see below), such as public health, the government, and HIV and STD messages. Some examples in each category follow.

Blaming Those at Risk

In 2001, the Los Angeles County Department of Health (LACHD) STD program held a meeting of representatives from federal, state, and local agencies to report on and discuss strategies for syphilis prevention among Los Angeles gay men. During the meeting, data were presented indicating that some HIV-positive gay men engaged in sex without condoms, though the men were aware of their HIV status. In addition, these men acknowledged that some of their partners were HIV negative or of unknown HIV status. This was presented in the context of risk behavior and decision making of gay men and the potential transmission of syphilis and HIV. In contrast, other data reflected that some men considered strategies to protect themselves by using condoms or other behavioral changes. However, an article in the *Los Angeles Times* on the presentations at the meeting stated that HIV-positive gay men "were knowingly engaging in unprotected sex although they could pass on the AIDS virus" (Bernstein 2001); the tone of the article implied intentional transmission of disease.

Another example of blaming those at risk is the focus on unthinking complacency as the driving force behind increasing unprotected sex and rising syphilis rates (Savage 2002). Men interviewed in rapid assessments, however, do not present such a clear and simple explanation. For example, complacency may appear as a lack of concern about becoming infected with HIV. But this was not simple complacency. Rather, it was resignation to the inevitability of becoming infected with HIV and a sort of fatalism (McGrath 1991, 1992).

> They see people living several years and not dying after two years. They see people in their forties and fifties leading healthy, normal lives. Figure if they get it, they get it. Like there are three [HIV negative] kids my age that want to sleep with me, to just get infected. One said he just wants to get it over with. He is actually trying because he's going to bareback parties. Most parties don't like bug-chasers. You have to be positive for two years, and they ask to see your records. My friend wants to get it over with so it's [seroconversion] one less worry that I have to worry about. He's twenty-one. I try to talk to him about it, but if I talk too much he stops talking to me. (HIV-positive twenty-three-year-old gay man)

Blaming Systems

In the assessments, we encountered a wide range of systems, organizations, or factors that were blamed for the recent syphilis increases among gay men. Some of these included the government or public health system, AIDS organizations, community-based organizations (CBOs), private health-care providers, old prevention messages, condom messages, and drug use.

Blaming the Public Health System

One type of blame that has the potential to lead to social disruption is blaming the government, including the public health system. Funding decisions at the federal, state, and local levels can create a competitive process for limited resources and may create a barrier to collaboration among government agencies or the organizations they fund. An effort to disseminate funds to target those who are most at risk for STDs/HIV has led to "little grants" going to various organizations, which has increased competition among those organizations. One respondent (a gay man and CBO project coordinator) noted, "Organizations sometimes shield ideas from one another to protect their funding," damaging collaborative efforts. Funding opportunities are limited, and there is competition between agencies for those funds, creating a structural barrier to collaboration. When government funding streams for HIV and other STDs were separated, it inadvertently created another structural and procedural barrier for collaborative efforts at the governmental and nongovernmental levels. Funding for STD services cannot be used for HIV services and vice versa. In addition, there are philosophical differences that separate STD from HIV services. On the surface, HIV services such as anonymous testing and patient-centered referral services privilege patient confidentiality above all else. STD services, such as partner notification (PN), superficially appear to privilege public health above individual privacy.[5] These system-level barriers were blamed for the increases in syphilis among gay men: "STD and HIV are divided. On this campaign, we've been saying that if we had the appropriate public health attitude about AIDS we wouldn't have this [syphilis] problem" (director of an HIV service organization).

In addition, the intense, widespread public health efforts to prevent HIV transmission among gay men that have overshadowed STD information has led some to question public health's commitment to STD prevention: "The health department does not care. They don't care about us [MSM] and STDs. The health department only likes to talk about AIDS around here" (twenty-year-old gay man).

During the assessments, local health department STD and HIV clinics were also blamed for the recent syphilis increases among gay men. In some communities, there was a perception of rude behavior, homophobia, and a need to "jump hoops" in order to be seen at the public clinics. Regardless of whether such perceptions were based in reality, a negative perception of public clinics in gay communities can result in avoidance of those clinics. Such avoidance may lead gay men to seek services from private health-care providers whose screening, case reporting, and partner services practices are often below practice guidelines or legal requirements (St. Lawrence et al. 2002). For those gay men who do receive care at public STD or HIV clinics, an unfriendly or threatening atmosphere may decrease their cooperativeness with public health missions.

For HIV medications, I go to the [local] county health department where some workers are rude and not friendly at all, which makes me feel uncomfortable when I go there. The STD control section is pathetic there. There are intervention people that preach to you about safe sex and scream at you when you tell them the truth that you had unprotected sex. They try to scare you, like one told me that I could be thrown in jail for having sex without a condom because of my [HIV-positive] status. One time I had syphilis and I refused to tell them anything or talk about my partners because they weren't nice. (HIV-positive thirty-year-old gay man)

Blaming Old Messages

Another type of blame revealed in the assessments was the use of "old" HIV prevention messages. Old messages are those that may be used too often and are overexposed to the point where some may ignore the messages while others lash out against these preventive efforts. Others believe that the old messages are too intrusive, as suggested by the same individual quoted in the preceding section:

Personally, I have "AIDS fatigue." I mean enough is enough. I do not want to be in a clinic getting examined all the time. It is a personal choice for males to accept or reject the messages out there. I guess I am really more tired of hearing about the misconception around HIV in the community. Like the way that doctors don't tell you the whole truth or contradict themselves. (HIV-positive thirty-year-old gay man)

One HIV-positive thirty-one-year-old gay man noted that, particularly as far as condoms are concerned, the general HIV prevention "message hasn't changed, and they [gay men] know the message." Some HIV prevention messages are also inappropriately used by gay men to prevent STDs. "A lot of guys also think if they aren't getting penetrated then they are free. They can give and receive oral sex [without condoms] all day long and not have to worry" (female medical assistant at an HIV care facility). Though these men understand that practices such as these put them at less risk for transmission of HIV, they do not consider the potential for STD infection or the possibility that an STD infection may increase the risk for HIV transmission by these otherwise "less risky" practices.

Blaming Drug Use

Alcohol and other drug use were identified as contributing to risky sexual behaviors among some gay men and thereby were implicated in the recent increases in syphilis. In contrast to much of the earlier injection drug use literature that focuses on "needle sharing," recent research has suggested that high-risk sexual activity may have a large role in HIV infection among gay men who are injection drug users (IDUs) (Strathdee et al. 2001; Strathdee and Sherman 2003). Thus, it was not surprising that some interviewees, exemplified by one of the leaders of a community work group, believed that drug use among gay men, whether IDU or non-IDU, "leaves them more vulnerable to unsafe [sex] practices."

Drugs were identified as contributors to risky sexual behavior among gay men, including the following: alcohol is a central nervous system (CNS) depressant that can reduce inhibitions. Methamphetamine (commonly referred to as "crystal" or "tina") is a stimulant that can cause feelings of euphoria and a "rush" (NIDA 2002). It is often used in combination with other substances, has been linked to increased sexual risk behaviors, and is related to higher rates of STDs in noninjection methamphetamine users among MSM in some urban areas (Molitor et al. 1998; Paul et al. 1993; Semple et al. 2002). 3, 4-methylenedioxy-methamphetamine (MDMA, "Ecstasy," or "X") is a synthetic psychoactive drug that can affect mood and sexual activity (NIDA 2006a). Gammahydroxybutyrate (GHB) is a CNS depressant that can produce euphoric and sedative effects (NIDA 2006b). Ketamine ("Special K") is an anesthetic that can cause dreamlike states and hallucinations (NIDA 2001). Sildenafil (Viagra) is a drug that sustains penile erection. Many men reported using these drugs alone or in a variety of combinations. As one respondent (a gay man and CBO project coordinator) said when talking about the reasons for drug use, "All your frustrations about being gay disappear." Another interviewee talked about the popularity of many drugs among gay men and their accompanying risks.

> Special K is popular, as well as alcohol and marijuana. GHB is on the rise. I think that "X" and alcohol play a significant role in increased risk behavior among gay men because feelings are heightened and men feel liberated to act out their fantasies without thinking of the possible health consequences. (prevention education manager at a CBO)

Social Stress

We suggest that social stress is at the root of some of these responses: specified risk behaviors, blame, flight, and isolation. When someone's social environment (such as community, family, friendship network) demands an
action or response that exceeds that individual's belief that she or he can
cope with the demand, then stress increases (McGrath 1970). When such a
threatening or burdensome environmental demand "can be traced back to
social structures and people's locations within them," social stress is heightened (Pearlin 1989: 242). The effect of HIV-related disease and death experienced by individuals living in gay communities in the United States has
created a social environment that is in itself stressful (Lang 1991; Martin and
Dean 1993). Ironically, gay communities that offered acceptance and support for gay men became a source of stress resulting from the devastation
of AIDS.

Simultaneously, the HIV epidemic has decimated some gay communities or social networks through the death of entire cohorts of gay men who
might have been at the core of those communities (Odets 1995). The word
"epidemic" conveys an impact focused upon a major community, as well as
"disease" and "death." Epidemics impact in social as well as physical ways.
The social fabric is torn as relationships are ended, one after another, by
death. Formal relationships among people, such as institutions in the community, are also shattered in this collision. The existing state of affairs no
longer exists. Only tattered fragments of the former community are left behind (Wallace 1988).

AIDS decimated particular gay subcultures or communities of gay men
in urban areas of North America through massive loss of members and dis-
ruptions of social networks (Berube 1988; Gagnon and Nardi 1997; Kramer
1989; Levine 1992, 1998; National Research Council 1993; Rubin 1997). Gagnon and Nardi (1997) report that among gay-identified men who would
have been twenty-five to forty years old in 1995, one in ten had already
died from AIDS. The rate is likely to be even higher for those in the cohort
concentrated in urban gay centers like New York City's Greenwich Village.
Gorman (1992) cites probability data from a study of gay men living in Los
Angeles gay enclaves in which respondents knew an average of eighteen
men with HIV-related infections. Many existing community institutions
were also interrupted and destroyed (Altman 1987; Cruikshank 1992; Levine
1992, 1998; Rubin 1997). "War" was a common metaphor that gay men used

to describe their experience of the AIDS epidemic (Gorman 1992). This wave of destruction stressed the social fabric and psychological well-being of members of these communities.

Communities Affected by the HIV Pandemic: Social Stress and Gay Men

Gay communities can provide a protective effect from stress for individuals identifying with one of the communities by providing coping resources in the form of supportive structures and values (Crocker and Major 1989; D'Emilio 1983; Morris et al. 2001; Newton 1993; Peterson et al. 1996; Thoits 1985). Meyer (2003) distinguishes between group-level and individual resources in coping with stress by defining "minority stress" as a form of social stress affecting lesbians, bisexuals, and gay men. The establishment and maintenance of a supportive gay community are important in coping with the stress resulting from the stigmatization of same-sex sexuality in society.

The story of AIDS, like that of the feminist and sexual liberationist movements, is one chapter that influenced the growth and development of gay communities in America. However, the development of gay communities is only one part of the story. It is eclipsed, in part, by the damage and in some cases the near destruction of gay communities incurred by the arrival of AIDS.

Surviving community members often incurred physical disabilities from their HIV infection. These surviving men also often lost their friendship networks and jobs (Bloom 1998; Lang 1991; Martin and Dean 1993; Odets 1995; Weiss 1989). Like other plagues and natural disasters, the HIV/AIDS epidemic has caused collective and individual trauma, which includes "shock, numbness, disorientation, guilt, and emotional depletion" (National Research Council 1993: 259).

Gay men experienced severe anguish and other psychological pain as a result of the AIDS pandemic (Martin et al. 1989; National Research Council 1993). Their communities had originated as a response to the stigmatization of same-sex sexuality in the larger society. The social response to AIDS in the larger culture revisited blame on those who survived (Gagnon and Nardi 1997; Gorman 1992). Herdt and Boxer (1992) write that as a result of this restigmatization of same-sex sexuality, many gay men once again reexperienced much of what they had previously dealt with in coming out as gay, along with experiencing extensive morbidity, mortality, and loss of supportive social networks because of AIDS—support that could help to buffer this stress.

If these larger social concerns of community loss, disease, and stigmatization are considered stressors, then risk behavior is the outcome resulting from social stress (Albee 1984; Cohen et al. 2000; Perry and Bloom 1998; Wallace 1988). McGrath (1992: 73), in discussing the AIDS epidemic, provides an example of increased risk in terms of resignation to the inevitability of infection leading to diminished attempts to protect others. The following discussion expands on this example and provides additional examples to support our hypothesis.

Sources of Social Stress

Some informants contacted in rapid assessments of communities undergoing increases in syphilis among gay men suggest that the HIV/AIDS pandemic and the deaths of core community members have left their community fragmented and without easily identifiable leadership. Others note cliquishness within communities of gay-identified men. In addition, some state that it is difficult to identify safe spaces for men who are coming out or who are new to the local gay communities. It is much easier to locate the more sexually charged social environments such as bars, bathhouses, and Internet sex sites. Importantly, most of the communities that were assessed had a gay and lesbian community center and had social groups based on the commonalities of participants—including religious groups and sports groups. However, for those men who are less established in the local gay community, and especially for those who believed that their gay community was cliquish, bathhouses, bars, or other widely advertised sexual venues may have offered a greater degree of acceptance through alcohol, drugs, and anonymity.

Some ethnic communities, such as African American, Asian American, or Latino populations, continue to be reported as homophobic with complex issues of sexual identity ranging from those men who identify as heterosexual despite engaging in sex with other men to those who are openly gay. Men who remain in these communities are reported to feel pressure to marry and have children. Some men cope by leading double lives with a family in their home community and sexual encounters in the gay community (or that geographic area where gay venues are clustered).[6] Men from such ethnic backgrounds who seek to become members of their local gay communities also experience the effects of community fragmentation and cliquishness previously mentioned.

Informants report diminished public health resources. For example, one county health department in a large urban area has decreased its number of STD clinics from thirty to fewer than ten over the past decade.[7] This trend has also included increased privatization of health care. In addition, informants have noticed that there is a reduced visibility of HIV/AIDS within gay communities. Informants described the mid-to-late 1980s as a time when there was an abundance of AIDS awareness campaigns, AIDS benefit functions, widespread condom distribution, and an overall focus on HIV/AIDS prevention in the gay communities, often with the support of public health organizations. This was coupled with a change in community norms, where HIV prevention strategies and condom use in particular were generally expected of gay men engaging in sex.

The Biological Impact of Social Stress

McGrath (1991) proposed a model by which to assess the impact of social responses to disease. Responses that decrease the biological impact are termed "biologically appropriate" (or "bioappropriate"), while those that increase the biological impact are not bioappropriate. In her model, McGrath measured biological impact in terms of increasing or decreasing disease transmission. As she noted, there are essentially four ways to control disease: eliminate the source of infection; eliminate "adequate contact" (such as unprotected contact from skin to skin, or skin to mucous membrane) required for transmission; decrease infectivity of the hosts, vectors, or environments; and decrease the susceptibility of uninfected persons. Therefore, the biological impact of a specific response can be assessed by considering its impact on these four means of disease control.

McGrath (1991) identified three issues regarding the potential role of social responses to disease in reducing a disease outbreak. First, the term "bioappropriate," when applied to social responses, does not connote intentionality. That is, the responses are often undertaken for social, rather than biological, reasons, and therefore their impact on the disease outbreak may be secondary to other impacts (see also Dunn and Janes [1986] regarding "deliberate" versus "nondeliberate" health behaviors). Second, McGrath noted that there may be a conflict between the biological appropriateness of a response for individuals and for the group. For example, going away from a location that is experiencing an epidemic may be efficacious in terms of interrupting the chain of transmission, but may produce negative consequences for the group by removing key persons within that social group. Finally, she noted that although social responses can serve to alleviate a disease outbreak, outbreaks can end for biological reasons (such as the rapid depletion of susceptible individuals).

McGrath (1991) identified a continuum of responses to disease throughout history, ranging from responses that are part of the existing repertoire through increasingly disruptive responses, such as flight and rejection of authority systems. As the disease and the responses continue, social group function may be severely disrupted, leading to social disintegration, with a subsequent increase in the negative biological impact. The greater the extent to which the social group can maintain normal social function, the more likely that the impact of the epidemic will be mitigated.

McGrath (1992) applied this model of social disruption to the HIV epidemic. She identified several responses to AIDS, including scapegoating (resulting in ostracism, stigma, and blame), resignation to the situation, use of alternative therapies, political mobilization, and conducting research. She argues that the bioappropriateness of responses to the AIDS epidemic can be evaluated according to whether they achieve one of the four ways of halting disease transmission. She calls for field-based tests combining epidemiologic and ethnographic research to assess the degree to which responses to AIDS are mitigating the epidemic.

McGrath's model was proposed as a means to understand the bioappropriateness of interventions for a single disease. Our use of McGrath's model differs in that we are comparing social responses to one disease (HIV/AIDS) in view of the bioappropriateness of the response for prevention of a second disease (syphilis). By doing so, we are able to examine sexual risk in a broader context of STD prevention.

Social Responses to HIV/AIDS

Gay men have enacted a number of strategies in response to the challenges of the HIV/AIDS pandemic. Some behaviors reported by our respondents serve to reduce their risk for syphilis, while other strategies may have no effect on syphilis transmission risk. For example, a number of men talked about limiting their sex partners to those with an HIV status concordant to their own. Though some may acknowledge the possibility of infection by additional strains of HIV when sexual partners are HIV positive, men report a general relaxation in the use of condoms when they are having sex with other men who share their HIV status. In addition, MSM often report having multiple or serial sexual partners. Regardless of whether a partner's HIV status is known, MSM generally report that there is no use of protective barriers, such as unlubricated or flavored condoms, for oral sex.

Thus, when syphilis is introduced in MSM populations, the same strategies that might have limited HIV transmission serve to spread syphilis. In other words, oral sex poses a relatively small risk for transmitting HIV (clearly much less than anal sex), but it can easily serve to transmit syphilis. HIV seroconcordancy of sexual partners eliminates the risk for initial HIV infections but does nothing to reduce transmissibility of syphilis. In terms of McGrath's criteria for bioappropriateness of social response, the former responses to the HIV pandemic have not eliminated the source of syphilis, eliminated contact with the source of infection, decreased syphilis infectivity, or decreased syphilis susceptibility in those who are uninfected. Importantly, the presence of syphilis may serve to increase HIV infectivity when men of discordant or unknown HIV status have sex, thus bringing greater complexity to determining the bioappropriateness of these behaviors for HIV prevention.

Implications

Syphilis among gay men is a looming threat to gay communities and may be an indicator of increasing syphilis rates in the general population. Fichtner and colleagues (1983) have noted that an increase in syphilis morbidity for gay men historically heralded syphilis epidemics within the general population during the 1960s and 1970s. Reasons for this are not clearly understood, but consideration of this would warrant caution in a tightly focused response targeting only syphilis reduction and only gay men. In view of limited resources, there exists a temptation to devote all resources available to the increasing rate of syphilis among gay men. Other local populations at risk for syphilis such as homeless persons, migrant and seasonal farmworkers, or drug users should be evaluated to identify increases in syphilis early and provide intervention as needed.

Recommendations made as part of the RAP highlight attention to a range of short-term to long-term concerns. This broad range of recommendations is chosen to increase the sustainability of syphilis case reduction with the idea that immediate actions might help to control the current situation. But if longer term issues identified in RAP (that is, risky sexual behavior, poor health-care utilization, social stress, stigma, isolation, and community fragmentation) are not addressed, the environment remains ripe for additional outbreaks.

A second concern is that increases in syphilis may also indicate a need to address broader concerns of gay men's health in general. Assessments in Los Angeles, greater Fort Lauderdale, Seattle, and Philadelphia have all shown that depression, substance abuse (particularly methamphetamine), and other health and social concerns are closely tied to risky sexual behavior, and in some instances directly with increased rates of syphilis. The recent attention paid to this at the Gay Men's Summit meetings over the past several years provides a forum for such a discussion.[8] One county health department collaborated with a community organization to initiate a gay men's health clinic in the neighborhood that serves as a center for local gay men and lesbians, with a number of gay-owned retail and entertainment businesses. The initial response to this clinic has been very positive.

Finally, analysis of these responses indicates a need for continued scientific efforts to identify, evaluate, and, as necessary, intervene in social responses to the HIV/AIDS pandemic. By understanding the nature of risk behaviors such as escapism, isolation, blame, and accusation as responses to social stressors, STD prevention interventions can be more appropriately developed, sustained, and modified over time. More specifically, McGrath's (1991) model of categorization can be applied to sexual risk and protective behaviors based on the bioappropriateness of these behaviors for STD prevention. This clear and concise framework serves to expose which existing health behaviors facilitate prevention and which are ineffective or even serve to paradoxically fuel STD transmission.

Notes

1. Highly active anti-retroviral therapy (HAART) and combination therapies.

2. Also called dedicated HIV clinics, where services are restricted to providing HIV/AIDS care.

3. Referring to intentional unprotected anal sex; sometimes used to describe unprotected sex with a partner of unknown HIV status, or unprotected sex between HIV serodiscordant men.

4. Gay men receiving treatment for HIV or aware of existing HIV infection prior to their infection with syphilis were a significant component—40 to 70 percent—of syphilis cases in these urban areas with increased gay men's syphilis rates.

5. STD testing is confidential, and privacy rights are protected as they would be in any health-care setting. However, some STDs (particularly syphilis) require public health efforts of partner notification. This requirement is based on sound epidemiologic science relating to biological aspects of the disease, including the ease of transmission and

severity of sequelae. During partner notification, contact information of sexual partners is elicited from the infected person, and partners are notified, often in person, in an effort to bring them in for treatment. At no time is the name of the index case disclosed. While some states require partner notification for HIV, others do not, basing the latter policy on protection of the anonymity of the infected person. The emphasis on anonymity is based upon historical discrimination and stigmatization of persons infected with HIV. At one time, this anonymity was the norm in public health, and many HIV/AIDS service organizations (and other individuals and groups) continue to remain supportive of anonymity. This divergence in the emphasis of public health versus individual privacy and anonymous testing remains a fundamental difference between STD prevention in public health and community- and public health–based HIV prevention.

6. The term "gay community" is often used to describe the population of gay-identified (and sometimes other) men in a particular geographic area regardless of whether there is an actual community, multiple gay communities, friendship networks, geographic districts of gay-oriented venues, or other combinations of these or related groups of people.

7. Also called categorical STD clinics whose services are restricted to providing STD care.

8. As of January 2005, there have been four Gay Men's Health Summit meetings, consisting of plenary speakers, workshops, and breakout sessions. The summits have addressed a wide range of health concerns for gay men, including HIV/AIDS and STDs, substance use, nutrition, mental health, spirituality, homophobia, physical fitness, and political activism.

References

Albee, G. W. 1984. Prologue: A model for classifying prevention programs. In *Readings in Primary Prevention of Psychopathology*, ed. J. M. Joffe, G. W. Albee, and L. D. Kelly, ix–xviii. Hanover, N.H.: University Press of New England.

Altman, D. 1987. *AIDS in the Mind of America*. Garden City, N.Y.: Anchor.

Bernard, R. 1988. *Research Methods in Cultural Anthropology*. Newbury Park, Calif.: Sage.

Bernstein, S. 2001. Anti-syphilis campaign has impact, but worries remain. *Los Angeles Times*, January 19.

Berube, A. 1988. Caught in the storm: AIDS and the meaning of social disaster. *Out/Look* 1: 8–19.

Bloom, F. R. 1998. Searching for meaning in everyday life: Negotiating selves in the HIV spectrum. *Ethos: Journal of the Society for Psychological Anthropology* 25(4): 454–79.

Centers for Disease Control and Prevention (CDC). 1999. Resurgent bacterial sexually transmitted disease among men who have sex with men—King County, Washington, 1997–1999. *MMWR* 48: 773–77.

———. 2000. Outbreak of syphilis among men who have sex with men—Southern California, 2000. *MMWR* 50: 117–20.

———. 2001. Provisional cases of selected notifiable disease, United States, weeks ending August 17, 2002, and August 18, 2001. *MMWR* 51: 746–54.

———. 2002. Primary and secondary syphilis among men who have sex with men—New York City, 2001. *MMWR* 51: 853–56.

———. 2003. Primary and secondary syphilis—United States, 2002. *MMWR* 52: 1117–120.

Chen, J. L., D. Kodagoda, A. M. Lawrence, and P. R. Kerndt. 2002. Rapid public health interventions in response to an outbreak of syphilis in Los Angeles. *Sexually Transmitted Diseases* 29(5): 277–84.

Ciesielski, C., and H. Beidinger. 2000. Emergency of primary and secondary syphilis among men who have sex with men in Chicago and relationship to HIV infection. Paper presented at the Seventh Conference on Retroviruses and Opportunistic Infections, Chicago, February 2.

Cohen, D., S. Spear, R. Scribner, P. Kissinger, K. Mason, and J. Wilden. 2000. "Broken Windows" and the risk of gonorrhea. *American Journal of Public Health* 90(2): 230–36.

Crocker, J., and B. Major. 1989. Social stigma and self-esteem: Self-protective properties of stigma. *Psychological Review* 96: 608–30.

Cruikshank, M. 1992. *The Gay and Lesbian Liberation Movement*. New York: Routledge.

D'Emilio, J. 1983. *Sexual Politics, Sexual Communities: The Making of the Homosexual Minority in the United States, 1940–1970*. Chicago: University of Chicago Press.

Dunn, F. L., and C. R. Janes. 1986. Introduction: Medical anthropology and epidemiology. In *Anthropology and Epidemiology*, ed. C. R. Janes, R. Stall, and S. M. Gifford, 3–34. Boston: D. Reidel.

Farmer, P. 1992. *AIDS and Accusation: Haiti and the Geography of Blame*. Berkeley: University of California Press.

Fichtner, R. R., S. O. Aral, J. H. Blount, A. A. Zaidi, G. H. Reynolds, and W. W. Darrow. 1983. Syphilis in the United States: 1967–1979. *Sexually Transmitted Diseases* 10(2): 77–80.

Gagnon, J. H., and P. M. Nardi. 1997. Introduction. In *Changing Times: Gay Men and Lesbians Encounter HIV/AIDS*, ed. M. P. Levine, P. M. Nardi, and J. H. Gagnon, 1–19. Chicago: University of Chicago Press.

Gorman, M. 1992. The pursuit of the wish: An anthropological perspective and gay male subculture in Los Angeles. In *Gay Culture in America: Essays from the Field*, ed. G. Herdt, 87–146. Boston: Beacon Press.

Herdt, G., and A. Boxer. 1992. Introduction: Culture, history, and life course of gay men. In *Gay Culture in America: Essays from the Field*, ed. G. Herdt, 1–28. Boston: Beacon Press.

Kahn, R. H., J. D. Heffelfinger, and S. M. Berman. 2002. Syphilis outbreaks among men who have sex with men: A public health trend of concern. *Sexually Transmitted Diseases* 29: 285–87.

Kramer, L. 1989. *Reports from the Holocaust: The Making of AIDS Activism*. New York: St. Martin's.

Lang, N. 1991. Stigma, self-esteem, and depression: Psycho-social responses to risk of AIDS. *Human Organization* 4(2): 228–30.

Laumann, E. O., J. H. Gagnon, R. T. Michael, and S. Michaels. 1994. *The Social Organization of Sexuality: Sexual Practices in the United States.* Chicago: University of Chicago Press.

Levine, M. P. 1992. The life and death of gay clones. In *Gay Culture in America: Essays from the Field,* ed. G. Herdt, 68–86. Boston: Beacon Press.

———. 1998. *Gay Macho: The Life and Death of the Homosexual Clone.* New York: New York University Press.

Martin, J., and L. Dean. 1993. Effects of AIDS-related bereavement and HIV-related illness on psychological distress among gay men: A 7-year longitudinal study, 1985–1991. *Journal of Consulting and Clinical Psychology* 61(1): 94–103.

Martin, J., L. Dean, M. Garcia, and W. Hall. 1989. The impact of AIDS on a gay community: Changes in sexual behavior, substance use, and mental health. *American Journal of Community Psychology* 17(3): 269–93.

McGrath, J. E. 1970. *Social and Psychological Factors in Stress.* New York: Holt.

McGrath, J. W. 1991. Biological impact of social disruption resulting from epidemic disease. *American Journal of Physical Anthropology* 84: 407–19.

———. 1992. The biological impact of social responses to the AIDS epidemic. *Medical Anthropology* 15: 63–79.

Meyer, I. 2003. Prejudice, social stress, and mental health in lesbian, gay, and bisexual populations: Conceptual issues and research evidence. *Psychological Bulletin* 129: 674–97.

Molitor, F., S. R. Truax, J. D. Ruiz, and R. K. Sun. 1998. Association of methamphetamine use during sex with risky sexual behaviors and HIV infection among non-injection drug users. *Western Journal of Medicine* 168: 93–97.

Morris, J. F., C. R. Waldo, and E. D. Rothbloom. 2001. A model of predictors and outcomes of outness among lesbian and bisexual women. *Journal of Orthopsychiatry* 71: 61–71.

National Institute on Drug Abuse (NIDA). 2001. *Hallucinogens and Dissociative Drugs: Including LSD, PCP, Ketamine, Dextromethorphan.* Research Report Series. National Institutes of Health (NIH) Pub. No. 01-4209.

———. 2002. *Methamphetamine Abuse and Addiction.* Research Report Series. National Institutes of Health (NIH) Pub. No. 02-4210.

———. 2006a. MDMA (Ecstasy). *NIDA InfoFacts.* February. Rockville, Md.: National Institutes of Health.

———. 2006b. Rohypnol and GHB. *NIDA InfoFacts.* June. Rockville, Md.: National Institutes of Health.

National Research Council. 1993. *The Social Impact of AIDS in the United States.* Washington, D.C.: National Academy.

Newton, E. 1993. *Cherry Grove, Fire Island: Sixty Years in America's First Gay and Lesbian Town.* Boston: Beacon Press.

Odets, W. 1995. *In the Shadow of the Epidemic: Being HIV-Negative in the Age of AIDS.* Chapel Hill, N.C.: Duke University Press.

Paul, J. P., R. Stall, and F. Davis. 1993. Sexual risk for HIV transmission among gay and bisexual men in substance abuse treatment. *AIDS Education and Prevention* 5: 1–24.

Pearlin, L. I. 1989. The sociological study of stress. *Journal of Health and Social Behavior* 30: 241–56.

Perry, M., and F. R. Bloom. 1998. Perceptions of pesticide associated cancer risks among farmers: A qualitative assessment. *Human Organization* 57(3): 342–49.

Peterson, J. L., L. Folkman, and R. Bakeman. 1996. Stress, coping, HIV status, psychosocial resources and depressive mood in African American, gay, bisexual and heterosexual men. *American Journal of Community Psychology* 24: 461–87.

Rubin, G. 1997. Elegy for the Valley of Kings: AIDS and the leather community in San Francisco, 1981–1996. In *Changing Times: Gay Men and Lesbians Encounter HIV/ AIDS*, ed. M. P. Levine, P. M. Nardi, and J. J. Gagnon, 101–44. Chicago: University of Chicago Press.

St. Lawrence J. S., D. E. Montano, D. Kasprzyk, W. R. Phillips, K. Armstrong, and J. S. Leichliter. 2002. STD screening, testing, case reporting, clinical and partner notification practices: A national survey of U.S. physicians. *American Journal of Public Health* 92: 1784–788.

Savage, Dan. 2002. I'm complacent, you're complacent. http://www.thestranger.com 12(1), accessed September 19, 2002.

Scrimshaw, S. C. M., M. Carballo, M. Carael, L. Ramos, and R. G. Parker. 1991. *HIV/ AIDS Rapid Assessment Procedures: Rapid Anthropological Approaches for Studying AIDS Related Beliefs, Attitudes, and Behaviours*. Cambridge, Mass.: Harvard Center for Population Studies.

Semple, S. J., T. L. Patterson, and I. Grant. 2002. Motivations associated with methamphetamine use among HIV+ men who have sex with men. *Journal of Substance Abuse Treatment* 22: 149–56.

Strathdee, S. A., N. Galai, M. Safaiean, D. D. Celentano, D. Vlahov, L. Johnson, and K. E. Nelson. 2001. Sex differences in risk factors for HIV seroconversion among injection drug users: A 10-year perspective. *Archives of Internal Medicine* 161: 1281–288.

Strathdee, S. A., and S. G. Sherman. 2003. The role of sexual transmission of HIV infection among injection and non-injection drug users. *Journal of Urban Health* 80(4): 7–14.

Thoits, P. 1985. Self-labeling processes in mental illness: The role of emotional illness. *American Journal of Sociology* 91: 221–49.

Wallace, R. 1988. A synergism of plagues: "Planned shrinkage," contagious housing destruction, and AIDS in the Bronx. *Environmental Research* 47: 1–33.

Weiss, R. 1989. Uncertainty and the lives of persons with AIDS. *Journal of Health and Social Behavior* 30: 270–81.

Whittier, D. K., J. S. St. Lawrence, and S. Seeley. 2005. Sexual risk behavior of men who have sex with men: Comparison of behavior at home and at a gay resort. *Archives of Sexual Behavior* 34(1): 95–102.

3

Treatment, Adherence, and Self-Preservation

LAURA D. STANLEY

Imperfect adherence to using HIV medications can decrease treatment efficacy and limit treatment options. Given the well-known importance of adherence in slowing viral replication and disease progression, many HIV care and treatment professionals are understandably frustrated when their patients do not properly adhere, take "drug holidays," or refuse treatment altogether. Since the consequences of noncompliance are regarded as incompatible with self-preservation, health-care professionals typically conclude that persons unable or unwilling to adhere to their treatment are in denial about their illness, have addiction issues, or are self-destructive. However, clinical assumptions that link poor adherence with ignorance, denial, or self-destructive tendencies overlook the psychosocial costs of adherence. My ethnographic research with twenty HIV-positive gay men in San Diego, California (1997–1999), considers several psychosocial costs of adherence and concludes that, paradoxically, decisions to selectively adhere or reject medications altogether are often motivated by a desire for self-preservation. Indeed, many of these HIV-positive men consider conventional HIV therapies "disempowering" and a greater threat to their long-term survival than the disease itself.

This chapter focuses on the experiences of HIV-positive gay men because research demonstrates that men are less likely to adhere to treatment than are women (Roca et al. 2000), and all of the persons living with HIV/AIDS (PLWHAs) in my sample who selectively adhered or refused conventional HIV treatment altogether were gay men. Sixteen of the twenty men had started combination therapy; four had decided not to take any medications. Of the sixteen taking medications, nine men admitted to intentionally skipping doses.

The men who were most careful about adherence had all suffered a serious AIDS-related complication. Having almost died, these men had a more immediate understanding about how adherence supports long-term survival than did PLWHAs who began treatment while feeling well. Research exploring the relationship between disease severity and adherence also concludes that PLWHAs who have not yet suffered any serious AIDS-related complications believe they have more treatment options and a greater sense of control over their health than PLWHAs who have almost died (Gao et al. 2000). In this chapter, I focus on this former group of HIV-positive men as I discuss how they experience the psychosocial costs of treatment and why they would deliberately choose adherence strategies most would consider maladaptive. In particular, I discuss two psychosocial reasons why PLWHAs would choose to risk long-term survival by intentionally skipping doses or rejecting medications altogether:

1. The ritualized practices associated with the culture of HIV care and treatment challenge the American norm of the autonomous self. Most particularly, the daily medication regimens and quarterly rituals measuring T cell and viral load counts can transform one from an "agent" into a "patient." These routines usurp an otherwise autonomous existence and impose an "illness-centered" or "HIV-centric" identity. Moreover, if treatment is offered before one feels ill, the strict regimens of combination therapy exaggerate seropositivity as the most salient aspect of one's self. For the men in my study, the potential benefits promised to those who perfectly adhere are not commensurate with the anticipated costs.

2. PLWHAs also reject potentially life-saving medications because they regard the medical establishment as "disempowering." Consequently, they choose not to take anti-retroviral medications in order to remain "empowered." Critically, these men hold self-empowerment as key to their long-term survival. My research also suggests that PLWHAs who reject conventional medicine on these grounds often grew up in families and faiths critical of their same-sex sexuality. PLWHAs who characterize their early familial and religious experiences with family and religion as "authoritarian," "demoralizing," and "disempowering" may also regard other social institutions similarly. Therefore, these men often turn to alternative healing forms such as prayer, meditation, and/or New Age metaphysical strategies to treat their HIV disease *and* to preserve their "endangered" self—the self that HIV status and its accompanying illness identity often fragments and obscures (Green and Sobo 2000). The remainder of this chapter illustrates how these two psy-

chosocial costs—dependency and disempowerment—can influence individual treatment decisions and adherence behaviors.

Compromised Identities: Autonomy, HIV, and the Sick Role

Anthropologists have argued that the notion of a distinct and bounded Western self that is autonomous and self-directed is oversimplified and exaggerated (Hollan 1990; Lutz 1987; Shweder and Bourne 1984). Still, the values associated with this model of self—independence, autonomy, and self-reliance—are valorized in American culture and assumed synonymous with male identity. The idealized "American" representation of self thus supplies the experiential self with a compelling cultural model for self-actualization (Geertz 1973). As such, a "naturalized" relationship exists between the virtues of autonomy, self-reliance, and risk. As I illustrate, PLWHAs who risk their long-term survival by rejecting medications often do so to preserve their endangered, if idealized, sense of self.

American society generally devalues social dependency and applauds self-sufficiency (Bellah et al. 1985). HIV disease suggests an illness identity for PLWHAs that conflicts with this idealized "American" self. And while any chronic illness can threaten these aspects of self, HIV is unique for several reasons. First, unlike cancer or heart disease treatments, HIV treatment success depends upon strict and lifelong adherence to often complex medication regimens; missing doses diminishes treatment efficacy and limits remaining options. PLWHAs also take an average of eight to sixteen pills per day [editor's note: at the time of this writing in late 2003]—some of which must be taken with food, others on an empty stomach. Additionally, some medications must be refrigerated, while others must be taken at precise intervals but not in combination with others. In short, perfect adherence favors the well-organized personality.

The side effects that can accompany treatment,[1] the bureaucratic entanglements (meetings with case workers and social service agencies), and the seemingly endless medical procedures (drawing blood, phenotyping, and genotyping) also limit autonomy and reinforce the notion that one is "sick." This illness identity can be especially demoralizing to one who does not yet feel ill. Furthermore, PLWHAs cannot stop their medications once their viral load is undetectable. Hence, PLWHAs are always labeled "ill" regardless of how they feel or what their outcome measures reveal. Thus, adhering to combination therapy invites PLWHAs to indefinitely assume an illness identity. Adherence, then, means more than just regularly taking one's pills; it also means eliminating denial as a psychological option. PLWHAs who begin combination therapy no longer dwell in a liminal position between secular and medical worlds. Taking these medications transports them across a symbolic threshold where adherence ritually confirms their status as PLWHAs and reinforces a complex and unique illness identity. For example, many PLWHAs I interviewed thought that the rituals associated with adherence reduce HIV-positive persons to physiological measurements of their immunity. That is, PLWHAs with "good numbers" are assumed to be "compliant," while "poor numbers" suggest that they have "failed." The problem is that PLWHAs also come to view themselves in similar terms and become dependent upon their latest lab reports to confer identities of health or illness.

Additionally, newly acquired disability and unemployment statuses may further compromise one's sense of autonomy and self-sufficiency. Because medication costs are often prohibitive,[2] PLWHAs lacking private health insurance must accept state or federal disability status in order to manage their illness and pay for medications. Indeed, doctors or caseworkers may actually encourage their HIV-positive patients to quit work to minimize immune-suppressing stressors from their lives. However, many PLWHAs feel discredited by this label and regard disability as yet another source of stigma, while unemployment can further erode self-esteem.

"Blake," for example, quit his job in order to manage his illness in 1989, soon after he was diagnosed with HIV. Although he initially benefited from his new status, Blake later felt it was demeaning:

> When I was on disability I could stay home all day and just take care of myself. But, after awhile, I felt really useless. Even though I was really sick sometimes, I also know that part of it was an excuse. As long as I was sick, I didn't have to plan for a future. Crazy as it sounds, planning on dying is a lot easier than planning on living.

Health-care professionals have also observed that PLWHAs on extended disability frequently invest in the sick role to the detriment of other, more vital aspects of self. And, as Blake suggests in the passage above, casting off the sick role can be quite difficult. Blake has become habituated to a life that revolves around doctors' appointments, medications, illnesses, and social services. Consequently, "HIV disease" has become Blake's primary point of self-reference: "HIV is who I am. I don't know who I am anymore without it." No longer just a facet of identity, HIV has become his identity. Having lost his sense of self-reliance, Blake retrospectively wonders if remaining part of the workforce might have been better for his long-term health than allowing himself to become "disabled."

However, many PLWHAs find it very difficult to resist the illness identity that HIV care and treatment can introduce. On the one hand, taking medications reinforces the notion that one is ill; on the other hand, rejecting medications can compromise long-term survival and incur community disapproval. Moreover, because American norms of individuality valorize autonomy—and sickness subverts it—underlying cultural expectations suggest that any real person deserving of respect should be striving to regain his or her autonomy or "nonsick" status.

Talcott Parsons's discussion of the "sick role" (1951) helps illustrate this point. Parson asserts that if ill persons are to retain their social status, they must seek the help of the socially identified authority and put themselves under that authority's care to demonstrate their desire to get well. And therein lies the paradox: our American norm of autonomous personality requires those who are sick to give up their autonomy; otherwise they are not worthy of respect. American culture understands and tolerates illness as long as the patient is doing everything in his or her power to heal—as dictated by the dominant standard of care. According to this analysis, PLWHAs who reject conventional treatment are also rejecting the dominant value system of those caregivers who seek their restoration to health. In other words, these PLWHAs are choosing maladaptive ways of being sick, and those who explicitly make this choice run the risk of losing community approval. Consequently, individuals for whom the psychosocial costs of adherence are too burdensome have a strong incentive to resolve this paradox.

Preserving Autonomy

Some PLWHAs resolve this dilemma of needing to be both cooperative yet autonomous ostensibly by buying into the medical establishment's dominant value system while simultaneously recovering their independence by subverting it. "David's" perspective epitomizes this point. David was diagnosed with HIV shortly after he seroconverted in 1996. Although he did not feel ill, his doctor advised him to start medications immediately before the virus had an opportunity to multiply. David complied with his doctor's recommendation but was soon nauseous and exhausted:

> I truly believe that if I didn't have to take them my life would be perfectly normal, and I'd be perfectly healthy and happy right now. It would be the same as before when I was negative. It's strictly the medications that have screwed everything up. I wouldn't be tired. I could travel anywhere. The meds are an inconvenience. So, I've cut back on them—only my doctor doesn't know. It's a big secret.

By secretly altering the ritual his doctor has prescribed, David subverts the traditionally patriarchal doctor-patient relationship while maintaining the illusion of compliance. He also resists the power of the medications to ritually transform him into a "patient." In short, David asserts a sense of control over his life by keeping his adherence decisions a "big secret" from his doctor.

However, David also accepts the personal risk that his decision to selectively adhere incurs. He is aware of the link between poor adherence and drug resistance (and thus a more rapid progression from HIV to AIDS), yet chooses to downplay this risk. David explains that the quality of his life is more important than the quantity of his life; thus, for David, following his "gut feeling" is the right thing to do:

> Most people worship the ground that doctors walk on and take whatever they say as the word of God. I know [my doctor] is a lot more knowledgeable about pharmaceuticals than I am, but if the meds are really interfering with my everyday existence then I am going to try and figure something out. My gut feeling is that I'll be fine and everything will be OK. If not, maybe I'll die a little sooner, but I want to make the final decision. *I'll do it my way, and that's important* [emphasis added].

David's desire for self-sufficiency clearly trumps the prolonged life that proper adherence promises:

> Not taking these medications, this is what I choose to do, even knowing what the possible consequences are. It's a chance I'm going to take. That is my whole outlook on life. That's also the way I was thinking when I was out having unsafe sex before I became positive. No matter what I do in life there will be pros and cons.

In other words, David's sense of self is inextricably linked to risk and autonomy, as is true for many American men. Conversely, he and others like him see dependence and compliance as infantilizing. For David, then, noncompliance is about self-preservation. Complete adherence interferes with his quality of life, and, for him, a prolonged life of diminished quality is too high a cost.

Another way that PLWHAs subvert their system dependence is by seeing a general practitioner rather than an HIV specialist for non-HIV-related illnesses. "Victor," for example, is a thirty-eight-year-old dancer who has been HIV positive for eight years. He has never had an AIDS-defining illness and continues to work. Although he takes his medications, Victor decided to cut his daily dose in half and take only his evening medications. His regimen, he explains, makes him feel sick while he otherwise feels fine. Further, because he is healthy, Victor avoids going to his HIV specialist for what he considers trivial maladies:

> If I have a bad cold or flu, I go to a regular physician rather than my [HIV] specialist and I never mention that I have HIV. As soon as you do, they stop looking at you like a normal person and see you as a walking virus, and start interpreting every cough and sneeze as HIV-related, and it's not. I just hate that. I am not a virus.

Victor thus resolves the dilemma that treatment presents for him by selectively adhering and seeing an HIV specialist only for what he believes are HIV-related issues. In this way, Victor minimizes the centrality of his HIV infection and regains his agency.

"Robert" also rejects the sick role. Robert explains that, whenever possible, he very conscientiously avoids the culture of HIV care and treatment in order to keep a "sick" and "victimized" identity at bay. Most emphatically, Robert rejects "the whole disability mentality"—a state of mind he considers self-destructive:

> I know people who've never had any HIV-related illnesses who quit work and immediately go on SSI when they [are diagnosed]. They get all this attention from special programs and services and want to stay in the role of victim. I've never been one to sit around and pity myself. If I quit work and sit at home collecting disability and doing nothing, I will die—*Robert will die* [emphasis added]. I don't need it or want it as an identity. And, I don't want any excuses for people taking care of me. I am in the living.

To preserve the self an HIV-centered identity threatens to destroy—the representation he self-consciously displays to the world as "Robert"—this man does not take anti-retrovirals. By avoiding the culture of HIV care and treatment, Robert thus rejects the illness identity it can introduce.

The experiences of these men provide insight into the link I am proposing between the decisions some PLWHAs make to imperfectly adhere or refuse HIV medications altogether and a desire to preserve the "autonomous self." For these men, the loss of autonomy, self-reliance, and, indeed, the subjective boundaries of personhood are too high a price to pay for the possibility of a few more years of life. Moreover, these are the values that, for many, make life worth living. For better *and* worse then, committing to medications and the health-care system through which they are administered reinforces an identity that conflicts with many PLWHAs' idealized sense of self.

Moreover, there is a contradiction inscribed in the norm of male autonomous identity and the treatment regimes prescribed by treatment professionals. American culture largely reifies the notion of self based upon self-directed activity—the ability to invent self and activity at will. Yet the medical profession insists upon a treatment regimen that imposes the harshest discipline upon these individuals. The result is cognitive dissonance. Individuals are torn between their desire for survival and their desire to survive in terms of the identities they have crafted for themselves. To submit to the medical profession's recommendations requires them to seemingly abandon this self-valued identity. Confronted by this dilemma, many individuals—like Robert—find the cost of a prolonged life too dear.

Opting Out

The life trajectory of gay men often requires confronting and rejecting moral authority. Indeed, their self-identity and life story are often self-consciously crafted as narratives of such rejection. Consequently, submitting to medical authority is a particular challenge for some gay men. Not only does it require them to abandon their painfully constructed notions of a self founded upon autonomy, but they are also precisely the people with the most cognitive resources to resist medical authority. As we shall see in this section, the techniques learned in their life histories help them reject medical authorities and posit their own medical universe. Indeed, this very rejection can even extend to the gay community's own norms.

For example, some PLWHAs avert an illness or HIV-centered identity by refusing to take HIV medications altogether. Rather than objecting to the illness identity that treatment and adherence can introduce per se, these PLWHAs object to what they characterize as the loss of control and dependence that, to them, intrinsically accompanies a foray into the world of conventional medicine. In short, they regard the institution of conventional medical as "disempowering." Instead, these PLWHAs believe that their positive thoughts and self-determined actions will best help them protect what Green and Sobo (2000) call the "endangered self"—the self HIV status often fragments and obscures—and nurture an "empowered self"—the self they hold as key to long-term survival. Moreover, these PLWHAs believe that resilience and self-empowerment are intimately linked. All described other PLWHAs who, they believed, died prematurely because they allowed themselves to become dependent upon their doctors' recommendations instead of their internal sources of strength. "Richard," who has been HIV positive since 1985, insists:

> The people who don't drop dead are just too damned mean. . . . These are the ones who are still in the game. Those who go down are the namby-pamby ones who say, "Well, the doctor told me I should do it, so I guess I should do it." The self-empowered ones do a lot better. You have to believe in yourself.

Accordingly, Richard frames surviving HIV disease as a product of mind over matter: "I think that the mind is far more powerful than Western medicine. I think you can actually set your head on a course . . . and manipulate your numbers in any direction you choose."

PLWHAs like Richard who reject conventional medications altogether consider biomedical approaches to treatment "disempowering" and believe that taking medications would undermine their chances of survival. Rather, they believe that the best way to promote resilience and survive HIV disease is by setting their own treatment course—much as they have set their own life course. Doing so, they hold, will preserve their "empowered" or idealized sense of self.

However, as previously stated, these men are not in denial about their disease, nor do they use self-destructive behaviors to cope with HIV. To the contrary, these men prioritize their health-care strategies and do so in ways consonant with their alternative understandings of self in relation to society. For instance, in lieu of conventional therapies, many of these men incorporate prayer, meditation, acupuncture, herbal regimens, and New Thought/New Age spiritual philosophies. Indeed, many of these men subscribed to the belief systems of ministers Marianne Williamson and Louise Hay. Both Williamson and Hay are New Thought/New Age ministers who have large gay followings, and almost all of the gay men I interviewed—regardless of their position on medications—had at least read Hay's (1987) book, *You Can Heal Your Life*, if not dabbled in Williamson's (1996b) *A Return to Love: Reflections on the Principles of a Course in Miracles*. In fact, every home I visited had a copy of at least one of these books in its library.

Both Hay's *You Can Heal Your Life* and Williamson's *A Return to Love* specifically frame HIV as a primarily spiritual rather than medical problem and emphasize the importance of self-empowerment in healing HIV infection. Both Hay and Williamson also locate the power to heal within the self and caution PLWHAs against getting caught up in the medical establishment's "hallucination of AIDS." For example, in the following excerpt from her *Principles of Healing* (1996a) lecture-on-tape series (specifically tailored toward people living with HIV/AIDS), Williamson asserts:

> All of the viruses and physical illnesses that we have, actually were hanging out in the mind for a long time before they were hanging out in our bodies. If we think that the virus did not come from our mind then we are missing the point entirely. It is the fact that we believed in this world so strongly to begin with that was the problem, so the answer is not going to come from believing in the virus. A cure for AIDS is not going to come about because of medicine, because medicine is of this world. If God didn't create the virus, then it doesn't really exist. It's just a hallucination. What you are here to be saved from is from your own negative thinking. Diseases come from the mind. We have to understand that we did make AIDS. The entire, loveless human consciousness made it up. How do we change this? The *Course in Miracles* says we simply change our minds.

In other words, Williamson suggests that PLWHAs are responsible both for their illness *and* their healing. Thus, she teaches, the power to heal cannot reside in the hands of powerful others, institutional authorities, or drug therapies but dwells only within the self.

"Jack's" story illustrates how one's decision to reject conventional HIV treatment can stem from a rejection of moral authority and a drive toward self-preservation. Jack, age forty-two, began following Williamson's spiritual philosophies after he was diagnosed with HIV in 1990. For the last several years, Jack has made monthly and sometimes weekly pilgrimages from San

Diego to Los Angeles to hear Williamson speak. Accordingly, he also rejects the widely accepted biomedical position that HIV causes AIDS and, leaning heavily on Williamson's philosophies, has decided against taking conventional HIV therapies.[3] Jack maintains:

> According to "The Course," when you are constantly judging and being judged, you experience constant guilt, blame, and shame, and that creates all kinds of diseases. HIV can be a very negative identity for people. It generates negative attention, and that negative attention further validates the system and serves to keep everyone in their roles [as victims]. Our job is to face our vulnerabilities, because that's where our power is.

I suggest that Jack's emphasis on self-empowerment stems from the feelings of helplessness that characterized most of his childhood. Growing up in an authoritarian Catholic home, Jack describes his mother as "physically and emotionally abusive" and his father as "abandoning and neglectful." Both his family and the Church, Jack recalls, made him feel "small, weak, worthless, and bad." Perhaps not coincidentally, Jack's characterization of the Judeo-Christian God is similar to his description of his parents:

> The Church I knew was frightening and guilt-provoking. God was a source of pain for me. I knew He was judgmental and disappointed in me. He was distant and nonresponsive. Fear, anger, blame, Hell, damnation . . . I always felt victimized by that deity.

Consequently, Jack left both home and the Church at age seventeen in search of a more spiritually nurturing path and more inclusive communities of support. He also began using recreational drugs with increasing frequency. Jack claims that he spent much of his adult life seeking to negate the idea that he is morally flawed and to overcome "feeling like a victim." In short, Jack seeks self-empowerment:

> Our culture is patriarchically determined. It has to be in control, and to stay in control and maintain power, it has to keep the victim in his role. My family kept me in that role, but I am not the victim. That's not my *true self* [emphasis added]. I am unlearning that false impression.

Thus, Jack scrupulously avoids subscribing to institutional belief systems that, like the Church and his family, portray him as weak, dependent, and "broken" or use fear to motivate his behavioral changes. Stigmatized and rejected by these mainstream institutions, Jack has spent a lifetime honing skills that allow him to cope with an outsider identity. Significantly, Jack's prior life experiences predispose him to maintain his agency at all costs.

Jack's prior life experiences with institutionalized prejudice and discrimination also predispose him to frame the doctor-patient relationship as disempowering and abusive because it fosters dependence, limits autonomy, and mirrors the dynamics most characteristic of his painful childhood:

> The first empowered decision I ever made in my life was to not take the medications. I told the doctor that I didn't want to fix what wasn't broken. He said, "But you are broken." I was livid! I was sick of that abusive mentality being projected onto me. I have a direct role in what happens to me.

Therefore, as victimization and institutional control go hand-in-hand, Jack must reject the latter if he is to avoid the former:

> I'm antiauthoritarian. I don't live my life in fear anymore. I am not going to buy into the whole negativity of the multibillion dollar AIDS industry. One needs to own their power. If I were to take medications it would be like saying, "Give me the answers! Control me!" All that negativity was polluting my system. By not taking the medications I am giving myself a chance to heal. I choose to live in the living, and not in the dying. This is my path, and it is extremely nurturing.

In order to preserve his "true" but endangered self, Jack refuses medications. Significantly, it is this "true" self that protects him from the "powerful others" who threaten his self-reliance and, indeed, his dignity.

Despite his stance against medications, Jack prioritizes his health care. He quit using drugs when he was diagnosed with HIV and for the first time in his life is attending college: "When I thought it was a death sentence, I didn't see the point. Now that I know that I am in control, I want to see how far I can go." In other words, this sense of self-empowerment inspires Jack to invest in his self-care. Going to college symbolizes and makes visible this changed perspective to both Jack and the world around him.

"Steven," age forty-five, also rejects conventional HIV therapies in order to remain "self-empowered." Steven, who follows the teachings of Louise Hay, believes that taking medications cultivates an "AIDS-consciousness," which, in turn, courts disempowerment. What Steven is also rejecting is the illness identity that can often accompany an HIV diagnosis. Steven believes that taking medications is tantamount to relinquishing one's sense of control or "giving up one's power." Critically, Steven also links disempowerment with giving up on life:

> What most disturbs me is when people become dependent on their doctor instead of going within to find the answers. You lose once you do that. I am more afraid of losing my freedom by taking medications and giving up my power to the medical world than I am of dying.

Because his life is framed in terms of freedom, Steven associates disempowerment with death and believes that living with HIV disease depends upon claiming and maintaining his power:

> People die from AIDS because they give up on themselves. They become apathetic and succumb to a victim's mentality. You have to have a direct role in what happens. One needs to own one's own power.

Steven's belief in an internalized sense of control directs his self-care. While he does not take HIV medications, Steven meditates on a daily basis, has given up recreational drug use, and drinks alcohol only moderately. He also quit his high-paying job as a graphic designer in order to pursue his creative passion—painting. By "listening to his heart," Steven manages his HIV disease on his own terms and thus maintains his autonomy.

"Paul," who has been living with HIV for more than fifteen years, is perhaps most representative of the attitude of those who reject medications:

> Protease-schmotease!! I'm comfortable with the choice I've made not to take medications. I have lived my life as long I have because I followed my own path. . . . I'll follow my own path to the end. This is where God has led me. I have no regrets even if I die tomorrow. It's an individual choice. You have to listen to that voice above all else.

Clearly for PLWHAs like Paul, a life worth living is defined in terms of autonomy and self-reliance. Indeed, according to this worldview, quantity of life is inextricably linked to life quality. Long-term resilience in the face of this disease then depends upon adhering to these values. Unsurprisingly, the treatment choices of PLWHAs follow from this predilection.

My research with these PLWHAs further suggests that a rejection of conventional medical authority is often linked to a general rejection of other authoritarian social institutions. In particular, all of the PLWHAs who refused anti-retrovirals on the grounds that taking medications is disempowering came from families and faiths that framed their sexual choices or orientations as "against God." These men grew up hearing that they would ultimately suffer because of their sexual orientation. Even though most of these men had long since extracted themselves from the Church (and their families) in search of more inclusive communities of support, the vestigial remains of their early religious beliefs and painful family experiences continued to inform their adult attitudes about religion and other mainstream social institutions. Thus, when diagnosed with HIV, these men tended to struggle with the notion that AIDS is a punishment from God for immorality. I suggest that these men were able to resolve the dissonance introduced by this cultural construction by rejecting the influence of powerful social institutions—in this case, medications and conventional HIV treatment—and asserting their self-reliance in this time of great psychological vulnerability. Moreover, their prior life experiences with institutionalized discrimination and stigmatization as gay men have shaped an outsider identity that stresses the importance of autonomy as an adaptive strategy for coping with adversity.

Refusing Treatment/Rejecting Authority

Gay men who grew up in families and faiths critical of their same-sex sexuality typically take one of two paths in order to resolve the moral conflict that same-sex sexuality initially presented for them. On the first path, they reject only the distressing particulars of these condemning belief systems—that is, same-sex sexuality is sinful and that they are morally flawed. However, because they did not challenge the moral authority of these frameworks as a whole, when they become ill, they tend to see HIV as a just consequence for their lifestyle. And regardless of sexual orientation, persons who internalize the notion that AIDS is a punishment from God frequently escalate self-destructive behaviors and/or refuse medical care because they do not believe that they deserve to get better. Men who take the second path, however, tend to view their childhood experiences as coextensive with moral authority per se, and thus reject the total authoritarian logic of these belief systems as well as the distressing particulars. Still, these men also continue to see authoritarian institutions as more harmful than helpful and authority figures as a source of psychological abuse, moral condemnation, and disappointment. They then take great pains to establish and maintain a sense of self separate from and independent of "powerful others."

In short, my research suggests that some PLWHAs reject institutional solutions in favor of self-empowerment paradigms and alternative healing strategies because they believe that the power to heal or delay the onset of AIDS does not—indeed, cannot—reside in the medical model but must reside within one's self. In this context, rejecting conventional treatment makes sense; taking medications requires one to trust and depend on the wisdom and benevolence of powerful others—in this case, HIV specialists and medical institutions. In order to preserve self, one must retain control over one's circumstances, and self-sufficiency must not be relinquished to those who, in the past, have abused this trust. In other words, these men trust the sociocultural logic of autonomous personality more than they trust the offerings of conventional medicine. They have long since concluded that trusting powerful others can compromise their long-term survival. Accordingly, these men are generally inclined to avoid traditional institutional settings—especially in times of high psychological vulnerability—and may reject conventional HIV treatments or even the entire theory that HIV causes AIDS.

As I have shown, these men equate a loss of autonomy with a loss of self. And, significantly, from their perspective, it is *this* loss—and not HIV—that precipitates death. Therefore, in order to understand why some PLWHAs defer or refuse potentially life-prolonging medications, we also must understand "the ways in which people use risk reflexively (either by avoidance or acceptance) to establish a sense of self. The links between risk and identity are fundamental to an understanding of risk behavior and each individual's risk behavior has to be set within the context of the constraints, restrictions and priorities related to who s/he is" (Green and Sobo 2000: 50).

The PLWHAs I have discussed here all make their decisions about treatment and adherence in the context of their individual constraints, restrictions, and priorities—and each asserts strong arguments for the treatment decisions he has made. Moreover, these PLWHAs have learned that authoritarian institutions and belief systems constitute dangerous social landscapes and are not to be trusted—especially when one's life is at stake.

Yet it is not just the medical community that constitutes a problematic authority for PLWHAs. The gay community also collectively functions, and can be perceived, as a similar authority by PLWHAs. For instance, the gay community explicitly rejects sociocultural constructions that link AIDS and immorality. However, many HIV-positive gay men harbor deep-rooted fears and anxieties concerning this link. Because the politics of AIDS discourages open dialogue about "AIDS as punishment" and frames such representations as a right-wing attack on gay sexuality, these men do not openly discuss their fears among peers. Indeed, the "ideal type" of gay man within this community is well educated and politically astute; he vehemently rejects such antigay rhetoric. To do otherwise is to risk being labeled a traitor to one's community.

However, when this community frames the link between AIDS and immorality as a hostile polemic rather than as a deeply rooted cultural proposition, it discourages gay men from directly confronting and constructively coping with their very real spiritual anxieties. In other words, talking about AIDS in any terms other than a value-neutral disease stripped of all metaphoric inference is to imply that one distinguishes between—and therefore has judgments about—"innocent victims" and "deserving deviants." "Paul," a gay HIV-positive political activist, articulates this dilemma:

> Most of us outwardly deny it, but we still carry the messages we learned as children around with us; that we are bad and abnormal. Many of us feel on some level that HIV is a punishment from God. Fear and hopelessness leads many of us to be self-destructive, especially those of us raised in strong damnation religious traditions. We avoid dealing with it because it scares us. Deep in our hearts, we are afraid that the right-wingers may be right.

Moreover, such internalized—and unexamined—homophobia can seriously impact treatment and adherence decisions. Men who experience guilt and self-blame after they are diagnosed often cultivate deep states of denial. Such denial can lead to self-destructive behaviors like substance abuse or poor self-care. Additionally, PLWHAs who have internalized these doubts often isolate themselves, suffer with depression or anxiety, and/or deny themselves medical treatment or social support.

Hence, while the morally neutral political AIDS discourses espoused by the gay community attack mainstream bigotry and challenge homophobia, they fail to address the very real spiritual fears internalized by many PLWHAs. For PLWHAs whose experiences predispose them to struggle with the link between AIDS and immorality, then, the existing institutional responses to AIDS may limit as much as they liberate. These gay men may then also turn away from the "moral authority" of the gay community at a time when they most need its resources.

Conclusion

The veiling of moral evaluation behind a "value-free professional context" and the general lack of consideration given to the patients' problems of meaning are directly relevant to the contemporary treatment of AIDS.

Dissatisfied with the inability of conventional medicine to address their most heartfelt concerns or consider their core spiritual values, many of the PLWHAs discussed in this chapter gravitated toward nonconventional, alternative treatment approaches that stressed mind-body integration and a connection to spiritual powers greater than themselves. They also strongly believed that personal empowerment was essential to controlling their disease progression.

Furthermore, these PLWHAs assigned a different meaning to health than did the medical profession. Rather than the eradication of HIV from their body (or a low viral load and a high T cell count), these PLWHAs often defined healing as a sense of "wholeness" or personal empowerment. In other words, healing was defined in terms of "quality of life." Because they think the medical establishment diminishes, belittles, or simply ignores the importance of their spiritual or existential beliefs, they have turned away from it. And for many PLWHAs, the death of the experiential and idealized sense of self is a much greater loss than mere physical demise. My research leads me to conclude that some "maladaptive" PLWHAs who reject medications, interrupt their treatment schedules, or "forget" doses value a more independent—if potentially abbreviated—existence over one that makes seropositivity the most salient aspect of self. For many PLWHAs, the very qualities that frame their identity—autonomy, spontaneity, and self-reliance—are compromised by submitting to medical discipline.

My research also reveals that PLWHAs consider what they stand to lose—not only what they may gain—when considering to adhere to or forgo combination therapies (see also Russell et al. 2003; Wright 2000). Hence, decisions about treatment and adherence are best understood in terms of individual motives, preferences, and limitations. While I do not advocate incomplete adherence, my research suggests that choices that honor one's sense of control, even when these choices are eticly (that is, from the outsider's or scientific view) defined as "bad," may support self-preservation on some level—especially in times of great uncertainty. As HIV directly challenges one's sense of control and self-reliance, behaviors and attitudes that promote meaning, connection, and commitment to life, even when not medically recommended, may have some positive therapeutic implications if they assuage anxiety, fear, and hopelessness and promote an active engagement with one's self-care.

Both the medical and the gay communities want to help PLWHAs. But the way that they market their services establishes them as authorities in a fashion that, ironically, undercuts their efforts. Consequently, we need more cultural analysis of the predicament of PLWHAs. As we have seen, many gay men often come to self-definition through their opposition to authority. If we truly want to help such PLWHAs, then we need to understand this particular antiauthoritarian life history. Not only is more research required to map the contours of this issue, but both the medical and gay communities must take this cultural landscape more seriously. For gay men, effectively treating AIDS is not just a technical problem but a profoundly cultural issue.

Notes

1. Common side effects include nausea, vomiting, rashes, explosive diarrhea, gastro-intestinal distress, fatigue, nightmares, peripheral neuropathy, and lipodystrophy.

2. In 1998, the annual cost of double combination therapies ranged from $4,836 to $9,276 (U.S. dollars) per person, while the annual cost of triple combination therapies ranged from $7,944 to $11,916 and up to $20,224 if Ritonavir is also added (Floyd and Gilks 1998).

3. A rejection popularized by microbiologist Peter Duesberg in the late 1980s and throughout the 1990s.

References

Bellah, Robert N., Richard Madsen, William M. Sullivan, Ann Swidler, and Steven M. Tipton. 1985. *Habits of the Heart: Individualism and Commitment in American Life.* New York: Harper and Row.

Floyd, Katherine, and Charles Gilks. 1998. Cost and financing aspects of providing anti-retroviral therapy: A background paper. Online conference paper hosted by the AIDS Economics Web Site: www.worldbank.org/aids-econ/arv/floyd/index.htm.

Gao, X., D. P. Nau, S. A. Rosenbluth, V. Scott, and C. Woodward. 2000. The relationship of disease severity, health beliefs and medication adherence among HIV patients. *AIDS Care* 12(4): 387–98.

Geertz, Clifford. 1973. *The Interpretation of Cultures.* New York: Basic Books.

Green, Gil, and Elisa Sobo. 2000. *The Endangered Self: Managing the Social Risks of HIV.* London: Routledge.

Hay, Louise. 1987. *You Can Heal Your Life.* Santa Monica, Calif.: Hay House.

Hollan, Douglas. 1990. Cross-cultural differences in the self. *Journal of Anthropological Research* 48(4): 283–300.

Lutz, Catherine. 1987. Goals, events, and understandings in Ifaluk emotion theory. In *Cultural Models in Language and Thought*, ed. D. Holland and N. Quinn, 290–312. Cambridge: Cambridge University Press.

Parsons, Talcott. 1951. *The Social System.* New York: Free Press.

Roca, B., C. J. Gomez, and A. Arnedo. 2000. Adherence, side effects and efficacy of stavudine plus lamivudine plus nelfanavir in treatment-experienced HIV-infected patients. *Journal of Infection* 41: 50–54.

Russell, C. K., S. M. Bunting, M. Graney, M. T. Hartig, P. Kisner, and B. Brown. 2003. Factors that influence the medication decision making of persons with HIV/AIDS: A taxonomic exploration. *Journal of the Association of Nurses in AIDS Care* 14(4): 46–60.

Shweder, Richard, and E. J. Bourne. 1984. Does the concept of person vary cross-culturally? In *Culture Theory: Essays on Mind, Self, and Emotion*, ed. R. Shweder and R. A. LeVine, 158-199. Cambridge: Cambridge University Press.

Williamson, Marianne. 1996a. *Principles of Healing*. Taped Lecture Series. Santa Monica, Calif.: Hay House.

———. 1996b. *Return to Love: Reflections on the Principles of a Course in Miracles*. New York: Harper Collins.

Wright, M. T. 2000. The old problem of adherence: Research in treatment adherence and its relevance for HIV/AIDS. *AIDS Care* 12(6): 703–10.

4

Gay Men, Language, and AIDS

WILLIAM L. LEAP AND SAMUEL COLÓN

A definition of language is always, implicitly or explicitly,
a definition of human beings in the world.

Raymond Williams, 1977

People are still having sex, lust keeps on lurking
Nothing makes them stop, this AIDS thing's not working

—LaTour, 1991

Studies of AIDS, culture, and gay men have not paid much attention to how gay men talk about AIDS, nor have they given much priority to language-centered research when trying to document the effects of the AIDS pandemic on gay men's lives.[1] Granted, Caron (2001), Farmer (1990), Patton (1991), Sontag (1988), Treichler (1988), and others have shown how discussions of AIDS are always embedded within broader assumptions about marginality, risk, fear, and blame. Gay men's discussions of the pandemic have, at times, been referenced in these works. And Adam et al. (2000), Koblin et al. (2003), Mansur and Palmer-Vanton (2001), Vinke and Bolton (1997), Vinke et al. (1992), Zia et al. (2003), and others have shown how gay men's responses during interviews and on questionnaires provide insights into their knowledge, attitudes, and practices (KAP) about AIDS. All of these studies are concerned with language in specific ways, yet their primary interests still lie outside of the linguistic terrain—in the first group, with the nonneutral meanings assigned to AIDS in the light of those assumptions; in the second group, with the details of AIDS-related KAP. For this reason, what gay men have to say about AIDS may be cited as anecdotal evidence supporting a project's research claims. But how gay men talk about AIDS and the significance of those linguistic practices remain unidentified and unexplored.

This chapter argues that these omissions are problematic when viewed in terms of the basic tenants of anthropological linguistic theory and in terms of the questions about AIDS and gay experience that research has yet to answer. Indeed, the nonneutral meanings associated with AIDS are deeply embedded within conversation and storytelling, asking questions, argumentation and debate, and verbal and nonverbal negotiation of sexual opportunity and sexual risk, and through other forms of social experience thoroughly embedded in linguistic practice. And gay men's AIDS-related KAP are also closely tied to the workings of similar discursive practices and to their outcomes.

Rather than using gay men's remarks about AIDS simply as a source of supportive anecdote, this chapter argues in favor of a more tightly focused use of linguistic data in studies of AIDS and gay experience. After outlining assumptions about text analysis (the approach to linguistic research on which this discussion is based), the chapter describes how several studies have used gay men's talk about AIDS to support their arguments and presents some reanalysis of textual material from some of these studies to indicate what issues could have been addressed if the focus on language in those projects had been more richly defined. Research incorporating such a richer linguistic focus is also examined to heighten these contrasts and to suggest directions that future research might follow to equally productive ends.[2]

Defining Text

The starting point for the discussion of language of interest to this chapter is *text*—that is, a particular "moment" of language use by a particular group of speakers within a particular social and historical setting.[3] A text can be as simple as an act of greeting or naming, but more typically text refers to a conversation, a story, a speech, or some other form of language/social interaction. Whatever its detail and function, a text is always situated and bounded. That is, because it occurs in particular contexts, a text is influenced by the backgrounds and experiences of the speakers who produce it, by the topic or topics under discussion within the textual moment, and by other social and cultural assumptions relevant to that setting. That these influences are attested in the linguistic form of the text, as well as in its content, is a central theme of this chapter, and so is the need to address issues of textual form in studying gay men's AIDS-related language use.

Why Text Matters: Language, Text, and Gay Identity

The phrase "gay men" is not without difficulty in this discussion, however. Other chapters in this volume have shown that male-centered same-sex desires, practices, and identities may take on a wide range of expression cross-culturally; there is no single script defining what "gay man" means, either cross-culturally or within specific cultural settings.[4] Similarly, recent research in sexuality studies argues that gay identity (or any claim to sexual identity for that matter) is not a predetermined timeless category, but something created in context, and something that can be renegotiated as the context begins to change. Moreover, these studies suggest, while gay identity may be an important component of a person's self-description, other features of social experience may be more important in that regard, including race, ethnicity, age, or class background. This is particularly the case when managing distinctions between public and private identities, or mediating differences between acceptable and "spoiled" identities.[5]

Given that text is so closely tied to conditions "at the site" in the sense just explained, it is not surprising to find that meanings of gay identity often gain expression through forms of text-making, and that conversation, storytelling, asking questions, sexual negotiation, and the other linguistic practices of interest to this chapter are, at the same time, key elements in such text-making. By keeping language in the foreground in studies of AIDS and gay experience, AIDS research is able to consider how gay identities are formed in the midst of discussions of AIDS and to trace how the particulars of these identities intersect in each case with other components of the AIDS-related KAP also in formation at the site.

This is an important mode of inquiry, since we know from the language of gay men's personal advertising, from narratives in gay autobiography, and from other textual sources that HIV status intersects unevenly with gay identity.[6] Some gay men are "out and proud" about being HIV positive; others are comfortable mediating serodiscordant relationships (where one person is HIV positive and the other is not); while others make explicit that they want sexual and social interaction only with HIV-negative persons like themselves. These are three different formations of "gay identity," each responding to the AIDS pandemic and its discursive meanings in specific and contrasting ways; there are, of course, other responses to be listed here as well. And given the interests of this chapter, these are also three distinct forms of AIDS-related "gay voice"—commentaries about the lived experience of the pandemic and about the speaker's place within that experience as he understands it. Certainly, clarifying AIDS-related gay voice is consistent with the goals of AIDS research, as defined elsewhere in this volume. As this chapter confirms, attention to linguistic practices—to text-making—is an especially effective research strategy to that end.

Language: From Word to "Talk"

But has an analysis of language included in studies of AIDS in gay experience addressed questions of gay voice? Indeed, what issues have been the focus of concern in such an analysis?

The earliest studies of gay men, language, and AIDS had a very specific focus: AIDS was a biomedical condition that had just begun to be identified and had previously not yet been named. Terminology proposed to that end gave the biomedical condition a particular gay visibility—for example, Gay Related Immune Deficiency (GRID) and "gay bowel syndrome"—and so did the placement of "homosexuals" at the head of the list of those groups (the "four H's") assumed to be at greatest risk of AIDS-related infection.[7]

In effect, these studies demonstrated the emergence of a language of AIDS that was being used to establish gay men's connections to the pandemic and to demonize them because of it.[8] Shilts's (1987) descriptions of the struggles to close the gay bathhouses in San Francisco during the early years of the pandemic made clear that some gay men also accepted this argument and were adopting the linguistic practices that articulated it.

The negative positioning of gay men reflected through this usage prompted the studies of AIDS, marginality, and blame referenced above. Here, as in the studies of terminology, the discursive power of language was confirmed on a broad scale, but the particulars of linguistic practice were still ignored. An important exception in this regard was Farmer's (1990) careful tracing of how "sending sickness" and the assumptions about sorcery that surrounded this practice provided a framework for explaining HIV illness in rural Haiti. Here, general messages about blame intersect with specific networks of accusation and the content of the gossip through which accusations were framed. Here, as Farmer's work powerfully reveals, talk about AIDS directly indexed other components of the everyday experience of the pandemic in rural Haiti. Nothing paralleling Farmer's focus on linguistic practices and their consequences had appeared in print by 1990 insofar as gay men, language, and AIDS were concerned.

Language as Text: Studying What Gay Men Have to Say about AIDS

By 1990, gay men had already begun to develop ways of talking about AIDS. Some of these linguistic practices allowed discussions of AIDS framed in strongly phrased political terms. Others allowed discussions of AIDS while keeping the specifics of diagnoses and symptoms shielded from public scrutiny. The focus of language and AIDS research during the 1990s began to shift away from a broadly defined nonneutral discourse and toward descriptions of this interface between AIDS, gay experience, and gay voice.

In truth, this shift in research position was not entirely based in AIDS research needs. By this time, scholars in such fields as anthropology, cultural studies, women's studies, lesbian/gay studies, and sociology were already using oral narratives, written documents, and other forms of text as the basis for social analysis, and the earliest interests in AIDS-related gay voice cannot be divorced from that intellectual trend. Supported by that trend, and by interests in augmenting the insights generated by quantitative inquiry, AIDS researchers began to supplement fixed-alternative questionnaires with more creative data-gathering techniques, many of which allowed respondents' discussions of AIDS experiences in their own words to become part of the project database. The following summaries suggest the range of interests addressed in these projects and indicate how gay men's remarks about AIDS became helpful points of reference in each inquiry.

Levine and Siegel (1992) used discussions of sexual safety emerging during face-to-face interviewing as the focus for their analysis, and they reviewed the stories and related commentary to identify the respondents' "subjective perceptions" (1992: 52) about unsafe sex, as well as their familiarity with the conventional arguments about safety and risk. Here, an important finding was the respondents' repeated references to the "uncontrollable urges . . . which [respondents] dubbed passion or 'horniness'—which overwhelmed their intent to use protection" and their insistence that such unbridled passion was not typical of their usual behavior but due, instead, to "powerful biological needs and drives" (Levine and Siegel 1992: 62). As in all instances where people derive sexual attraction from innate needs and drives, Levine and Siegel's analysis of their respondents' remarks shows how the respondents use this argument to avoid accepting responsibility for participating in unsafe sexual activity or for any of the consequences stemming from those practices.

Henriksson and Månsson (1995) were part of a project that trained a group of male research assistants in ethnographic research, and then asked them to visit several video clubs in a Swedish urban area to engage in participant observation on-site and to prepare written field note descriptions of their experiences. Henriksson and Månsson use the information in the field notes, and the written statements themselves, as evidence showing that gay men's sexual encounters are structured by personal, symbolic, and sexual considerations. Thus, these remarks suggest, attempts to "change attitudes" about sexual safety are forced to contend with a much broader range of concerns than sexual practice alone.

Coxon (1996) reports on a project that asked gay men in Cardiff and London (United Kingdom) to keep written diaries of their sexual activities, and he used the entries in those diaries, amplified by follow-up interview discussions, as a focus for further analysis. Among other details, the diaries describe multiple instances where the respondents' well-intended commitments to safer-sex activity became upstaged by the desirability (in the terminology inspired by the diaries, the "fuckability") of their sexual partners. The diary entries are after-the-fact reflections, in the sense addressed below. Even so, the entries call into question whether unsafe sex should be described simply in terms of an irrational experience of relapse.

Dowsett (1996) conducted a series of interviews with twenty men over a period of three years and shows how "their own tales" about their lives as gay men "demands that the social process of being homosexual be recognized as a historically constructed sexual and collective practice" (1996: 11). What emerges from their stories is a sense of gay sexuality very different from that suggested by the neatly defined categories proposed in lesbian/gay theory. His respondents are not "camp," or "butch," or "top," or "bottom," or members of a homogeneous (or even heterogeneously defined) "gay community." Instead, each of the stories Dowsett presents demonstrates both "the historical formation of a homosexually active man and . . . the contribution of sexual experience to the creation of [that] sexuality" (Dowsett 1996: 28). Importantly, "HIV/AIDS is drawing a cordon around [these men's] social and sexual possibilities" (Dowsett 1996: 28), so the respondents' life stories repeatedly force Dowsett to ask how the AIDS pandemic is becoming part of the historic formation defining homosexuality as individual gay men experience it. Specific episodes from the life stories and discussions of those episodes provide Dowsett with the data he needs to answer that question.

Turner (1997) collected sexual life stories from seven gay men from West Hollywood, California. His review of the respondents' accounts of their experiences with sexual risk led him to question whether "relapse" effectively described what respondents are reporting about those experiences. Instead, he sees stronger connections between respondent narratives as models of "negotiated safety," and cites additional comments from his respondents to suggest—here very differently from Levine and Siegel (1992) and similar to Coxon (1996)—that gay men's participation in sexual risk may be more conscious than AIDS education models have previous allowed, and therefore more susceptible to change if intervention is targeted appropriately.

Text Analysis: Reclaiming Significance in Hindsight

While the concerns of these projects differ somewhat, they share a common interest in exploring the effects that the AIDS pandemic has had on gay men's lives. Gay men's depictions of their pursuit of sexual risk taking, their attempts to negotiate sexual safety, their disclosure or concealment of their HIV status, their reactions to illness (their own or that of their friends or lovers), and other remarks about AIDS provided the necessary documentation. The job of the researcher was to report it and draw generalizations from it.

None of the projects assumed that the respondents' remarks contain unbiased, objective descriptions of their real-life experiences. As is always the case with personal narratives and commentary, the remarks have been tempered by after-the-fact enthusiasm, embarrassment, insight, and regret. This meant, however, that the remarks contain indications of how the respondents *now* make sense out of the AIDS-related experiences they are revisiting through their storytelling. This position is similar to one adopted by other researchers who were asking questions about the validity of narrative at this time. Kleinman has referred to this aspect of the storytelling process as "retrospective narratization" (1988: 50–51). Lewin termed it the communication of "cultural" rather than "descriptive significance" (1993: 11). Plummer cited the "self-consciousness at work [in sexual storytelling] that scans the past life for clues to one's sexual being" (1995: 33). And Yoneyama (1999) described the matter succinctly in her phrasing within the title of her monograph, the "Dialectics of Memory."

The point is, "rather than attempting a literal reconstruction of history in textual terms, narratives allow us to explore how narrators themselves interpret their own history and to assess the significance that the narrators assign to such details" (Leap 1996: 139). As the examples just reviewed suggest, research projects that focused on experiences as reported in gay men's narratives and other texts about AIDS proved to be helpful in that regard.

Language as Text: Studying Textual Form

Focusing on experiences as reported in narratives was, in another sense, a source of limitation for these projects. Because researchers were using narratives as a source of anecdote and documentation, there was no reason to look beyond the content of the respondents' statements and to consider the details of textual form. Textual form was beginning to capture the attention of researchers interested in language and sexuality—particularly, researchers interested in drawing connections between sexual topic and linguistic practice in gay men's text-making, and to see how gay men's descriptions of their identity as sexual persons became positioned within those connections.[9]

In one of his first papers on gay men's English, Leap (1991, 1996: 141–50) examined a group of HIV-positive gay men's explanations for how they contracted their HIV. Ordinarily, as studies of life-story narratives had shown (Linde 1993), when speakers talk about their personal experience, they organize their remarks in terms of "what *I* did" and "what *I* accomplished." Such remarks appear to be suspended, however, when speakers begin to describe how they contracted HIV. Here, as Example 1 suggests, speakers shift from "what I accomplished " to "what happened to me," and from "things I did" to "things someone else did to me, without my consent or control." Similarly, speakers move some other individual, usually, "the one who gave me the virus," into the primary position in this segment of the conversation.

Example 1 (Leap 1991: 278–79)

> I: investigator—a health-care professional
> R: respondent—a middle-age white gay-identified man, HIV positive, symptomatic, receiving hospital care for multiple AIDS-related infections
>
> I: Where do you think you got the HIV?
> R: The person I was living with.
> I: Where did he get it?
> R: His travels.
> I: Was he, did he have many partners?
> R: I really couldn't say; I believe so.
> I: Did you have many partners?
> R: No. Uh, none.
> I: Do you have any friends with HIV?

R: Not to my knowledge.

I: Do you know many people with AIDS?

R: No, not that I know of.

I: How about friends, do they treat you . . .

R: I have not told my friends.

I: You've kept this a secret?

R: Yes . . . as far as the disease itself, it is not worth what I have to go through.

I: Say that again.

R: The severity of the illness. If I knew this was what it was all about, I would not have gotten involved.

I: What could you have done to protect yourself?

R: I would not have gotten in the gay lifestyle.

I: Do you feel that people have a choice between a gay lifestyle and a straight lifestyle?

R: I did, because I was primarily a bisexual.

I: Were you ever married?

R: Yes, seven years.

I: Can you tell me about your ideas when you switched from primarily heterosexual to primarily homosexual?

R: Oh, [I thought at the time that] this is a new experience. Let me try this out. Let me try this also.

Assigning responsibility for one's HIV-positive status to some other party is not unique to gay men's use of language regarding AIDS. Discussions of HIV/AIDS are often framed through references to "the other," regardless of the sexuality of the speaker (Clatts and Mutchler 1989; Farmer 1990; Patton 1991), whose mysterious qualities make members of the category easier to fear, pity, or hate. But besides providing a focus for blame, references to "the other" serve an additional function in discussions like that in Example 1. Bringing "the other" into the text makes it easier for the respondent to avoid acknowledging participation in risk-related behavior and to argue that his HIV status was something over which he had no control. Thus, we have the respondent's suggestion that he did not have many sex partners, while insisting that the person he was living with was the source of his infection. At a later point in the interview, when AIDS is no longer the foregrounded theme in the discussion, the respondent indicates a much more enthusiastic participation in gay sexual experience: "Oh, this is a new experience. Let me try this out. Let me try this also." And with that, he expressed much more responsibility for the management of his own sexual behavior.

References to "the other" can be labeled and described in various ways, but may also be encoded in textual form. In Example 1, the respondent positions "the person I was living with" as the source of his HIV infection, leaving the specifics of their relationship (personal and sexual) as information to be read into the text by the interviewer. The respondent did not use phrases like "lover," "boy friend," "sex partner," or "fuck buddy," which would have acknowledged their sexual activity and perhaps suggest that they shared other moments of intimacy. Leaving out such references strengthens the message, already encoded through pronouns and verb choices, that the respondent positions his roommate as the active, irresponsible party, and the respondent sees his own HIV status as a result of the roommate's willful indiscretion.

Similar arguments appear in descriptions of needle-sharing practices collected from injecting drug users in the Seattle area during the late 1980s, which Leap (1990) examined. One group of respondents interviewed for this project described their involvement in activities such as needle sharing and freely indicated that these activities were the likely sources of their HIV infection. Judging by a review of comments in these interviews, many of the respondents in this category were heterosexual women.

A second group of respondents, whose comments indicate that many were gay or bisexually identified men, took the stance suggested in Example 2 (see below). They admitted to sharing needles and indicated they had concerns about AIDS, but did not report that sharing needles placed them at any risk for HIV infection. If anything, sharing needles with friends became an act of trust.

Example 2 (Leap 1990: 151)

> I: *investigator—researcher, University of Washington*
> R: *respondent—white gay man, late twenties, HIV positive, interview*
>   *occurred in the late 1980s*
> I: Did you share needles?
> R: Yes, I did.
> I: When would you share needles?
> R: I basically had my own needles. I'd share with other people that
>   would come in and want to buy drugs and if I were out of points

that I was selling and they want to be hit up or something, you know I'd always rinse the point, rinse the needle and tell them that it was used. It was mine and [I would] tell them that they were taking their chances. . . .

I: Would you use needles with a group of people?

R: No. I would share my needles, basically, if I knew the person. I shared with the people that I knew of, that I remember that I shared my needles with.

I: What was your reluctance about sharing needles?

R: Fear of AIDS. Those were basically people that I ran with, hung out with, dealt with.

These respondents reacted very differently to needle sharing by other persons who were present in injecting drug use settings, but not otherwise known to the respondents. Unlike the case reported for the "people that I ran with, hung out with, dealt with," these unfamiliar persons "took their chances" when they used needles that the respondent had already used. He warns them, the respondent insists, though they apparently paid his comments no heed. Their failure to share in his "fear of AIDS" reinforces their status as "other" in the text, and thereby renders the status of his friends as familiar parties and therefore as persons who are protected from HIV infection.

The distinction between "familiar" and "other" at work here is encoded in Example 2 through the juxtaposition of specific phrases—for example, "it was mine" and "they were taking their chances"; "fear of AIDS" and "those were basically people that I ran with, hung out with, dealt with"; as well as the juxtaposition of the discussion of needle sharing by customers (which occurred in the first part of the transcript of the complete interview) and the discussion of needle sharing with friends (which occurred later in the original transcript). These are content references, but their location within the text and their positioning in relation to each other are equally important components of the message they express. Location and positioning, like pronoun function and verb choice, are additional features of textual form.

*   *   *

Does the Form of the Text Matter?: Hector Carrillo's
The Night Is Young

Carrillo's (2002) analysis of sexual narratives that he collected during the 1990s, while he was studying sexuality, socialization, and HIV prevention in Guadalajara, Mexico, offers considerable attention to textual form.[10] He explains that he chose Guadalajara as the site for his fieldwork because he wanted to work in a metropolitan center that was outside of the United States but closely connected to the U.S. political economy and sexual culture, at a site that had long-standing associations with male same-sex behavior, and in a setting that was familiar to him and would be accepting of him as a Mexican-born U.S. resident and gay-identified man. Guadalajara met all of these criteria. But by choosing Guadalajara, Carrillo recognized that his own assumptions about Mexican same-sex cultures (as well as his experiences with gay life in the United States) were likely to influence his participation in the interview process. So he needed a plan for data gathering and analysis that would foreground respondents' understandings of the sexual and provide opportunities for them to describe sexual experiences in terms of those understandings.

For these reasons, rather than determining in advance whose voices should be included in the inquiry, Carrillo decided to interview a broad range of local residents, women as well as men, some of whom were primarily same-sex identified. Others described their sexual identity and sexual attractions in more fluid fashions. By doing this, gay men's stories about their lives in Guadalajara could be studied in context, not as detached, isolated narratives.

Further, instead of citing discrete segments of the interviews to provide anecdotal support for particular arguments, Carrillo treated his questions as well as the respondents' answers as part of his research data, and included both in the write-up of his research findings. By doing this, he restores a sense of the conversational flow by presenting this exchange as if it were part of a nonfictional narrative rather than extracted from a courtroom transcript. Where appropriate, and continuing this theme, he added his own reflections on the issues, speaking now as the researcher/observer working at a distance from the interview setting, in contrast to the researcher/participant in the interview context while in the field.

For example, speaking about what Carrillo (2002: 247) describes as the "intuitive, silent assessment that often informed decisions about [negotiated risk and harm reduction] with any given sexual partner," Gonzalo (one of

Carrillo's respondents) said: "The thing is that if you are really expecting to carry on a [sexual] relationship, you have to put it [the condom] on. If I am not sure of my situation and the other person's, despite how much I want him, [I don't do it]." Gonzalo added that these remarks "applied to situations in which sex is tied to love, because when it is just passion perhaps you don't even care. [The passion increases so much] that you are not interested [in condoms] and do not protect yourself'" (Carrillo 2002: 247). Carrillo (2002: 247) continues:

> Two years before the interview, Gonzalo experienced a great passion upon meeting a stranger at a gay disco. . . . "After embracing, kissing, touching, passion erupted and they [Gonzalo's reference to the partner] suggested, Let's go to my hotel. I thought about it for just a moment, not long, and I said to myself, this guy is from out of town and he won't come back. There will be no other opportunity. We went to their hotel, to his room . . . where we *estuvimos* [literally 'were,' meaning 'we had intercourse']. When it happened, . . . I did not have protection."

Carrillo interrupts the flow of Gonzalo's narrative to note:

> According to Gonzalo's account, they never uttered the words, "Let's have sex." Sex was always indirectly implied, which allowed for the silent flow . . . of sex to happen and provided a potential exit should one of the two decide not to continue with the encounter. Gonzalo used these indirect references to sex even in his account of the experience as he used the word "*estuvimos*" as an indirect way of saying we had intercourse. (2002: 247)

Carrillo's description of the interview continues: "I asked Gonzalo whether his partner had condoms available. 'No, there was nothing there to use for protection. But . . . the relationship took place anyway'" (2002: 247).

Carrillo adds a further commentary: "Again note that 'the relationship took place'; it is not something that he and his partner did (or were responsible for); it took place, it happened to them" (2002: 248).

Then he continues his description of the question-and-answer exchange:

> "Did you think at any time in making this decision whether there was any danger?" . . . I asked him.

"Yes but I did not really consider it. I tried anyway to not finish inside this person . . . to avoid any situation. And, in fact, it happened quickly, and we finished later by masturbating."

"Were you ever worried about this after the encounter?"

"Yes it worried me, but not much because, I don't know if I am wrongly informed, but I understand that, although there is risk as well for the one who penetrates, the risk is higher for the one who is penetrated. So given that I did not finish, maybe there was no opportunity [for me to get infected]." (Carrillo 2002: 248)

Carrillo identifies his respondents by name each time the respondents' remarks on a topic are quoted. Next, Carrillo uses conversations about specific sexual encounters that he held with individual respondents, not written narratives or other sources of information, as the entry point for eliciting more detailed comments from the respondent about experiences of safe/ unsafe sex.

Carrillo is especially attentive to the segments of the sexual narrative that are specified directly in the text and to the segments that are indicated less directly. Gonzalo's use of "*estuvimos*," "we were," as the representation for "we had intercourse," instead of a verb that identifies the sexual practice more precisely, is one example. A shift in pronoun usage from what "we" did to a subjectless "the relationship took place" in references to moments of unprotected intercourse is another. Additionally, there is the shift from "I" and "we" references to a more subject free "there was no opportunity" in Gonzalo's answer to Carrillo's question about unprotected anal sex and danger.

Carrillo is also attentive to instances where his respondents use contrasts in terminology to indicate boundaries of real-world experience. Gonzalo distinguishes sex dominated by *la pasion* from sex that (in Gonzalo's words) is "tied to love." An English speaker (or a speaker of Mexican Spanish unfamiliar with sexual culture in Guadalajara, for that matter) might not think that an anonymous sexual encounter like the one Gonzalo described in the remarks above would be "tied to love." But such was the case, according to the distinction developed throughout Gonzalo's remarks and encoding specifically the wording of this exchange. That is, there was sexual excitement, but *la pasion* did not preclude entirely Gonzalo's reported awareness of the need for condom use and for other forms of safer-sex-related practices. As the passage on unprotected anal sex suggests, Gonzalo is aware of the need for safety. He reports structuring his sexual activity accordingly—even if he retains some questions as to whether his action was entirely successful.

Implications

This chapter is not suggesting that AIDS researchers should become linguists. Rather, it invites AIDS researchers to look more carefully at the "talk" that they collect from gay men during their research so that their analysis will more effectively analyze gay men's understandings about AIDS experience.

The features of textual form that will direct researchers to those understandings include, but are not limited to: pronoun functions, verb choices, speaker claims to position within the text (narrator, object, actor), references to "the other"—in contrast to speaker experience—as a focus for guilt and blame, and other contradictory messages encoded within single sentences or at different locations within the text. Admittedly, none of these features is unique to the ways that gay men talk about AIDS in English or any language. But these features do not need to be unique to meet the interests of this chapter. They need only be significant—that is, they need to be associated with a noticeable difference in textual message when they occur within textual practice. Judging by the evidence reviewed in this chapter, these features of textual form are significant.

Paying attention to features of textual form reveals gay men's understandings about AIDS-related experiences in ways that studies of content alone are unable to provide. It is important to note that such a broadening of research interests need not require dramatic changes in data-gathering techniques. Responses to survey instruments and other structured interviews can serve as texts for purposes of the analysis proposed here. What will have to change, however, is the belief that linguistic data are useful as forms of illustration but not as sources of information in their own right. Verbatim quotation, without considering how the remarks were constructed or what implications should be inferred from the presence (or absence) of particular features, presents limited insights. AIDS research needs to meet much higher standards. Certainly, there are issues that figure prominently in today's agendas for AIDS research and education that stand to benefit greatly from such inquiry.

For example, judging by the textual evidence reviewed in this chapter, gay men may be able to distinguish between high-risk sexual behaviors that result from a "deliberate relapse" from those that result from "negotiated safety." However, again judging by the textual evidence, gay men describe this distinction as unfolding somewhat ambiguously within the erotic moment, with what might begin as cautious negotiation spilling into relapse, and what begins as relapse reshaped as negotiated safety (Carrillo's retelling of Gonzalo's story). This may be a case where the researcher's classification of risk and the categories used to orient AIDS education are out of touch with the lived experience of gay men's sexual practice. We might wonder whether the intent of the distinction between "relapse" and "safety" (Adam et al. 2000) could be more effectively described if it were phrased along the lines described by Coxon's "fuckability," Carrillo's "*la pasion*," or some other categorization that was more responsive to how gay men actually talk about AIDS and sexual pleasure.

But remarks endorsing AIDS research that foregrounds "how gay men really talk about AIDS" have to be tempered by realistic assessments of the politics that govern AIDS policy making, AIDS education policies included. U.S.-based AIDS policies continue to define sexual safety in terms that are largely out-of-step with vernacular understandings of sexual risk and risk reduction. Attention to the referencing of safety and risk as disclosed in gay men's sexual narratives makes this point emphatically. Those references, and the linguistic forms through which they are expressed within those narratives, suggest that gay men's negotiation of sexual enjoyment is often a well-informed practice, and that if sexual risk taking overwhelms safer-sex practices, risk taking speaks to an endorsement of other types of priorities rather than a failure to understand the dynamics of "relapse."

Language-centered research, guided by a commitment to examine the form as well as content of gay men's talk abut AIDS, can make this point and can document it with the sorts of examples of gay men's narratives examined in this chapter. Language-centered research can make this point by unpacking the assumptions about AIDS embedded within "abstinence-only" or "procreation-biased" sex-education materials, as compared to material developed by more radical, populist health activist sources. Such inquiry will force confrontation of the fact that sexual decision making cannot be reduced to formulas or managed by slogans, and play up how little we understand about gay men's sexual practices or about the understandings of sexual desire, object choice, and subjectivity that inform them. Why basic questions about male same-sex desire are still unanswered, more than twenty-five years into the pandemic, is also certainly worth asking.

Notes

Our thanks to Doug Feldman for inviting us to submit this chapter for this volume and to Roger Lancaster for his careful reading of earlier drafts of the manuscript.

1. This chapter is based on a review of sources published between 1985 and 2002 and identified in online databases (e.g., FirstSearch, ArticleFirst, OVID, JSTOR, ProQuest); we used different permutations of the following terms to locate the online citations: AIDS and language, AIDS and discourse, vernacular talk and AIDS, AIDS and intimate communication, AIDS and policy, HIV/AIDS educational materials. We also reviewed relevant citations in bibliographies of publications related to language and AIDS, particularly Adam et al. (2000), Myrick (1999), and Solomon (2002). We focused attention on English-language sources, since much of the material we identified during the literature review for this chapter was written in English and describes discussions of AIDS as they take place in English.

2. We are concerned in this chapter with considerations related to spoken-language text. This definition of text, and the mode of inquiry connected to it, applies just as readily to written languages, sign languages, visual languages in various formats, and communication in nonverbal formats.

3. Halliday (1978) and Fairclough (2003) provide a formal statement of this position. Leap (1996) connects this position to studies of gay men's English.

4. See also Blackwood (1986) and Herdt (1994, 1997).

5. Lancaster (1992) provides a workable statement of this argument. Goffman (1963) remains the classic discussion of "spoiled identity." The linguistic implications of these claims are outlined in Cameron and Kulick (2003) and Eckert and McConnell-Ginet (2003); they are further refined in Boellstorff and Leap (2004), Bucholtz and Hall (2003), and Morrish and Leap (2005).

6. To cite only one example, compare the different positionings of "author" vis-à-vis AIDS in O'Hara's *Autopornography: A Memoir of Life in the Lust Lane* (1997) and in Wojnarowicz's *Close to the Knives: A Memoir of Disintegration* (1991).

7. The "four H's"—"homosexuals, heroin addicts, Haitians, and hemophiliacs"—was an early attempt to create a category that would specify persons deemed at greatest risk from HIV infection, thereby creating a larger category of people who, not being part of the "four H's," were deemed not likely to be at risk.

8. See, for example, Lancaster (1983), Murray and Payne (1989), and Shilts (1987). Additional studies from this period are listed in the bibliographies in several chapters in Feldman (1990).

9. Much of this work was framed in terms of U.S. English settings, and came to be known as studies of "gay men's English." Studies of similar topics relevant to other language traditions also appeared during this time, as did studies of lesbian/same- sex-identified women's linguistic practices; see Leap (1995) and Livia and Hall (1997). A more recent profile of these research interests can be found in Leap and Boellstorff (2004). Critiques of this work are outlined in Cameron and Kulick (2003) and Kulick (2000).

10. Carrillo's exploration of HIV/AIDS and sexual practices in Guadalajara is one of several studies that have appeared since 2000 that examine gay men, language, and AIDS outside of English-speaking settings. Other studies include Solomon's (2002) detailed analysis of the emerging language of AIDS in Israel and the uneasy relationship between Israeli gay speech and the authority of the nation's medical/educational code; Manalansan's (2003) exploration of loneliness and connectedness in Filipino *bakla*'s conversa-

tions about AIDS; Higgins's (1999) tracings of AIDS activism and the formation of gay community in Montreal; and Provencher's (2004) explorations of the tensions between AIDS and sexual citizenship for gay men in France.

References

Adam, Barry D., Alan Sears, E. Glenn Schellenberg. 2000. Accounting for unsafe sex: Interviews with men who have sex with men. *Journal of Sex Research* 37(1): 24–35.

Blackwood, Evelyn, ed. 1986. *The Many Faces of Homosexuality: Anthropological Approaches to Homosexual Behavior*. New York: Harrington Park Press.

Boellstorff, Tom, and William L. Leap. 2004. Introduction: Globalization and "new" articulations of same-sex desire. In *Speaking in Queer Tongues: Globalization and Gay Language*, ed. William L. Leap and Tom Boellstorff, 1–22. Urbana: University of Illinois Press.

Bucholtz, Mary, and Kira Hall. 2003. Theorizing identity in language and sexuality research. *Language in Society* 33: 469–515

Cameron, Deborah, and Don Kulick. 2003. *Language and Sexuality*. New York: Cambridge University Press.

Caron, David. 2001. *AIDS in French Culture: Social Ills, Literary Cures*. Madison: University of Wisconsin Press.

Carrillo, Hector. 2002. *The Night Is Young: Sexuality in Mexico in the Time of AIDS*. Chicago: University of Chicago Press.

Clatts, Michael, and Ken M. Mutchler. 1989. AIDS and the dangerous other: Metaphors of sex and deviance in the representations of a disease. *Medical Anthropology* 11(2–3): 105–14.

Coxon, Anthony P. M. 1996. *Between the Sheets: Sexual Diaries and Gay Men's Sex in the Era of AIDS*. London: Cassell.

Dowsett, Gary W. 1996. *Practicing Desire: Homosexual Sex in the Era of AIDS*. Stanford, Calif.: Stanford University Press.

Eckert, Penelope, and Sally McConnell-Ginet. 2003. *Language and Gender*. New York: Cambridge University Press.

Fairclough, Norman. 2003. *Analysing Discourse*. London: Routledge.

Farmer, Paul. 1990. Sending sickness: Sorcery, politics and changing concepts of AIDS in rural Haiti. *Medical Anthropology Quarterly* 4(1): 6–27.

Feldman, Douglas A., ed. 1990. *Culture and AIDS*. Westport, Conn.: Praeger.

Goffman, Erving. 1963. *Stigma: Notes on the Management of Spoiled Identity*. Englewood Cliffs, N.J.: Prentice-Hall.

Halliday, M. A. K. 1978. Language as social semiotic. In *Language as Social Semiotic*, 108–26. London: Edward Arnold.

Henriksson, Benny, and Sven-Axel Månsson. 1995. Sexual negotiations: An ethnographic study of men who have sex with men. In *Culture and Sexual Risk: Anthropological Perspectives on AIDS*, ed. Han ten Brummelhuis and Gilbert Herdt, 157–82. Newark, N.J.: Gordon and Breach.

Herdt, Gilbert, ed. 1994. *Third Sex, Third Gender: Beyond Sexual Dimorphism in Culture and History*. New York: Zone Books.
———. 1997. *Same Sex Different Cultures: Exploring Gay and Lesbian Lives*. Boulder, Colo.: Westview Press.
Higgins, Ross. 1999. *De la clandestinite a l'affirmation: Pour un histoire de la communaute gai montrealise*. Montreal: Comeau and Nadeau.
Kleinman, Arthur. 1988. *The Illness Narratives*. New York: Basic Books.
Koblin, Beryl, Margaret A. Chesney, Mark J. Hersnik, Sam Bozeman, et al. 2003. High risk behaviors among men who have sex with men in 6 US cities: Baseline data from the EXPLORE Study. *American Journal of Public Health* 93(6): 926-932.
Kulick, Don. 2000. Gay and lesbian language. *Annual Review of Anthropology* 29: 243–85.
Lancaster, Roger. 1983. What AIDS is doing to us. *Christopher Street* 75: 4–54.
———. 1992. *Life Is Hard: Machismo, Danger, and the Intimacy of Power*. Berkeley: University of California Press.
LaTour, (William). 1991. "People Are Still Having Sex." Single. Polygram Records.
Leap, William L. 1990. Language and AIDS. In *Culture and AIDS*, ed. Douglas A. Feldman, 137–58. Westport, Conn.: Praeger.
———. 1991. AIDS, linguistics, and the study of nonneutral discourse. *Journal of Sex Research* 28(2): 275–88.
———, ed. 1995. *Beyond the Lavender Lexicon*. Newark, N.J.: Gordon and Breach.
———. 1996. *Word's Out: Gay Men's English*. Minneapolis: University of Minnesota Press.
Leap, William L., and Tom Boellstorff, eds. 2004. *Speaking in Queer Tongues: Globalization and Gay Language*. Urbana: University of Illinois Press.
Levine, Martin, and Karolynn Siegel. 1992. Unprotected sex: Understanding gay men's participation. In *The Social Context of AIDS*, ed. Joan Huber and Beth E. Schneider, 47–71. Newbury Park, Calif.: Sage.
Lewin, Ellen. 1993. *Lesbian Mothers: Accounts of Gender in American Culture*. Ithaca, N.Y.: Cornell University Press.
Linde, Charlotte. 1993. *Life Stories: The Creation of Coherence*. Berkeley: University of California Press.
Livia, Anna, and Kira Hall, eds. 1997. *Queerly Phrased: Language, Gender and Sexuality*. New York: Oxford University Press.
Manalansan, Martin F., IV. 2003. *Global Divas: Filipino Gay Men in the Diaspora*. Durham, N.C.: Duke University Press.
Mansur, Lalljee, and Emma Palmer-Vanton. 2001. Communication and consistency: AIDS talk and AIDS attitudes. *Journal of Psychology* 135(1): 87–100.
Morrish, Liz, and William L. Leap. 2005. Sex talk: Language, desire, identity and beyond. In *Language, Sexualities, and Desires: Cross-Cultural Perspectives*, ed. Helen Sauntson and Sakis Kyratzis, 17-40. London: Palgrave Press.
Murray, Stephen O., and Kenneth W. Payne. 1989. The social classification of AIDS in American epidemiology. *Medical Anthropology* 10: 115–28.

Myrick, Roger. 1999. In the life: Culture-specific HIV communication programs designed for African American men who have sex with men. *Journal of Sex Research* 36(2): 159–70.

O'Hara, Scott. 1997. *Autopornography: A Memoir of Life in the Lust Lane*. Binghamton, N.Y.: Harrington Park Press.

Patton, Cindy. 1991. Containing African AIDS: From nation to family. In *Nationalisms and Sexualities*, ed. Andrew Parker, Mary Russo, Doris Sommer, and Patricia Yaeger, 218–34. New York: Routledge.

Plummer, Ken. 1995. *Telling Sexual Stories: Power, Change and Social Worlds*. London: Routledge.

Provencher, Denis. 2004. Vague French Creole: (Gay English) cooperative discourse in the French gay press. In *Speaking in Queer Tongues: Globalization and Gay Language*, ed. William L. Leap and Tom Boellstorff, 23–45. Urbana: University of Illinois Press.

Shilts, Randy. 1987. *And the Band Played On*. New York: Viking Penguin.

Solomon, Harris. 2002. Skirting around: Towards an understanding of HIV/AIDS educational materials in modern Israeli Hebrew. In *Language and Sexuality: Contesting Meaning in Theory and Practice*, ed. Kathryn Campbell-Kibbler, Robert J. Podesva, Sarah J. Roberts, and Andrew Wong, 225–47. Stanford, Calif.: Center for the Study of Language and Information.

Sontag, Susan. 1988. *AIDS and Its Metaphors*. New York: Farrar, Strauss and Giroux.

Treichler, Paula. 1988. AIDS, homophobia, and biomedical discourse: An epidemic of signification. In *AIDS: Cultural Analysis/Cultural Activism*, ed. Douglas Crimp, 31–70. Cambridge, Mass.: MIT Press.

Turner, Dwayne C. 1997. *Risky Sex: Gay Men and HIV Prevention*. New York: Columbia University Press.

Vinke, Jon, and Ralph Bolton. 1997. Beyond the sexual monad: Combining complementary cognitions to explain and predict unsafe sex among gay men. *Human Organization* 56(1): 38–46.

Vinke, Jon, Ralph Bolton, Rudolf Mak, and Susan Blank. 1992. Coming-out and AIDS-related high risk sexual behavior. *Archives of Sexual Behavior* 22(6): 559–85.

Williams, Raymond. 1977. *Marxism and Literature*. London: Oxford University Press.

Wojnarowicz, David. 1991. *Close to the Knives: A Memoir of Disintegration*. New York: Vintage.

Yoneyama, Lisa. 1999. *Hiroshima Traces: Time, Space and the Dialectics of Memory*. Berkeley: University of California Press.

Zia, Maria Cecilia, Carol A. Reisen, and Rafael M. Diaz. 2003. Methodological issues in research on sexual behavior with Latino gay and bisexual men. *American Journal of Community Psychology* 31(3–4): 281–91.

5

Diffusion of Effective Behavioral Interventions for HIV Prevention for Men Who Have Sex with Men

From Academia to the Gay Community

CHARLES COLLINS AND CAMILLA HARSHBARGER

Several researchers have identified an increase in risk-taking behaviors by men who have sex with men (MSM) and rates of HIV infection that continue to be unacceptably high.[1] Valleroy and colleagues (2001) demonstrated alarming rates of HIV infection among young MSM in seven cities. Rates were as high as 15 percent for Latinos and 30 percent for young African American MSM. Results of a study conducted in four cities between 1997 and 1999 showed the rate of new HIV infections among MSM to be nine times higher than that of heterosexual men, and the rate among Latino and African American MSM was almost twice that of white MSM (Linley et al. 2002). In addition to high rates of HIV infection, Chen and colleagues (2002) recently reported increasing rates of unprotected anal intercourse among MSM in San Francisco.

To prevent new HIV infections in MSM, the Centers for Disease Control and Prevention (CDC) must help build the capacity of their prevention partners to use evidence-based HIV prevention practices. The national diffusion and implementation of evidence-based behavioral interventions for MSM to facilitate and maintain safer sexual behaviors is an important strategy for reducing the spread of HIV. With no vaccine or cure in the foreseeable future, we suggest that the widespread diffusion of evidence-based behavioral interventions to change HIV sexual risk behaviors (Collins et al. 2004) is an effective strategy for decreasing the spread of HIV in MSM populations.

The effectiveness of proven behavioral interventions in reducing HIV risk behavior is recognized among public health officials and behavioral

scientists (NIH 1997). There is also evidence that community-based organization (CBO) administrators and program staff believe that theory-based
prevention interventions are effective at reducing HIV risk (DiFranceisco
et al. 1999). Although investigators conducting systematic reviews of the
HIV prevention literature found HIV behavioral interventions for MSM,
as a whole, to be efficacious in reducing HIV-related sexual risk behaviors
(Herbst et al. 2005; Johnson et al. 2002), the data from different types of
behavioral interventions for MSM were aggregated for these reviews. Very
few prevention interventions focusing on MSM have, individually, demonstrated efficacy. If we are to meet the prevention needs of this population,
more evidence-based interventions for MSM need to be implemented. For
example, in the CDC's *Compendium of Effective HIV Prevention Interventions with Evidence of Effectiveness*, only five interventions for MSM populations meet the CDC's rigorous requirements for proof of efficacy (CDC
1999). In a recent efficacy review of the 2000–2004 literature, the CDC's
HIV/AIDS Prevention Research Synthesis (PRS) Project team determined
that only three additional interventions directed at MSM were efficacious
(Lyles, Kay, et al. in press). Additionally, prevention service providers report
challenges and barriers to implementing these evidence-based prevention
interventions; these challenges include staff training and retention, recruitment of potential clients to participate in interventions, and evaluation of
the interventions (DeGroff 1996).

Few behavioral interventions deemed efficacious are implemented by
prevention providers in practice settings under real-world conditions (Clark
1995). Prevention programs for MSM are implemented within a community
context that typically differs from the research setting, and we have limited
understanding of how to translate these efficacious interventions into real-
world settings. Additionally, traditional methods of diffusion of behavioral
science, such as presentations at professional meetings and articles in journals, are not accessible to most CBO prevention providers (DeGroff 1996).

During our three years of diffusing efficacious behavioral interventions
to CBOs that provide prevention services to MSM, we observed a vary-
ing range of trust for research-driven, evidence-based interventions. Some
CBOs assert that researchers are out of touch with, or misunderstand, community-level politics and economies. Other CBOs question the funding for
research grants instead of funding for their own program budgets, and they
question whose work has the greatest impact among populations vulnerable
to sexually transmitted diseases (STDs), HIV, and hepatitis. Because of their
separation from academia, underserved or stigmatized communities can be

especially distrustful of interventions developed in the academic community.

Throughout this chapter, we use the term "MSM" to refer to persons whose same-sex sexual behaviors place them at an increased risk for HIV infection. We use the term "gay community" to refer to the social networks where men who identify as gay or bisexual interact with friends, social contacts, lovers, and other sexual partners. We use the term "non-gay-identified MSM" to refer to men whose sexual behaviors with other men may place them at risk for HIV infection. However, because they do not self-identify as gay, they may be only marginally connected to the social networks of the gay community.

Most HIV prevention service providers, such as health departments and CBOs, have been slow to implement evidence-based interventions. CBOs that serve the gay community have not traditionally been consumers of evidence-based programs. Furthermore, fewer than half of the CBOs that responded to a national survey (Somlai et al. 1999) reported offering workshops to their clients to facilitate HIV risk assessment at the personal level or to teach risk-reduction skills. Both activities are central to HIV prevention and are common elements of most efficacious interventions for MSM (Herbst et al. 2005).

Providers of HIV prevention in gay communities may not be getting adequate guidance or the necessary incentives to implement evidence-based prevention interventions. This may be partly due to a lack of familiarity with the research. Some HIV/AIDS divisions of state health departments (Arizona, Maryland, Massachusetts, New Jersey, and Texas) are requiring community-based prevention providers to implement evidence-based interventions. However, mandating is easier than actually ensuring implementation. Unless adequate training, technical assistance, and other capacity-building resources are provided to prevention staff, these efforts may fail.

A diffusion system integrated into the current HIV prevention public health infrastructure is needed to support the adaptation and subsequent implementation of evidence-based HIV prevention practices. Adaptation is the process of adjusting the intervention to new risk populations, venues, communication channels, and health messages without changing the core elements or intent of the intervention. This type of change in developing HIV prevention services infrastructure and systems among community-based prevention providers is expensive. Consideration must be given to the increases in labor and to the challenge of promoting change and innovation in an existing prevention program.

A community-based prevention provider serving a gay community that is considering adopting an evidence-based program must complete a complex process of thoroughly reviewing the new technology and comparing it with the provider's current practice. If there are advantages to the new prevention practice, the provider must also be able to learn how to successfully compete for funding necessary to carry out the intervention. In addition, CBO decision makers must deal with barriers to adopting evidence-based interventions. These include staff resistance to change, lack of participation by target risk populations, lack of interest or support from the communities and administrative gatekeepers, poor communication with researchers, adaptation to coincide with cultural perspectives, practices of racial and ethnic minority communities, and insufficient resources. Decision makers must also consider whether the evidence-based intervention tested in one location can be adapted from this venue to another and still be effective (DeGroff 1996; DiFranceisco et al. 1999).

In HIV prevention work, converting the intervention's scientific language, theory, and protocol into user-friendly terms for prevention providers in the field is called "translation." Those who take on the role of "science translator" of evidence-based interventions for MSM communities must find a way to link research to HIV prevention practices in gay communities. To be successful, these translators must speak the language of behavioral science as well as the language of community practice. This means they must bring knowledge of both behavioral science and the application of services to communities.

Terminology such as "sampling frame," "randomization," "instrument design," "effect size," "statistical significance," and "multivariate analysis" means little to community practitioners. Similarly, academic researchers sometimes overlook concerns of community prevention practitioners, such as whether the target audience actually enjoyed the intervention activities and the time burden involved in participating in the intervention sessions. The work of the science translators is easier if the gay community perceives the translators as advocates for community-based HIV prevention in the gay community.

There is a vast difference in how a community perceives a science translator whose primary intention is to bring quality prevention services to the stigmatized and inadequately served community and a researcher whose primary intention is to pilot an intervention with multiple communities to test the generalizability of the theory or the efficacy of the intervention. The rigorous focus on internal validity necessary for addressing efficacy may convey messages to the community that make the community members suspicious of the intent of the intervention. For example, many prevention providers have an open "all comer" approach to services; however, researchers must ensure that intervention recipients are somewhat homogeneous and thus qualify for the intervention as specified in the intervention protocol. Research protocols may exclude subjects based on a priori selection criteria, but prevention providers rarely exclude clients for prevention services unless they are intoxicated, disruptive, or violent. This is just one example of the differences between behavioral research and prevention services that have the potential to stimulate distrust in communities. The work of the science translator may be easier if the translator is familiar with research and practice distinctions so as to better articulate the underlying concepts to community members. The work of the science translator may be further facilitated if the science translator identifies with or is personally connected to the underserved community by gender, race, ethnicity, language, or sexual orientation (Trickett 1998).

The diffusion of evidence-based programs requires an approach that fosters clear communication channels and strong collaborative efforts among HIV prevention providers, researchers, and other stakeholders. Building strong collaborations between prevention researchers and CBOs that deliver HIV prevention programs to gay communities and improving the availability of capacity-building resources and technical assistance to these agencies are ways to enhance the successful transfer of behavioral interventions to the field (Kelly et al. 2000; Neumann et al. 2000; Sogolow et al. 2000).

In this chapter, we review community-level and group-level interventions that are currently being used in HIV prevention activities. Each evidence-based HIV/STD prevention intervention has core elements that fundamentally define its nature. These core elements, which are derived from theory, a logic model, the researcher's experience, and empirical evidence, are most likely to account for the intervention's main effects (Kelly 2004). Core elements must be closely followed so that implementers such as CBOs and health departments are more likely to have program outcomes similar to the outcomes in the original research. The CDC sets parameters for each intervention so that prevention providers can adapt interventions to local conditions, yet maintain the core elements.

Diffusion of Effective Behavioral Interventions

Diffusion of behavioral interventions usually takes place through "technology transfer." Technology transfer in the field of HIV prevention is the process of disseminating interventions that have evidence of efficacy for implementation and continued use in program application. The implementation often requires the additional provision of training and technical assistance (Neumann and Sogolow 2000). The CDC diffuses evidence-based interventions on a national level. The diffusion program is built on the foundation of the HIV/AIDS PRS Project (Lyles, Crepaz, et al. in press; Sogolow et al. 2002) and the Replicating Effective Programs (REP) project (Neumann and Sogolow 2000).

The CDC initiated the HIV/AIDS PRS Project to inventory prevention research studies and to analyze the efficacy of HIV prevention interventions (Sogolow et al. 2002; Lyles, Kay, et al. in press). The CDC's PRS Project team used rigorous evaluation criteria to initially identify twenty-four interventions with evidence of efficacy. These interventions are described in the *Compendium of Effective HIV Prevention Interventions with Evidence of Effectiveness* (CDC 1999). When this document was later updated, eight evidence-based interventions were added (Kay et al. 2003). More recently, the PRS team reviewed the 2000–2004 literature and identified eighteen interventions that met the PRS best-evidence criteria for efficacy (Lyles, Crepaz, et al. in press). The CDC's REP project pilot tests interventions from the *Compendium* in communities and packages them for diffusion to communities (Neumann and Sogolow 2000).

In 2001, the Institute of Medicine recommended that the CDC rapidly transfer HIV prevention technology to communities and make this effort an essential component of the national HIV prevention plan (Institute of Medicine 2001). In response to the recommendation, the CDC started the Diffusion of Effective Behavioral Interventions (DEBI) project in 2002 to diffuse HIV/STD prevention interventions to CBOs and health departments nationwide. Interventions for DEBI were selected from the *Compendium* and the REP project for diffusion to prevention providers through a training program supported with technical assistance to trainers and implementers. Introducing DEBI required extensive strategic planning and partnership building with stakeholders, including intervention researchers, trainers, technical assistance providers, contractors, and staff from CBOs, health departments, several divisions of the CDC, and other governmental agencies.

"Efficacious" Does Not Always Mean "Effective"

The term "efficacy" is used to describe research results that indicate that an STD/HIV prevention intervention produced a significant outcome and resulted in the desired behavior change—usually a reduction in risk behavior in a specified population in particular locations. "Effectiveness" refers to the evaluation of an implementation of an intervention across multiple sites and under real-world conditions that shows desired outcomes (Flay 1986). While rigorous clinical trials can be used to evaluate intervention efficacy, the true test of large-scale intervention effectiveness in a community is the adoption of the intervention and measurable outcomes in real-world settings (Institute of Medicine 2001). Whereas in an efficacy study the research team is primarily concerned with internal validity (that is, the association of the independent variables with the dependent variables) in an effectiveness study the research team is concerned with external validity (that is, the generalizability of effects over populations, venues, or other treatment conditions). Because there is typically less control in real-world settings, implementation of an efficacious intervention does not mean that it will be effective in broad public health practice (Glasgow et al. 2003). The lack of evidence of effectiveness is a consideration when selecting interventions for potential diffusion.

In typical efficacy studies, little attention has been focused on how interventions could be realistically carried out in various and differing program settings (Clark 1995). An intervention that is efficacious in a research trial is not necessarily effective when implemented by community prevention providers. Little attention has been directed to helping HIV prevention providers successfully adapt evidence-based interventions (Kelly et al. 2000), or to increasing the scientific understanding of the organizational factors that affect implementation in community settings (Miller 2003). Glasgow and colleagues (2003) have made strong arguments that the absence of such research impedes the transfer of behavioral interventions to public health practice. We found this to be true during our three years of diffusing interventions. Many CBOs are sophisticated consumers and ask such critical questions as: "In how many cities was this intervention shown to be efficacious?" and "If this intervention was shown to be efficacious ten years ago, what guarantee is there that it still works?"

To address their skepticism, we used the following line of reasoning when we communicated with CBOs that doubted the effectiveness of the interventions we proposed to diffuse. Except for two interventions that have had broader success, the interventions under consideration for diffusion effectively reduced HIV-related risk in one and sometimes two clinical trials or quasi-experimental designs. The two exceptions are the Popular Opinion Leader, which has repeatedly been found to be efficacious in a range of cities and populations (Kelly et al. 1991; Kelly et al. 1992) and has been adapted to populations beyond those in Kelly's original research (Miller et al. 1998), and the AIDS Community Demonstration Project (ACDP 1999), which was found to be efficacious in a multisite study with multiple risk populations. We stressed that there is no guarantee that the interventions, even when implemented exactly as intended, will work every time and in every situation. This is especially true when diverse communities working in fluid political and funding environments implement the interventions. These interventions do, however, have a better chance of reducing HIV-related risk than interventions that were never shown to be effective. This is the basic rationale that we used to move forward with diffusion of behavioral interventions that have been shown to be efficacious but have not yet been established as effective.

Practical Barriers Encountered during Diffusion

We encountered five practical barriers during diffusion. First, some CBOs did not provide incentives for participation in behavioral interventions. Second, some interventions were conceptually complex or difficult to implement, or both. Third, some agencies lacked the capacity to implement complex interventions. Fourth, some CBOs could not bear the costs of some of the interventions. Fifth, difficulty in adapting the intervention to local conditions and populations was an immediate and persistent theme.

Most of the group-level interventions were designed as behavioral research that required subjects to participate in multiple group-level intervention sessions and to be followed up after the study to determine the longer-term outcomes of the intervention on risk behaviors. To obtain higher levels of both consistent participation and follow-up, providers conducting most of the group-level interventions used incentives for participation and follow-up assessments. However, paying incentives comparable to those paid in research settings is frequently beyond the resources of many HIV prevention providers serving the gay community.

Many of the interventions were conceptually complex or difficult to implement, or both. Prevention providers demonstrate a broad range of agency capacity to implement an evidence-based behavioral intervention.

However, there is a likely relationship between agency capacity and the ability to adopt and successfully implement a complex intervention.

Another barrier was cost. The funds required to appropriately implement the interventions typically exceed the budgets that most prevention providers allocate to this type of activity.

Additionally, agencies may not be adequately prepared to adapt interventions to meet the needs of their target populations while maintaining fidelity to the core elements and integrity of the intervention. HIV prevention technology diffusion systems are new, and technical assistance from experts or researchers may not be readily accessible. We have little understanding of the ability of evidence-based interventions to successfully undergo the transformation of adaptation in communities, or whether this transformation will dilute effectiveness.

Effective Interventions for Diffusion to MSM Populations

The process of diffusing evidence-based behavioral interventions and building the capacity for implementing them in field settings is a large and complex task. We considered the following five interventions listed in the CDC's *Compendium* that have been proven efficacious for MSM:

Popular Opinion Leader (POL) by Kelly and colleagues (1991);
AIDS Community Demonstration Project (ACDP) (Community
    PROMISE) by the ACDP Research Group (1999);
Mpowerment by Kegeles and colleagues (1996);
Small Group Lecture Plus Skills Training (Valdiserri et al. 1989); and
Behavioral Self-Management and Assertion Skills (Kelly et al. 1989).

We summarize each of the interventions considered and explain the decision on whether to move forward with diffusion activities.

Popular Opinion Leader (POL)

The POL intervention (Kelly et al. 1991) is a community-level intervention.[2] The POL model is based on the premise that sexual behavior change in the gay community can occur if enough respected peers (that is, popular opinion leaders) within the gay community endorse the desired behavior with peers in casual conversations. Kelly based the POL model on Everett Rogers's (1983) diffusion of innovation theory, which suggests that opinion leaders within a community can bring about changes in norms when they adopt, endorse, and diffuse the behavior change messages through peer networks.

Ethnographic methods are used to identify popular members of the target population. These persons, referred to as "popular opinion leaders" (POLs) or simply "opinion leaders," are recruited to participate in the intervention and are trained to communicate HIV risk-reduction messages to their peers through casual conversations. After several groups of POLs have been recruited and trained, they are supported by agency staff in conducting intervention activities. Opinion leaders diffuse safer-sex messages throughout the gay community by using social networks. These safer-sex messages eventually will strengthen community safer-sex norms.

The POL intervention was a leading candidate for national diffusion by the CDC's Divisions of HIV/AIDS Prevention because results of multiple studies have shown this intervention could reduce the prevalence and frequency of high-risk sexual behaviors of men who socialize in gay bars in midsize U.S. cities (Kelly et al. 1991; Kelly et al. 1992; Kelly et al. 1997). Very small towns may not have the gay male social networks that are necessary for the diffusion of the safer-sex norms. Larger cities or gay resort towns, such as Provincetown, Massachusetts, and Key West, Florida, have so many gay tourists that diffusion of safer-sex norms can be hampered by the movement of tourists into and out of the target community. In the target communities, from baseline to follow-up, the intervention consistently resulted in an approximately 30 percent increase in condom use by the gay community for anal intercourse. In the control cities, an increase in condom use was not demonstrated in the gay community.

The decision to select POL for national diffusion was further strengthened by a replication study of the POL with male sex workers in three male hustler bars in New York City (Miller et al. 1998), which provided further evidence of the adaptability of the POL intervention.

Miller and colleagues (1998) reasoned that the patrons of specific gay bars form a subset of a social network within the larger gay community, and the intervention messages and norms the POLs convey could be diffused by this smaller social network within the larger New York City gay community. Miller and colleagues (1998) provided evidence that, when implemented correctly—that is, specific social networks are identified within the larger community and POLs are recruited from those networks—the POL intervention was adaptable to large cities as well as midsize cities. Two other events influenced our decision to include POL in the DEBI project: the

CDC had also selected the POL model for the REP process, and Kelly and colleagues (Neumann and Sogolow 2000) had created a POL intervention kit.

During the preparation of materials to promote POL, reports on the effectiveness of POL interventions for gay men in the United Kingdom indicated that the intervention did not lead to a reduction in HIV risk behavior. POL was implemented in gay gyms in London (Elford et al. 2001a, 2001b) and in gay bars in Glasgow and Edinburgh, Scotland (Flowers et al. 2002), but without success. These results raised questions: Was POL no longer viable in the gay community? Did the British researchers make implementation errors that would explain the failure to find intervention effects? If the implementation methods of the British researchers were well identified with process measures, we could use this information to strengthen POL training materials and to help ensure that U.S. agencies did not make similar implementation errors.

Kelly (2004) concluded that "neither of the UK studies constituted true or adequate tests of the POL intervention and its conceptual foundations." Kelly reviewed the work of the British researchers and found that their programs did not incorporate many of POL's core elements. Kelly notes that in the study by Flowers and colleagues (2002), a small number of men and women, including personnel from an AIDS organization, were paid as part-time outreach workers to distribute written health education material. Additionally, these employees had not been identified as opinion leaders within the target population. In response to these lapses in the POL protocol, we ensured that the DEBI POL training materials on recruitment included appropriate methods for identifying potential opinion leaders and that they discouraged using agency employees in this role.

Kelly (2004) further noted that in the research conducted by Elford and colleagues (Elford et al. 2001a, 2001b; Elford et al. 2002), most contacts within the target community consisted of providing brief information about AIDS rather than a personal endorsement of safer-sex practices. Only a small number of the opinion leaders were recruited, trained, and maintained by the project. To deal with these gaps, we ensured that the DEBI POL training curricula fully addressed the issues of delivering POL prevention messages, estimating the size of the target population to be reached by the intervention, and emphasizing the need to recruit 15 percent of that population. The POL core element that addresses the need to recruit this percentage of the target population to endorse new behavioral norms appears to be essential to the success of the intervention. Recruitment of a large number of appropriate opinion leaders is needed to establish new sex behavior norms within a community.[3]

Kelly (2004: 144) states that "lack of knowledge about AIDS and risk-reduction steps rarely appear any longer as robust determinants of sexual behavior among MSM." He identifies determinants of sexual behavior by psychological factors such as perceptions about peer and sexual partner norms regarding safer sex, perceived vulnerability to HIV infection, and self-efficacy in being able to conduct safer sex within a range of conditions and partner types. In response to these findings, the DEBI POL training materials were revised to include information on HIV transmission and to ensure that the psychosocial aspects of risk-reduction messages were fully incorporated into training materials.

Community PROMISE

Community PROMISE (ACDP 1999) was implemented to reach diverse populations at high risk for HIV infection. One target group for the intervention was non-gay-identified MSM. When data were aggregated across all sites and risk groups, the intervention was found to successfully move target communities through the stages of change toward safer-sex behaviors. Role-model stories based on the experiences of non-gay-identified MSM that demonstrated movement toward safer-sex behaviors were disseminated through their social network by peer advocates of non-gay-identified MSM to other non-gay-identified MSM. Researchers at the sites where non-gay-identified MSM were studied (located in Denver, Colorado; Long Beach, California; and Seattle, Washington) found a significant increase in condom use for anal sex with nonprimary male sexual partners. However, the intervention was not efficacious for non-gay-identified MSM for condom use for vaginal intercourse with primary female sex partners (Goldbaum et al. 1999).

Community PROMISE, the only evidence-based intervention for non-gay-identified MSM in the *Compendium*, was selected for inclusion in DEBI for national diffusion. The STD/HIV prevention training centers in Dallas and Denver have offered training to CBO staff on how to implement the intervention for several years. Denver's STD/HIV Prevention Training Center implemented Community PROMISE for non-gay-identified MSM for five years (1991–1996). The ongoing project has been adapted to serve MSM sex workers, MSM who inject drugs, and, most recently, MSM noninjecting substance users. Although it does not have the name recognition of POL among CBOs, Community PROMISE is a compelling candidate as a prevention intervention within gay communities.

Community PROMISE intuitively appeals to communities because of the role-model stories, which are based on interviews with members of the target population. However, the appeal of such stories obscures the complexity of this community-level intervention, which requires mastery of multiple behavior change theories to create these stories and command of complex community survey sampling methods to assess intervention effects. The decision to move forward with diffusion of Community PROMISE was further facilitated by the development of the intervention kit through the REP process (Neumann and Sogolow 2000).

Mpowerment

Mpowerment (Kegeles et al. 1996) is a community-level intervention for young MSM. The intervention uses a range of strategies and activities to reach young gay men with health messages, to change sexual behaviors, and to develop gay community norms to support the maintenance of safer-sex behaviors. The intervention uses "social opportunity" as a tool for reaching the target audience. The researchers found that young gay men are motivated to engage in social opportunities to meet and interact with other young gay men. Thus, social opportunities became a component of the intervention.

The intervention uses formal and informal outreach, one-session groups, and social-marketing techniques to reach the target population. Formal outreach, defined by Kegeles and colleagues (1996) as outreach to specific identified venues at particular times and dates in the gay community, creates visibility for the intervention. Informal outreach, based on diffusion of safer-sex norms through gay community social networks, is facilitated through subtle communication skills and personal endorsement of safer-sex norms that are taught during the one-session "M-groups." The M-groups are skills-building sessions that teach the men how to practice safer-sex negotiation and correct condom use so that they can transfer these skills to other members of the young gay community. Research indicates that those who participate in the intervention significantly decreased their rates of unprotected anal intercourse. The decision to diffuse Mpowerment was facilitated by the development of an Mpowerment intervention kit that was funded through the REP process (Neumann and Sogolow 2000), the National Institute of Mental Health, and the University of California's AIDS Research

Program. In close collaboration with researchers Susan Kegeles and Greg Rebchook, the CDC has diffused Mpowerment nationally through DEBI.

Small Group Lecture Plus Skills Training

Valdiserri and colleagues (1989) delivered an intervention consisting of a lecture and skills training session given in a two-session, small-group format in a CBO setting. The cohort of MSM was 95 percent white; 33 percent had a college degree. The 60-to-90-minute lecture component, which was led by a gay health educator, reviewed HIV transmission and the clinical outcomes of HIV infection, the risks of specific sexual behaviors, the importance of risk reduction through safer-sex practices, correct condom use, and the interpretation of HIV antibody tests. The 140-minute skills training session was led by a psychotherapist with experience in counseling gay men. The skills training included role-playing, psychodrama, and group process (that is, facilitated discussions) to promote the social acceptability of safer sex. The counselor also presented strategies to reduce sexual risk behaviors and led a group discussion on male sexuality and personal relationships among gay men.

Two of the investigators, Ronald Valdiserri and Laura Leviton, expressed concerns that the intervention content might be outdated and that the conditions for delivering the intervention, which included use of a mental health professional, might not be easily replicated by CBOs serving the gay community. On the basis of these discussions, the intervention was not included in the DEBI project. The recommendation and rationale offered by the original researchers not to diffuse an intervention are key factors in deciding not to select a particular evidence-based intervention for diffusion.

Many Men, Many Voices

Many Men, Many Voices (MMMV) is an intervention adapted from the group-level intervention Behavioral Self-Management and Assertion Skills (Kelly et al. 1989). The intervention was adapted for African American gay men by the STD/HIV Prevention Training Center, University of Rochester School of Medicine and Dentistry, and Men of Color Health Awareness (MOCHA), both in Rochester, New York, and by People of Color in Crisis, a CBO in New York City. Because MMMV is a recent adaptation of an evidence-based intervention in the *Compendium*, we do not yet know if the adapted version of the intervention is efficacious. However, this intervention was selected for diffusion because of the demand for an evidence-based intervention for African American MSM. The urgency of the demand was supported by epidemiologic evidence indicating that African American MSM remain the subgroup within the MSM population most affected by HIV/AIDS (CDC 2001). An evidence-based intervention that had been adapted by and for African American gay men was expected to hasten the diffusion process of this intervention into the most affected communities.

Discussion

Four interventions, three of which were packaged through REP (Neumann and Sogolow 2000), were selected for diffusion through DEBI for MSM. Three were community-level interventions, and one was a group-level intervention. In two meta-analyses, Johnson and colleagues (2002) and Herbst and colleagues (2005) found that community-level and group-level interventions for MSM produce similar behavioral outcomes. In community-level interventions, the benefits for MSM who did or did not participate directly in the intervention were similar to the benefits experienced by MSM who directly participated in group-level interventions. Because of these similar outcomes and the potential to reach larger numbers of MSM at the community level, three of the four interventions selected for diffusion to MSM communities are at the community level—POL, Mpowerment, and Community PROMISE.

In communities where participation in facility-based interventions is not likely, there is a marked absence of community-level interventions that have the potential to reach large numbers of MSM (Johnson et al. 2002). Diffusion of community-level interventions for MSM is supported by the findings of Johnson and colleagues (2002). However, community-level interventions such as Mpowerment, which has the capability of reaching large numbers of people in the population at risk, are costly. Unfortunately, a community-level intervention has not yet been developed that can reach a large number of MSM, is capable of producing substantial behavior change effects, and can be delivered by the average HIV prevention provider. Mpowerment and Community PROMISE have the potential to succeed as community-level interventions. However, Mpowerment requires extensive agency resources for all intervention components, and Community PROMISE requires extensive capacity building to train agency staff how to develop stage-based role-model stories.

Although many evidence-based HIV prevention interventions for MSM can be adapted for ethnic minority MSM, few interventions have been developed with the collaboration of ethnic minority gay men, and few have been proven efficacious in outcome studies. MMMV is the first intervention to begin to meet these criteria, but its efficacy still needs to be evaluated.

All four of the selected behavioral interventions for MSM are dependent on an MSM social network, gay-identified or non-gay-identified. These social networks are the vehicle by which the intervention meets its behavioral change goals. Johnson and colleagues (2002: S125) found that community-level interventions "reached and influenced substantial proportions of the study populations, whether through direct exposure to the formal intervention mechanism or by informal social diffusion." The community-level interventions in DEBI—POL, Community PROMISE, and Mpowerment—depend on a social network for recruiting members of the target audience to participate in the intervention to ensure diffusion of safer-sex norms. The group-level intervention in DEBI—MMMV—depends on a social network for recruiting the target audience to participate in the intervention activities.

The historical context of an intervention's development, including socio-cultural and other factors, may influence the effectiveness of the intervention in MSM communities. Interventions developed before highly active anti-retroviral therapy (HAART) was available for people living with HIV are possibly based on an outdated public perception of the morbidity and mortality associated with HIV infection. Since HAART was introduced, the morbidity and mortality have been perceived to be more manageable (Moore and Chaisson 1999; Palella et al. 1998). This dramatic improvement in the management and treatment of people living with HIV affects the efforts of behavioral intervention staff in recruiting and retaining peer advocates, volunteers, and popular opinion leaders. It will be beneficial to learn how post-HAART conditions affect the current use of social networks as a vehicle for HIV prevention interventions in MSM communities and how these can be adapted based on this information.

Openly gay men rather than non-gay-identified MSM were the focus of three of the evidence-based HIV prevention interventions for MSM. Appropriate behavioral interventions other than Community PROMISE have not been developed specifically for this hard-to-reach segment of MSM, especially those who are ethnic minorities. However, this does not mean that non-gay-identified MSM cannot be reached by community-level interventions designed for openly gay MSM. Non-gay-identified MSM may be reached by the diffusion of norms and behaviors through the social networks where gay-identified MSM and non-gay-identified MSM commingle.

In community-level interventions such as POL, Mpowerment, and Community PROMISE, which can be diffused through gay male social networks, the benefits MSM will derive from the diffusion of safer-sex norms may be related to MSM's proximity to the center of the social network or the social interaction bonds they have with members of the network. When community-level interventions are diffused through the gay male social network, the farther away a particular gay man is from the center of this social network or the fewer social bonds he maintains, the less likely he will benefit from the diffusion of safer-sex norms. This outcome is a result of reduced exposure to these norms because of his position on the fringes of the MSM social network. When two non-gay-identified MSM engage in a sexual encounter, higher-risk sex may be more probable since neither is integrated into the gay community social network; therefore they have not benefited from diffusion of safer-sex norms strengthened by an effective behavioral intervention. Paradoxically, HIV infection risk may be increased in gay social networks where unsafe sex is the normative state or in gay social networks that have not been influenced by an effective behavioral intervention.

When a gay man who is integrated into the gay community and who can be reached with an effective community-level intervention has a sexual encounter with a non-gay-identified man, intervention expectations are that the safer-sex norms instilled in the gay man will be the predominant influence in the sexual encounter. However, this supposition has not yet been empirically demonstrated. A factor that may affect the safety of male-to-male sexual encounters is whether one or both men have been exposed to risk-reduction interventions. Other factors, such as attractiveness of sex partners, serostatus, male-to-male sexual roles and power dynamics, and intoxication, may also influence behaviors (Stall et al. 2000). More study is needed on these topics.

Another topic that requires more research is how a change in the primary sexual partner due to the break-up of a couple affects subsequent sexual risk behaviors with new sexual partners and transmission of STD/HIV. If relationship dynamics change the risk determinants for safer-sex behavior, then interventions may be needed that focus on different patterns of male-to-male sexual bonds. The gay community is a fluid phenomenon with individuals constantly coming into and out of the social network, thus requiring a range of effective behavioral interventions that are sustained by communities to maximize effectiveness.

Conclusion

Input from MSM communities and behavioral scientists who conduct intervention research and translate that research into real-world conditions is needed for the successful creation and diffusion of additional evidence-based interventions into real-world settings. Behavioral scientists have been and continue to be funded to design, implement, and evaluate behavioral interventions for MSM populations for efficacy. Yet more evidence about the effectiveness of these interventions is needed. An additional need today is to engage behavioral scientists in designing and implementing behavioral science diffusion systems to reach MSM populations.

The studies done in the United Kingdom increased the scrutiny placed on POL and other community-level interventions. We think this added scrutiny could help ensure that lessons learned from program implementation failure are used to strengthen the training of prevention providers in the United States on the implementation of POL and other HIV prevention models.

A strategic diffusion system must account for variance in the capacity of HIV prevention providers to implement evidence-based interventions. Such a system requires development of diffusion channels, such as training and technical assistance, that reflect the core elements of the behavioral research while helping providers adapt the intervention to specific community needs and resources. Prevention providers serving the gay community may be motivated to adapt evidence-based programs once they are convinced that such programs play an essential role in improving prevention practices. These providers know the at-risk populations they serve and the local resources and politics, but they must be instructed on how best to adapt interventions while maintaining the fidelity of the intervention. This community-level experience of the adaptation process could be of great value to other prevention providers as well as to the behavioral science community.

Scientists in the applied social sciences working in STD/HIV prevention build and use social networks of prevention providers, such as CBOs and health departments, to diffuse interventions that can reach social networks within at-risk populations. Gay male social networks within communities are also vehicles for diffusing the messages of effective evidence-based interventions and for promoting safer-sex norms. Through word-of-mouth endorsement of the intervention activities, this social network also facilitates the recruitment of members from the at-risk community to participate in these activities. The social network's communications about the intervention activities also help to legitimize and sustain group-level interventions. Collaboration on many levels is essential for an intervention to be effective in the community it is intended to serve.

Diffusion of evidence-based interventions to gay communities requires partnership with and endorsement by MSM-serving agencies. Social networks of agencies that serve the gay community can help to facilitate the flow of science into effective HIV prevention practice. Strategic diffusion at the national level and implementation of evidence-based interventions at the community level that engage behavioral scientists, the community at large, and the gay community are vital to improving or maximizing HIV prevention efforts. More study is needed on how to effectively bring together all the essential components of an intervention to ensure its successful implementation. An ongoing commitment to confront the dynamics of HIV prevention will strengthen our resolve to continue to develop effective interventions to reduce the number of new HIV infections.

Notes

1. The findings and conclusions in this chapter are those of the authors and do not necessarily represent the views of the CDC.

2. The POL has nine core elements (Kelly 2004) that are needed to be feasible for implementation by CDC-funded CBOs through the Divisions of HIV/AIDS Prevention. These are (1) having a well-defined target audience that can be reached in community venues and that allows estimates of the size of the at-risk population, (2) using ethnographic techniques to segment the population and to identify the potential opinion leaders, (3) recruiting 15 percent of the target population as opinion leaders for diffusion of norms to occur, (4) training opinion leaders on how to casually introduce safer-sex concepts in conversation with friends, (5) training opinion leaders on how to recommend practical risk-reduction steps to friends, (6) conducting weekly group sessions for skills building, (7) setting goals for opinion leaders on the number of peers they hope to reach with risk reduction endorsement, (8) reviewing and reinforcing opinion leaders' efforts, and (9) using a visual logo to start a conversation.

3. To ensure that HIV prevention providers understand the amount of effort this intervention requires, we have consistently used the following example: If a POL program wanted to influence male condom use with 1,000 Asian and Pacific Islander MSM in Oakland, California, they would need to recruit, train, and maintain 15 percent of this population as POLs. Thus, 150 men would need to be identified, interviewed, recruited, trained, and maintained. Some men would choose not to be interviewed, not to join the training, and not to remain active in the POL program, meaning that many potential

opinion leaders would be needed at the beginning stages of program implementation to ensure that 150 opinion leaders remain in the program. If fifteen potential opinion leaders are in each training cycle, and a training cycle takes five weeks, ten training cohorts are needed over a span of fifty weeks. The intervention may not reach the criteria level of 15 percent until after a year of program implementation.

References

AIDS Community Demonstration Projects (ACDP) Research Group. 1999. Community-level HIV intervention in five cities: Final outcome data from the CDC AIDS Community Demonstration Projects. *American Journal of Public Health* 89(3): 336–45.

Centers for Disease Control and Prevention (CDC). 2001. HIV incidence among young men who have sex with men—7 U.S. cities, 1994–2000. *Morbidity and Mortality Weekly Report* 50: 440–44.

Centers for Disease Control and Prevention (CDC), HIV/AIDS Prevention Research Synthesis Project. 1999. *Compendium of HIV Prevention Interventions with Evidence of Effectiveness*, 1–64. http://www.cdc.gov/hiv/pubs/hivcompendium/hivcompendium.htm.

Chen, S., S. Gibson, and W. McFarland. 2002. High level of unprotected anal intercourse between HIV serodiscordant men who have sex with men, San Francisco. Abstract No. TuOrC1148. Paper presented at the Fourteenth International AIDS Conference, Barcelona.

Clark, G. N. 1995. Improving the transition from basic efficacy research to effectiveness studies: Methodological issues and procedures. *Journal of Consulting and Clinical Psychology* 63: 718–25.

Collins, C., C. Harshbarger, and R. Sawyer. 2004. Broad diffusion of 12 effective behavioral interventions for HIV prevention. Abstract No. ThPeP8182. Paper presented at the Fifteenth International AIDS Conference, Bangkok.

DeGroff, A. 1996. Is prevention research reaching front line prevention programs? A descriptive study from San Francisco. Paper presented at the Eleventh International Conference on AIDS, Vancouver, British Columbia.

DiFranceisco, W., J. A. Kelly, L. Otto-Salaj, T. L. McAuliffe, A. M. Somlai, K. Hackl, T. G. Heckman, D. R. Holtgrave, and D. J. Rompa. 1999. Factors influencing attitudes within AIDS service organizations toward the use of research-based HIV prevention interventions. *AIDS Education and Prevention* 11: 72–86.

Elford, J., G. Bolding, and L. Sherr. 2001a. Peer education has no significant impact on HIV risk behaviors among gay men in London. *AIDS* 15: 535–37.

———. 2001b. Peer-led HIV prevention among gay men in London: Process evaluation. *AIDS Care* 14: 351–60.

Elford, J. A., L. Otto-Salaj, L. Williamson, G. and Bolding. 2002. Peer-led HIV prevention among homosexual men in Britain. *Sexually Transmitted Infections* 78: 158–59.

Flay, B. R. 1986. Efficacy and effectiveness trials (and other phases of research) in the development of health promotion programs. *Preventive Medicine* 15: 451–74.

Flowers, P., G. J. Hart, L. M. Williamson, J. S. Frankis, and G. J. Der. 2002. Does bar-based peer-led health promotion have a community-level effect amongst gay men in Scotland? *International Journal of STD and AIDS* 13: 102–8.

Glasgow, R. E., E. Lichtenstein, and A. C. Marcus. 2003. Why don't we see more translation of health promotion research to practice? Rethinking the efficacy-to-effectiveness transition. *American Journal of Public Health* 93(8): 1261–267.

Goldbaum, G. M., W. Johnson, R. J. Wolitksi, C. Reitmeijer, R. W. Wood, D. Kasprzyk, and D. Montano. 1999. Sexual behavior change among non-gay-identified men who have sex with men: Response to a community-level intervention. Unpublished data; for more information contact Gary Goldbaum at ggoldbaum@shd.snohomish. wa.gov.

Herbst, J. H., R. T. Sherba, N. Crepaz, J. B. DeLuca, L. Zohrabyan, R. D. Stall, and C. M. Lyles. 2005. A meta-analytic review of HIV behavioral interventions for reducing sexual risk behavior of men who have sex with men. *Journal of Acquired Immune Deficiency Syndrome* 39(2): 228–41.

Institute of Medicine. 2001. Committee on HIV Prevention Strategies in the United States. In *No Time to Lose: Getting More from HIV Prevention*, 68–79. Washington, D.C.: National Academy Press.

Johnson, W. D., L. V. Hedges, G. Ramirez, S. Semann, L. R. Norman, E. Sogolow, M. D. Sweat, and R. M. Diaz. 2002. HIV prevention research for men who have sex with men: A systematic review and meta-analysis. *Journal of Acquired Immune Deficiency Syndrome* 30 (Suppl. 1): S118–29.

Kay, L., N. Crepaz, C. Lyles, T. Griffin, J. Patterson, T. Sherba, J. Britton, J. Herbst, and the HIV/AIDS Prevention Research Synthesis Team. 2003. Update of the *Compendium of HIV Prevention Interventions with Evidence of Effectiveness*. Paper presented at the National HIV Prevention Conference, Atlanta, Georgia.

Kegeles, S. M., R. B. Hays, and T. J. Coates. 1996. The Mpowerment project: A community-level HIV prevention intervention for young gay men. *American Journal of Public Health* 86: 1129–136.

Kelly, J. A. 2004. Popular opinion leaders and HIV prevention peer education: Resolving discrepant findings, and implications for the development of effective community programmes. *AIDS Care* 16(2): 139–50.

Kelly, J. A., D. A. Murphy, K. J. Sikkema, T. L. McAuliffe, R. A. Roffman, L. J. Solomon, R. A. Winett, and S. C. Kalichman. 1997. Randomized, controlled, community-level HIV prevention intervention for sexual risk behavior among homosexual men in U.S. cities. *Lancet* 350: 1500–505.

Kelly, J. A., J. S. St. Lawrence, Y. E. Diaz, L. Y. Stevenson, A. C. Hauth, T. L. Brasfield, S. C. Kalichman, J. E. Smith, and M. E. Andrew. 1991. HIV risk behavior reduction following intervention with key opinion leaders of a population: An experimental analysis. *American Journal of Public Health* 81: 168–71.

Kelly, J. A., J. S. St. Lawrence, H. V. Hood, and T. L. Brasfield. 1989. Behavioral intervention to reduce AIDS risk activities. *Journal of Consulting and Clinical Psychology* 57: 60–67.

Kelly, J. A., J. S. St. Lawrence, L. Y. Stevenson, A. C. Hauth, S. C. Kalichman, Y. E. Diaz, T. L. Brasfield, J. J. Koob, and M. G. Morgan. 1992. Community AIDS/HIV risk reduction: The effects of endorsements by popular people in three cities. *American Journal of Public Health* 82: 1483–489.

Kelly, J. A., A. Somlai, W. J. DiFranceisco, L. L. Otto-Salaj, T. L. McAuliffe, K. L. Hackl, T. G. Heckman, D. R. Holtgrave, and D. Rompa. 2000. Bridging the gap between the science and service of HIV prevention: Transferring effective research-based HIV prevention interventions to community AIDS service providers. *American Journal of Public Health* 90(7): 1082–88.

Linley, L., D. Withum, H. Weinstock, J. Mei, K. Bell, J. Royalty, and M. Miller. 2002. Using STARHS to estimate HIV-1 incidence among patients attending STD clinics in selected U.S. cities, 1997–1999. Paper presented at the Fourteenth International AIDS Conference, Barcelona.

Lyles, C. M., N. Crepaz, J. H. Herbst, L. S. Kay, for the HIV/AIDS Prevention Research Synthesis Team. In press. Evidence-based HIV behavioral prevention from the perspective of CDC's HIV/AIDS Prevention Research Synthesis Team. *AIDS Education and Prevention.*

Lyles, C. M., L. S. Kay, N. Crepaz, J. H. Herbst, W. Passin, A. Kim, S. Rama, S. Thadiparthi, J. DeLuca, and M. Mullins, for the HIV/AIDS Prevention Research Synthesis Team. In press. Interventions with best evidence of efficacy: Findings from a systematic review of HIV behavioral interventions for U.S. populations at high risk, 2000–2004. *American Journal of Public Health.*

Miller, R. L. 2003. Adapting an evidence-based intervention: Tales of the hustler project. *AIDS Education and Prevention* 15 (Suppl. A): S127–38.

Miller, R. L., D. Klotz, and H. M. Eckholdt. 1998. HIV prevention with male prostitutes and patrons of hustler bars: Replication of an HIV prevention intervention. *American Journal of Community Psychology* 26: 97–131.

Moore, R. D., and R. E. Chaisson, 1999. Natural history of HIV infection in the era of combination antiretroviral therapy. *AIDS* 13(14): 1933–942.

National Institutes of Health (NIH). 1997. Interventions to prevent HIV risk behaviors. *NIH Consensus Statement* 15(2): 1–41. NIH Consensus Development Conference, Kensington, Maryland.

Neumann, M. S., and E. D. Sogolow. 2000. Replicating effective programs: HIV/AIDS prevention technology transfer. *AIDS Education and Prevention* 12 (5 Suppl.): S35–48.

Neumann, M. S., E. D. Sogolow, and D. Holtgrave. 2000. Supporting the transfer of HIV prevention behavioral research to public health practice. *AIDS Education and Prevention* 12 (5 Suppl.): S1–S3.

Palella, F. J., Jr., K. M. Delaney, A. C. Moorman, M. O. Loveless, J. Fuhrer, G. A. Satten, D. J. Aschman, and S. D. Holmberg for the HIV Outpatient Study Investigators. 1998. Declining morbidity and mortality among patients with advanced human immunodeficiency virus infection. *New England Journal of Medicine* 338(13): 853–60.

Rogers, E. M. 1983. *Diffusion of Innovations.* 2nd ed. New York: Free Press.

Sogolow, E. D., L. S. Kay, L. S. Doll, M. S. Neumann, J. S. Mezoff, A. N. Eke, S. Semaan, and J. R. Anderson. 2000. Strengthening HIV prevention: Application of a research-to-practice framework. *AIDS Education and Prevention* 12 (Suppl. A): S21–34.

Sogolow, E. D., G. Peersman, S. Semaan, D. Strouse, C. M. Lyles, and the HIV/AIDS Prevention Research Synthesis Project Team. 2002. The HIV/AIDS prevention research synthesis project: Scope, methods, and study classification results. *Journal of Acquired Immune Deficiency Syndromes* 30 (Suppl. 1): S15–29.

Somlai, A. M., J. A. Kelly, L. Otto-Salaj, T. L. McAuliffe, K. Hackl, W. DiFranceisco, B. Amick, T. G. Heckman, D. R. Holtgrave, and D. J. Rompa. 1999. Current HIV prevention activities for women and gay men among 77 ASOs. *Journal of Public Health Management and Practice* 5: 23–33.

Stall, R. D., R. B. Hays, C. R. Waldo, M. Ekstrand, and W. McFarland. 2000. The Gay 90's: A review of research in the 1990's on sexual behavior and HIV risk among men who have sex with men. *AIDS* 14 (Suppl.): S101–14.

Trickett, E. J. 1998. Toward a framework for defining and resolving ethical issues in the protection of communities involved in primary prevention projects. *Ethics Behavior* 8(4): 321–27.

Valdiserri, R. O., D. W. Lyter, L. C. Leviton, C. M. Callahan, L. A. Kingsley, and C. R. Rinaldo. 1989. AIDS prevention in homosexual and bisexual men: Results of a randomized trial evaluating two risk reduction interventions. *AIDS* 3: 21–26.

Valleroy, L. A., D. A. MacKellar, J. M. Karon, D. H. Rosen, W. McFarland, D. A. Shehan, S. R. Stoyanoff, M. LaLota, D. D. Celentano, B. A. Koblin, M. H. Katz, L. V. Torian, and R. S. Janssen. 2001. HIV prevalence and associated risks in young men who have sex with men. *Journal of the American Medical Association* 284(2): 198–204.

6

"Not One Inch"

The Ruthless Politics of Developing
an AIDS Community-Based Organization

DOUGLAS A. FELDMAN

Looking back now, I should have known better at the time. When I accidentally found out back in early 1987 that Mary Ann Carey, the district manager of Community Planning Board 9 in Queens, one of New York City's
five boroughs, was in the hospital for serious heart problems, she pleaded
with me that I not let her political enemies know about it. "Please, don't let
them know," she told me. "Let them think that it's something less serious. If
they find out it is my heart, they will use that against me. They will use my
health as an issue to try to get rid of me." I remember looking at her—a truly
courageous and caring woman—in disbelief at how anyone could actually
think that people would use someone's misfortune concerning their health
to undermine their position. By the end of that year, however, I knew exactly what she was talking about. Local-level politics in the central part of
the borough of Queens can get fairly ruthless. District 9 is located in central
Queens, covering Kew Gardens, Woodhaven, Richmond Hill, and northern
Ozone Park.

At times, it seems so very long ago. But at other times, it seems as if it
just happened yesterday. It was in 1986 that the idea for the AIDS Center
of Queens County (ACQC) began. The "official" history of the founding of
ACQC reads: "a dedicated group of concerned residents and professionals . . . nurses, social workers, religious leaders and members of the gay
community . . . organized to respond to the RFP [request for proposal from
the New York State AIDS Institute]. Their proposal was accepted and, with
a start-up grant of $160,000, the AIDS Center of Queens County came into
existence" (VolunteerNYC.org 2007). But that's not quite what happened.

Here's how it really happened. I attended an informational meeting held
by the New York State AIDS Institute in March 1986 in which the institute
had requested proposals for developing AIDS services in the Bronx, Brook-

lyn, and Queens (three of the five boroughs of New York City). As Health and Social Services Committee Chair of Community Planning Board District 9 in Queens, I was well aware of the scarcity of AIDS-related services in the borough.

At that time, Gay Men's Health Crisis (GMHC) had a few teams of buddy volunteers operating in the western half of Queens, while the Long Island Association for AIDS Care (LIAAC), the AIDS community-based organization serving Nassau and Suffolk counties, had one team of buddy volunteers operating in the eastern half of the borough. However, with over 1,000 people diagnosed with AIDS living in Queens at the time, people who wanted to visit a case manager or counselor would have to travel into Manhattan to the GMHC offices. Those coming from the central or eastern part of this borough of two million people would have to travel for at least an hour or more on a bus and subway, since there was no AIDS center located in Queens.

By then, as an applied and medical anthropologist, I had previously conducted a study of early behavioral change among gay men in New York City as a response to the new health crisis. I had conducted AIDS-related research in Rwanda, had attended a National Academy of Science workshop on HIV epidemiology, and had published my first edited volume on AIDS. I resigned that same month from my position as principal writer with the New York City Department of Finance so that I might work full-time as a research fellow at the Human Relations Area Files in New Haven, Connecticut, where during the spring and summer of 1986 we developed and submitted several research proposals on AIDS. I developed proposals for additional AIDS research in Rwanda, which were submitted to the National Institute of Mental Health (NIMH) and the National Science Foundation (NSF), and a proposal for an AIDS national hotline, and began a proposal for a Yale University/Human Relations Area Files joint AIDS research center. Unfortunately, none of these proposals were funded, so I continued part-time teaching at New York University.

I was personally and professionally committed to combating HIV/AIDS. I had conducted my doctoral dissertation research in sexually transmitted infection (STI) clinics on Long Island, and was now focusing on AIDS as an STI. Perhaps more important, during these early years of AIDS, as a gay person I was concerned with what the disease was doing to the gay community—to my community. Were we all going to eventually die from this epidemic? This crisis loomed as a veritable holocaust, and I was compelled to do something about it.

The Beginning of the AIDS Center

It was clear to me that the borough of Queens desperately needed an AIDS program, so I started working on the New York State AIDS Institute's request for proposals (RFPs) to develop one. I submitted the proposal through a Queens-based health organization, with the agreement that if it were funded, I would serve as the program director of the new AIDS program. Mel Rosen, the institute's director, and his assistant, Elaine Erhlich, met with us on the Friday before the Labor Day weekend to negotiate the details of the grant that would cover the new program. However, at the last moment, to my complete dismay and surprise, the director of the health organization declared her intention that we would only serve as a referral agency and not provide any real psychosocial services. This clearly was not what the institute wanted, and I knew it.

As everyone began to get up to leave, I realized that if I did not quickly come up with an alternative, all my efforts to secure an AIDS program based in Queens would have been in vain. I offered to rewrite the proposal to create a whole new AIDS community-based organization that would offer all of the needed services that the institute wanted and that was required in their RFP.

For a moment, Rosen and Erhlich stared at each other, rather bewildered. Then they looked back to me. "I can rewrite this proposal and give you exactly what you are asking for, create a new model AIDS organization that would solve the problem of inadequate services in this borough. I would serve as the new AIDS center's executive director," I told them. They cautiously sat down again, and we began to discuss it. I elaborated on what the AIDS center would do. They said that they would need the new proposal completed in four days, and they would take a look at it. "Consider it done," I said. I canceled my plans for that Labor Day weekend and had it to them by the day after Labor Day.

Our mission would be to provide case management for persons with AIDS (PWAs), an AIDS hotline, and a comprehensive HIV education program. We would launch a volunteer buddy program that would visit PWAs in their homes and provide assistance and companionship, and also provide individual and group counseling and other AIDS-related services.

I came up with the name "AIDS Center of Queens County" rather spontaneously. People in the borough of Queens never referred to Queens as "Queens County," but I was concerned that if we named it the "AIDS Center of Queens," antigay bigots would denigrate the organization's name. So

I added "County" to the end of the name. Besides, the acronym "ACQC" sounded like "ACDC," which was a popular term within the gay community for bisexual men at the time, and it had a catchy sound to it.

While Elaine Ehrlich immediately liked the proposal, for me, a nervous six weeks followed. I was told that there would be a fifty-fifty chance for it to be funded, and every week I was told the answer might come the following week. I was not working at the time, and the bills were coming in.

Finally, I got the word that the proposal was indeed funded with an initial grant of $157,000 beginning in mid-October 1986. I assembled a board of directors, incorporated the organization, submitted an application for 501.C3 nonprofit status, and began hiring staff.

One of our first hurdles was a prolonged seven-month delay in receiving our first check from the state of New York. I tried to resolve our growing cash flow problem by meeting directly with the directors of several hospitals in Queens and requested a cash donation. To my pleasant surprise, this was fairly successful and brought in several thousand dollars. We were told by the New York State AIDS Institute that LIAAC, the AIDS organization to our immediate east, could (with no risk to them) act as a conduit for our funds and speed up our payment from the state. However, the LIAAC board of directors, much to my disappointment, refused to assist us. Apparently, they saw no advantage in helping us, and may have seen us as a competitor for HIV clients in the eastern part of Queens, where they had been working. Nevertheless, we succeeded in getting a generous no-interest bridge loan from the United Way of New York, and later we obtained bridge loans from a commercial bank.

We had been working out of a two-room, 400-square-foot office during the day, which was generously loaned to us by one of our board members who used the office only during the evening hours. By April 1987, we were literally bursting at the seams, with chairs, people, and file cabinets. Our new office furniture was sitting in storage, we could not hold counseling sessions during the evening hours, and my health educator was threatening to quit unless I gave him a permanent desk to work at. After waiting for six months for our first actual check to arrive from the state, we finally had the money to move out to a new location, but nowhere to go. I immediately began looking for a 2,000-square-foot office in central Queens that we could quickly move into. But when they learned what the letters "ACQC" stood for, the offices were no longer available. One rental agent initially had four prospects lined up for me to visit, but when he mentioned to them that we were an AIDS center, the appointments were all canceled.

I eventually found a perfect space on an upper floor of an office building in an excellent location along Queens Boulevard close to a subway stop. At first the large rental management firm, Lefrak Management Corporation, was enthusiastic about renting to us, but when they learned we were an AIDS center, the offer was withdrawn, and they instead showed us a smaller, inadequate space in an apartment basement nowhere near public transportation. I filed an AIDS discrimination complaint against the rental firm with the New York State Division of Human Rights, and I was pleased to learn a year and a half later that we had won the case.

Finally, I located a space in the Richmond Hill section of central Queens. It was in front of a bus stop, was in the middle of a commercial area along Jamaica Avenue, was near an elevated subway stop, had parking in the rear of the building, was exactly 2,000 square feet, and was well within our budget. Located above a large hardware store, the space needed considerable renovation. It had formerly been occupied by a rock band and had graffiti all over the walls, and needles and syringes were found on the floors. I liked the symbolism of converting this makeshift "shooting gallery" into an AIDS service center. The landlord was willing to rent to us (as long as we put "ACQC, Inc." and not the word "AIDS" on our front door, which I told him was no problem), and so we signed the lease. City councilperson Arthur Katzman, one of our board members and an attorney, had reviewed the lease. Katzman was ideologically a progressive in a council district that was both conservative and progressive. He was a very astute politician trying to placate his conservative constituency, while remaining true to his strong progressive principles.

Renovations took longer than promised, but we finally moved in on May 26, 1987. During the next few days we were up and running in our new location, offering evening individual and group counseling, and we were able to do our buddy training in a more comfortable space during evening hours. Buddy training was a common service activity during the 1980s where healthy volunteers would become friends and assist AIDS clients. Everything was going along fine with our board members, deputy director, director of social services, volunteer coordinator, new health educator (the other one did resign even with a new desk and office), administrative assistant, office aide, a growing cadre of volunteers, an increasing number of HIV and AIDS clients, and myself.

Resistance against the AIDS Center

However, on June 19 I received a phone call from Arlene Perdone, president of the Richmond Hill Block Association, asking me if it was true that we had moved into "her neighborhood" without first obtaining the approval of her block association. I told her we had moved in, and no approval was required. The Richmond Hill Block Association is the same politically conservative group that had been instrumental in putting together, along with other nearby block associations, a massive demonstration two years earlier against an elementary public school in neighboring Ozone Park that allowed a child with AIDS to attend. The message that they sent was that it was acceptable to discriminate against persons, even children, with AIDS. The demonstration in 1985 received national media attention and helped increase membership and rejuvenate the political base of the local block associations. By June 23, I was getting calls from several of my board members saying that they heard that the Richmond Hill community was up in arms. Richmond Hill is a mostly Italian American and other white ethnic community of old private homes, and it had been declining during the 1980s. The opening scene with rows of houses in the 1970s television sitcom *All in the Family* was actually filmed in Richmond Hill, and this was certainly "Archie Bunker country." Perdone invited me to a community-wide meeting held at the Richmond Hill Block Association town hall located four blocks from our AIDS center on the following evening.

At the meeting, attended by about 150 worried and angry citizens (inadequately counterbalanced with only a few of our board members and staff), I explained our mission and responded to their concerns about AIDS. A major concern was what if a Richmond Hill high school student on his way to the high school a block away was solicited by an AIDS-infected "prostitute" from nearby Jamaica, Queens, hanging out in front of our building? Read "white" for the male high school student and read "African American" for the female sex worker. One of our key missions was to combat AIDS discrimination in the borough of Queens. Indeed, only a week or so earlier we had filed a complaint through the New York City Department of Consumer Affairs on behalf of our clients against eight dentists who were refusing to treat persons with AIDS. And now we were ironically finding ourselves the focus of AIDS discrimination. I approached this as an excellent opportunity to educate and inform the local community about AIDS and why AIDS discrimination should not be tolerated.

At one point during the meeting, an elderly man from the back of the room shouted out as I was speaking that I was a "fairy." This epithet, which was oddly archaic even at that time, at first stung deeply. What struck me was the reaction of the audience. This previously hostile audience all came to my defense, angrily insisting that I was not a "fairy," and they verbally condemned the man for unfairly suggesting it. I wanted to tell the audience that I am proud to be gay. But I did not. I knew that that would weaken our position, and it was more important at that time to win over their support for our AIDS center than to start lecturing them about gay rights.

Toward the end of the meeting, I thought that I was beginning to win over many in the audience. But Perdone concluded the meeting by saying that the Richmond Hill Block Association, the Richmond Hill Development Corporation, and the nearby Woodhaven Block Association were now at "war" with the AIDS center, which was soon to become pejoratively known as "Feldman's Center," and that she would not rest until we were out of Richmond Hill.

"We Will Not Budge One Inch": Holding Our Ground

The word from my board members, our funding source (the New York State AIDS Institute), and many of the key members of Community Planning Board District 9 was to "not budge one inch": this was a matter of principle and not subject to compromise. We were staying in Richmond Hill, no matter what. Our slogan rapidly became: "We are not budging one single inch!"

During the summer of 1987, the community began to choose sides. A coalition of Protestant churches held a meeting in July to support us in our efforts. Pastor Sonnenberg of the local Lutheran church and Reverend Bryer of the local Congregational church were especially helpful to us. Monsignor Leonard at the local Roman Catholic church, however, remained officially neutral, although he stayed active on the board of our adversary, the Richmond Hill Block Association.

Most of the community leaders from neighboring Kew Gardens (a predominantly Jewish and politically progressive area) and the Queens Borough president, Claire Shulman, were very supportive. At the time, I was amazed how a small nonprofit organization devoted to a single disease was able to rapidly become the center of political activity and concern in the borough. But then AIDS is not just another disease, and we were not just another small nonprofit organization. With AIDS, sex itself was no longer safe, and this made it very political, indeed.

The local weekly press in Queens was also mostly supportive and worked with me in getting out our message to the community. Nevertheless, during that summer, a rock was thrown through our second-story window; our front door was vandalized with a scrawled message: "AIDS Center Get Out!"; a repairman working in our parking lot was physically threatened; and two of our staff's personal cars were vandalized in our parking lot. A hardware store two blocks away put up a sign that read, "Shop here. We don't have an AIDS center above us!"

On July 12, I met with the local police captain and a representative of the block association to discuss the escalating violence. The woman from the block association started shouting at me during the meeting that I was "nothing but a do-gooder." "You're a do-gooder," she said in anger. I looked at her and replied: "What then, do bad?"

On July 27, I met with the block association's entire board to discuss the issue. State Assemblyman Anthony Seminerio was also there and made it clear that he wanted us out of Richmond Hill. Tony Seminerio was a politically powerful figure in central Queens. Just a few weeks earlier, he managed to pull strings to get a new wing for Jamaica Hospital (located in the eastern part of Richmond Hill) and had a huge three-story banner placed over the entrance to the dedication ceremony that said "SEMINERIO CITY." This was a politician with enormous clout. I tried to clarify what we did and how our helping people with AIDS was no risk to anyone in Richmond Hill. But I also made it clear that we still were not going to budge one inch. It remained a matter of principle, not subject to compromise.

Interestingly, their rhetoric focused against injecting drug users and sex workers, but not against gay men during this meeting and throughout the entire period of political opposition. The crack houses along Jamaica Avenue just east of Richmond Hill were a real perceived threat to the political leadership of Richmond Hill. There were no gay bars in Richmond Hill, and the gay world of Manhattan, Jackson Heights, and Brooklyn Heights at the time was merely a distant threat at the most.

When I arrived at the office a week later, my volunteer coordinator told me that she heard that there was going to be a demonstration by the gay community and that there would be a counterdemonstration led by Assemblyman Seminerio. I knew that the gay community in Queens was not well organized and that if people were coming from Manhattan, I would have heard about it beforehand. I made some well-placed phone calls down to City Hall and found out that it was the assemblyman himself who started the false rumor that there would be a demonstration by the gay community, just so that he could rally a counterdemonstration against us. I called and confronted Seminerio with what I had learned. He backed down, cursed at me over the phone, and called off the planned counterdemonstration. The news media did show up, however, and I appeared on the evening Channel 2 news to say, once again, that "we will not budge one inch." Clearly, these were volatile times, and the battle lines were drawn.

The following week I met with Richard Dunne and Tim Sweeney, then the director and deputy director, respectively, of GMHC, the largest AIDS organization in New York, to discuss strategy and policy. Word had it that Perdone was planning to hold a major demonstration against us sometime in mid-September, shortly after the schools reopened. Our landlord cautioned me that he heard a rumor that the Mafia was quite seriously out to get me, and strongly recommended that I keep a gun in my office. After giving it some thought, I decided against getting a gun.

I met with Monsignor Leonard at the Roman Catholic church on August 25, who urged us to try to find a way to reach a compromise. Katherine "Kitty" Cappelli, director of our board, called to tell me that she was under pressure by the head of Jamaica Hospital (where she was an infection control coordinator and nurse) to resign from our board, and that she found this "all very stressful." I urged her to "hang in there" and not to leave at this critically important time. She hesitantly agreed. A few days later I got a letter from David Rosen, the director of her hospital (and no relation to Mel Rosen of the New York State AIDS Institute), saying that they supported Assemblyman Seminerio in his view that we should move out of Richmond Hill. The letter, of course, was carbon copied to the assemblyman.

Selected members of our board (including City Councilperson Katzman and Community Planning Board 9 District Manager Mary Ann Carey), members of the Richmond Hill Block Association (led by Arlene Perdone), Assemblyman Seminerio, and Elaine Ehrlich (our project officer at the New York State AIDS Institute) met on September 1 at a neutral location to see whether any solution was possible. After an acrimonious meeting that went on for hours, and in an effort to hold off the inevitable demonstration against us, we agreed to compromise slightly. We agreed to do some limited counseling at a location in Jamaica, an African American neighborhood a few miles to the east of Richmond Hill. I strongly argued against this deal.

We blinked first. We budged that inch. But the board believed that we had no choice. Yet Perdone did not think that this was enough, and Seminerio was still calling for our complete relocation.

To boost our spirits and to further mobilize community support, we held an open house at our AIDS center on September 9. Violence was feared, and the police provided highly visible protection during and after the event. The open house, however, was a total success. Everyone who supported us— community and religious leaders, our volunteers, our board members, many of our clients, and even some neighborhood residents—showed up. Tim Sweeney (deputy director at GMHC) and Michael Hirsch (founder of Body Positive in New York, just shortly before his death) at the open house event offered to organize a candlelight march along Jamaica Avenue to counter any demonstration by the opposition. At the time, I said that that would not be a good idea, since the straight community would see it as "wimpy" and just reinforce their views that gay men are effeminate. Looking back now, perhaps we should have had the candlelight march after all.

And then . . . nothing . . . nothing happened. Day after day, I kept looking out of my office window expecting the demonstration organized by the block association, and nothing happened! What was going on? What happened to it?

Political Pressure

On September 23, I met with Mel Rosen, director of the New York State AIDS Institute, in his midtown Manhattan office. Kitty Cappelli met with him separately first. After she left, I went in. He asked me how I planned to solve the problem. I told him that we made a small compromise, and I saw no need to go any further. "Let them picket," I told him. He said, however, that that was no longer acceptable to the AIDS Institute. They were giving us $300,000 a year at this point, nearly all of our funding. He suggested that we compromise further by opening up a satellite office in Jamaica, Queens, where we would do all of our group counseling and all individual counseling for Jamaica residents. He would try to get an additional $25,000 for our budget to pay for the satellite office. "How come the shift in policy?" I asked. "Mr. Seminerio put pressure on David Axelrod" (the state commissioner of health), he answered. "But why should Axelrod be influenced by Seminerio? He is only one of 155 state assemblymen," I said. "True, but he sits on a powerful state committee, and was threatening to block all AIDS Institute funds for the coming year."

We held a special meeting of the ACQC board on October 6. Mel Rosen and Elaine Ehrlich attended. While we were waiting to begin, Rosen told me that he would be leaving his position as director of the AIDS Institute soon to become an associate director of Helen Hayes Hospital, a state psychiatric hospital in West Haverstraw, New York. I asked him, since that was the case, why didn't he challenge the commissioner on the issue. Certainly he was aware that this was a matter of principle. What would he have to lose? He confided to me that it was the commissioner who got him the better-paying position, and this was the payoff.

I had agreed that the board should support the proposal if we could get a verbal commitment for the $25,000 addition to our budget. If we got the additional funds, it would help us to expand our services; if, on the other hand, we had to absorb the new satellite center within our existing budget, it would represent both a symbolic loss and a need for us to curtail some planned services to pay for it. During the course of the meeting, however, Rosen said that he could not guarantee that we would get the extra funds. He also implied that he would defund us completely if we did not agree. I knew that this was a bluff. We were too important politically at this point to be defunded. But the board was thoroughly intimidated, and I was appalled that they lacked the backbone to stand up to him. It must have shown on my face, since Rosen asked me if there was something wrong. I then made a push for a more definite commitment for the $25,000. A demonic expression came over his face, and he responded by literally screaming at me as loudly as he could, right in front of our board members, who were both shocked and further intimidated, saying that I was responsible for everything that had gone wrong and that he would "make sure that I pay."

By the end of the meeting we did reach an agreement to go along with the compromise. A few weeks later we learned that we would receive the additional $25,000 after all.

The Growth of the Organization

During the next few months, things settled down to the business of further building up the functions of our AIDS center. We held a one-day borough-wide AIDS symposium attended by health providers and some of the leading politicians in Queens. I continued giving talks throughout the borough on AIDS and the AIDS center. We now had fifty volunteers on our HIV hotline, buddy program, and other projects. Our client load continued to grow, and we were now segmenting our support groups. Our health educator was providing workshops on HIV prevention to various groups. We put together our first ACQC newsletter. We were beginning to hold fund-raising events for additional administrative support and enhanced services.

The Power Struggle

I heard that Tony Seminerio was "out to get me," but I was not worried since I knew that as long as I maintained the support of my board, there was nothing he could do. During December 1987, the AIDS Institute evidently sought its revenge by putting us through a comprehensive audit and evaluation. For two weeks we had to nearly suspend all services so that we could complete the endless paperwork they demanded. The standards used were the same that were developed to judge large state hospitals and the GMHC, which are multimillion-dollar organizations with very sizable staffs. The auditors quickly issued a critical report, citing deficiencies when comparing us with GMHC, which at that time had been in existence for over five years and had an annual budget of $8 million. At the January 1988 board meeting, most of the board members dismissed the report as absurd, and remained very supportive of the rapid progress we had made against such adversity in so brief a period. However, Kitty Cappelli, the board chair, said that she was going to conduct her own evaluation of my performance.

Since October 1987, her attitude had shifted, and she often talked about the need for me to mend fences with Arlene Perdone and the Richmond Hill Block Association. She uncharacteristically began to carry with her to board meetings a briefcase filled with ACQC documents and recorded and questioned everything we were doing. I became suspicious that she may have been reporting back to her supervisor, the director of Jamaica Hospital, and perhaps other ACQC opponents. During February 1988, she thoroughly scrutinized all of my activities. While, previously, she could not get off from work during the day to visit the AIDS center, now she had plenty of time from her hospital duties to spend hours during weekdays to review what I was doing. I later learned that my deputy director, Gary Maffei, who knew that his position was temporary and scheduled to become defunded in March, was very cooperative with her in attempting to find, or invent, evidence against me.

On February 23, after months of quiet within the community, two men drove up in the late evening while I was still working in the office, fired a BB gun pellet through our front door, and quickly drove off. I believe that this was done by someone to intentionally create instability at the following night's board meeting.

The next day Cappelli sent out a message that only board members were permitted to attend that evening's board meeting. The representative from the borough president's office who usually attended the board meetings called me to ask what was happening. I told him I was not sure. Cappelli knew that a few of my strongest allies on the board were out of town and were not able to attend the meeting. At the meeting, she began by insisting that I leave the room since, as the executive director, I was not a board member. Behind closed doors, she then made a series of entirely false charges against me and demanded that I immediately be asked to resign. If not, she would immediately resign. From my closed office I could hear the venerable Councilperson Katzman first arguing that I should be given an opportunity to respond to these accusations, and then storming out of the building saying that he was resigning in anger and protest. Two of the board members entered my office and told me that I had a choice of either resigning immediately or being terminated immediately. I told them that I would not resign unless I had a chance to respond to the false and scurrilous charges. They told me that this would not be possible and that I was immediately terminated. Gary Maffei, the deputy director, become the acting director and eventually the new executive director.

I wrote a lengthy response to these trumped-up charges and mailed them to the members of the board. Over the next few weeks, half of the board resigned in my support. The *New York Times* published an article indicating that there had been a shift at the AIDS center, and suggested that the plan was now to move the center out of Richmond Hill, after all we had been through in keeping it there (Kingson 1988). In March, it was announced that Axelrod had awarded Jamaica Hospital with a contract for an eighty-six-bed in-patient facility, of which thirty-three beds were designated for patients with AIDS. Cappelli was immediately given a promotion to director of Infection Control Nursing at Jamaica Hospital. Shortly after, she resigned from the board of ACQC.

Most of the staff also resigned, since they found it very difficult working for the new executive director. During the summer, ACQC announced that it would be moving out of Richmond Hill, and I wrote an op-ed piece in *Newsday*, a daily newspaper, urging that this decision be reconsidered (Feldman 1988). In October 1988, however, ACQC made the move out of Richmond Hill. The legal case against the Lefrak Management Corporation was won, and, ironically, it was agreed that ACQC would move into the very same building along Queens Boulevard in Rego Park (about five miles away) that we had been excluded from earlier. I had filed two legal complaints against the ACQC board and a slander suit against Seminerio, but none of them was ultimately successful.

The Following Years

Mel Rosen died of complications from AIDS in 1992. David Axelrod had fallen into a coma and died in 1994. Councilperson Arthur Katzman, who was eighty-four in 1987, retired in 1991 and moved to Hawaii. He died in 1993 while in California. Anthony Seminerio remained an assemblyman for the same district in Queens for the New York state government until 2008, when he was forced to resign under corruption charges. He had become a notable talk radio show host on WABC in the New York City area, supporting conservative causes. He also became a part-time movie actor. I have since learned that he was a student at the New York State Institute of Technology during the mid-1970s at the same time that I was an adjunct professor teaching there. However, I do not recall and have not been able to ascertain whether he was in any of my classes at the time. He has stated that his animosity toward higher education stems from his political disagreement with one of his professors at that college back then. I do not know if I was that professor.

Elaine Erhlich left the New York State AIDS Institute in early 1992. Gary Maffei was forced to resign after it was learned that he had continually sexually harassed one of his male employees on the job. District Manager Mary Ann Carey is doing well twenty years after her hospital stay, and still is the district manager for Community Board 9. I am not certain what happened with the other people involved, but I am sure that life continues unchanged in the tumultuous world of central Queens politics.

I had conducted some consulting in Uganda and Bangladesh on AIDS during 1988, and moved to Miami at the end of that year to accept a faculty position in the University of Miami School of Medicine. Today, I am happy to hear that ACQC has grown into a major AIDS organization, the second largest in New York (Columbia University Mailman School of Public Health 2007), with a staff of over 140 people and a $9 million budget, serving 4,800 program participants. ACQC is located in eight offices in various sections of Queens, but, interestingly, not in Richmond Hill. Services now include case management, HIV education and prevention, housing, legal, mental health, primary medical care, and substance use prevention and harm reduction (AIDS Center of Queens County Official Web Site 2007). I am very glad that my work back in the late 1980s has led to the continuing growth of the ACQC today.

Acknowledgments

I would like to thank C. Todd White of the University of Rochester for reading and making valuable comments on an earlier version of this chapter.

References

ACQC: The AIDS Center of Queens County Official Web Site. 2007. www.acqc.org.

Columbia University Mailman School of Public Health. 2007. Sexuality and Health Track. www.mailman.hs.columbia.edu/popfam/sht/students/current.html.

Feldman, Douglas A. 1988. "Pariahs" of Richmond Hill. *New York Newsday*, September 8.

Kingson, Jennifer A. 1988. Shift of AIDS center forced in Queens, March 13. query.nytimes.com/gst/fullpage.html?res=940DE1DF113BF930A25750C0A96E948260.

VolunteerNYC.org. 2007. The mayor's volunteer center/United Way of New York City. www.volunteernyc.org/org/6404128.html.

7

The Varieties of Recovery Experience

HIV Risk and Crystal Meth Anonymous

THOMAS LYONS

The early part of recovery for those dependent on alcohol and drugs is a formidable challenge, since the newly sober person must change his or her habits, friends, and life. As part of the recovery process, many people in the United States are exposed to Alcoholics Anonymous (AA), or other twelve-step programs modeled after it, either voluntarily or mandated through courts or treatment programs. There is a vast literature on the extent to which these programs produce long-term abstinence (McCrady and Miller 1993; Timko et al. 1999). These studies often show that substance use outcomes are not predicted simply by group attendance, but by more complex measures of involvement (Montgomery et al. 1995).

Little is known, however, about how well these kind of programs work with newly prevalent drugs such as methamphetamine ("meth") and Ecstasy. For those who join twelve-step groups, a structure of meetings, sponsor, and "fellowship" is in place to deal with the difficulties of abstaining from alcohol or other drugs and the other life problems that come up and must be faced. One of these problems for many gay and bisexual men is HIV infection, either because they have the virus or must confront the possibility of contracting it. To the degree that it leads to abstinence from drugs, twelve-step involvement has an impact on HIV risk through injection drug use. This chapter examines how and to what extent these programs also have an effect on HIV risk through sexual behavior.

This question is important because gay and bisexual men who abuse drugs and alcohol are more likely to engage in sexual behavior that puts them at risk for HIV transmission (Paul et al. 1993; Shoptaw and Frosch 2000; Stall and Purcell 2000). Treatment studies of injection drug users (Gottheil et al. 1998; Magura et al. 1998) and stimulant users (Shoptaw et al. 1998) have found that treatment significantly reduces risky sexual behavior. A treatment program specifically aimed at meth users (Reback et al. 2004) succeeded in reducing meth use and HIV risk behavior one year after treatment. Rather than involving the twelve-step model, the intervention consisted of either cognitive behavioral group therapy, "contingency management" therapy (similar to positive reinforcement), or a gay-oriented intervention. Another study showed that substance abuse treatment on the twelve-step model reduced risky sexual behaviors (Stall et al. 1999). Reductions occurred soon after enrollment in a substance abuse program, but quickly leveled off. An enhanced program focusing on sexual risk taking did not do better in reducing sexual risk than a substance abuse program by itself.

However, no studies have looked at community-based, as opposed to treatment-based, twelve-step programs. Twelve-step programs such as AA and Narcotics Anonymous (NA) more closely resemble social movements or subcultures (for want of a better term) than formal treatment with professional staff. Little is known in the literature about AA and NA among particular populations such as immigrants, gays and lesbians, and HIV-positive individuals. In addition, although use of meth by gay and bisexual men has reached epidemic proportions (Gorman et al. 1997; Semple et al. 2002) and meth use is highly associated with unsafe sex, no study has been done of people addicted to crystal meth in the newly formed Crystal Meth Anonymous (CMA) twelve-step program. The question of to what degree abstaining from substances is associated with reduction in risky sexual behaviors has only begun to be explored.

Drug Abuse and HIV Risk

Meth users, particularly those who inject drugs or engage in unprotected anal sex, are at high risk for HIV transmission (Halkitis et al. 2001; Shoptaw et al. 2002). Ethnographic and other studies have linked the use of meth to unprotected anal sex (Clatts and Sotheran 2000; Gorman et al. 1997; Klitzman et al. 2000; Reback et al. 2004; Semple et al. 2002). To say that drug use "causes" risky sex by disinhibiting the person taking drugs, however, may be too simplistic (Clatts et al. 2001). Meth is used to enhance the sexual experience (Gorman et al. 1997; Semple et al. 2002) and to obtain a "time out" from stress, including the stress of living with HIV (Clatts et al. 2001; Semple et al. 2002). Rather than disinhibiting or increasing sexual drive incidentally, meth may be used intentionally for these effects.

The observed associations between meth use and sexual behavior most likely indicate complex underlying relationships. The association between substance use and risky sex may go in both directions—that is, sex may spur substance use. In focus groups with gay men in early sobriety, Paul and colleagues (1993) found that drug/alcohol relapse in sexual situations was quite common, and that the men needed specific training in having sex while sober. Drug use can also be part of the "partnering process"—that is, a means of attracting or keeping sex partners (Clatts et al. 2003). Men engaging in risky sex are following culturally and socially conditioned sexual scripts (Simon and Gagnon 1987) that govern their behavior in different contexts (for example, in bathhouses) or with different kinds of partners (for example, anonymous partners). Sexual scripts may help account for the finding that sex with primary partners is far more likely to be unprotected than casual sex (Clatts et al. 2003; Gorbach and Holmes 2003). Substance use is an additional important part of that context.

This chapter focuses on the subset of meth users who are attempting to abstain through participation in twelve-step programs. While certainly not representative of meth users as a whole or even of those who have quit, their stories shed light on possible mechanisms by which abstaining from substances may be linked to reduction in sexual risk behavior. In particular, I focus on a new twelve-step group, CMA. Twelve-step groups for lesbians and gay men are over thirty years old and were the first entities to recognize the particular problems of substance-abusing gay men and lesbians (Israelstam 1986; Zehner and Lewis 1983). There are now at least 500 gay AA groups in the United States (Bloomfield 1990). Closely modeled on NA and AA, CMA was founded in Southern California about eight years ago, and gay and bisexual men in large cities often attend CMA meetings.

Currently, CMA meetings are held in twenty-one U.S. cities and Canada (CMA 2005). While some meetings are in smaller towns, particularly in the West, many CMA meetings in larger cities are designated "Gay/Lesbian" or are held in twelve-step meeting places attended by gay men and lesbians (for example, in Atlanta, Chicago, Fort Lauderdale, Miami, and Washington, D.C.), attesting to the popularity of meth among gay men. Attendance at meetings is growing rapidly: one meeting in Chicago grew from five to thirty members in three and one-half months. (Whether this growth is because more users are reaching "bottom," the point where they ask for help, or because more are becoming aware of the meetings is unknown.)

The pilot data presented here are the result of twenty in-depth interviews with new members of CMA and observation of about fifteen CMA meetings, as well as AA and NA meetings. The interview participants were recruited through informal methods (approached at the end of meetings) and respondent-driven sampling. Each participant signed a consent form to participate. "Open" meetings were observed after the group gave unanimous verbal consent (see below). Participants interviewed had between one week and six months of "clean time" (that is, being off the drug). Eighteen were white, and two were African American. Of the seventeen who stated their age, the median age was forty, with a range from twenty-one to fifty-five. Ten of the respondents were HIV negative, eight were HIV positive, and two did not know their status. Each respondent was asked about his drug and alcohol history, sexual history—both while actively using and after entering the program—and opinions and attitudes about sex and recovery.

CMA meetings were observed, which took place three nights a week in a relatively affluent area of Washington, D.C. Unlike most AA meetings, very few of the attendees at CMA meetings I attended in Washington had more than one year of "clean time." This reflects the fact that it is a new program, that meth has only recently become a widespread drug of abuse in these cities, and also that the pattern of use of, and abstinence from, meth differs from that of alcohol or cocaine, as I describe below. Many CMA members also attend NA or AA.

A Note on Participant Observation in Twelve-Step Meetings

The twelve-step meeting is a kind of ritual in which, in theory, statements uttered within the "sacred space" are protected by anonymity. At the beginning of some meetings the chairperson reminds the group: "Whom you see here, what you hear here, when you leave here, let it stay here." The emphasis on anonymity makes participant observation problematic, since the researcher is there precisely to take away insights and even verbatim comments (anonymously, of course). In addition, the researcher's presence might affect what is said or compromise the therapeutic value of the meeting for some participants. Although "open" meetings can be attended by family and friends, by students writing reports on twelve-step movements, and by merely the curious, these attendees do not usually record statements made.

These problems are not unique to research on twelve-step groups. The research community and institutional review boards (IRBs) are very aware of them. The IRB evaluating this pilot project required that the researcher obtain unanimous verbal consent to his presence from the group at the beginning of the meeting. A second IRB required that the group leader obtain unanimous verbal consent from the group before the researcher entered the meeting. Alongside the important issue of gaining consent, however, the researcher must take time to make himself or herself and his or her project known to the participants before gathering any data, and to informally gauge their comfort level with his or her presence. In fact, it became clear that many of those recovering from addiction to crystal meth want research to be done on the problem, and they want CMA to be more widely known. They take for granted that the researcher's data will never be linked to the identity of participants. Hence it is my belief that studying twelve-step groups via participant observation has many difficulties, but they are not insurmountable, and this method is perhaps the only effective way to obtain information about a new twelve-step movement.

Mechanisms of Change in Twelve-Step Programs

Studies of how twelve-step programs work focus on the sharing of stories in meetings (Cain 1991; Jensen 2000; Kurtz and Ketcham 1992; Rappaport 1994; Rodin 1986; Steffen 1997; Wittmer 1997). The act of sharing or listening to these stories, with the social and emotional support gained inside and outside the meeting room (Bloomfield 1990; Cohen and Wills 1985; Gottlieb 1988), and the reassuring nature of the program's basic doctrines (Galanter 1993) are some of the key ingredients of the program's success. Twelve-step groups also have factors in common with other behavioral interventions, such as increasing self-efficacy (confidence in one's ability to carry out the behavioral change) (Morgenstern et al. 1997) and self-esteem (Christo and Sutton 1994).

Beyond attending meetings and abstaining from alcohol and drugs, the "program" is said to consist of a set of principles. These are based on the twelve steps of AA and include the slogans that are presented in member "shares" (statements usually under five minutes made by each member during the meeting) and sometimes written down and placed on the wall in meeting rooms. These serve as distillations of program philosophy, and, to the extent that group members adhere to them and repeat them, they are tokens of belonging to the group. Rather than discuss the program strictly in terms of the twelve steps, in this chapter I focus on elements of the "program" and the corresponding slogans, some arising from the steps and others not, that may be involved directly or indirectly in sexual decision making. These elements are: the emphasis on honesty, facing reality, making an inventory of one's character defects, the concept of "one day at a time," the fellowship that develops among CMA members, and spirituality. For each of these elements, I examine both how they are talked about—in meetings and informally—and how they are practiced, as reported in interviews. Do they affect sexual risk taking and disclosure of HIV status to sexual partners? More generally, does CMA attendance contribute to HIV prevention, and if so how?

Honesty

Perhaps the most important principle of twelve-step programs like AA and CMA is honesty. The program emphasizes being rigorously honest with oneself, first and foremost, and in admitting that one is powerless over drugs and alcohol. However, the concept extends to honesty in every area of one's life. The words "honest" and "honesty" recur three times in the first three sentences of "How It Works," a section of the "Big Book" read at most meetings and generally held to be the most important section of that text (Alcoholics Anonymous 2001: 58). The relevant phrase here is "rigorously honest." The program stresses honesty in everyday life and more particularly in facing one's past.

Honesty begins in the meeting room. Since the beginning of the epidemic, HIV, like same-sex sexuality itself, has been stigmatized, and disclosing one's HIV status has led to dismissal from employment, eviction from rental apartments, and discrimination by health-care providers. The HIV-positive participant can rely on the anonymity of the twelve-step program to protect himself or herself from disclosure of his or her status to the outside world. Honesty about HIV status in meetings means that those who are not aware of, or not "out" about, their status are encouraged to follow the example of those who do share information about their HIV status.

HIV-positive members of the programs also face the issue of whether they should disclose their HIV status to potential sexual partners. Active users of meth often do not disclose their HIV status to their sex partners (who are often fellow users). According to my informants, this trend is increasing, though data are scarce to back up this impression. "When we're talking about the crystal meth scene and sex, we're talking about a whole new generation of people who don't care. No one asks questions . . . and nobody says anything. So I gave up trying a long time ago." This respondent has identified a "negative feedback loop" between one's unwillingness to ask and to tell one's status (Reback et al. 2004; Zea et al. 2003). The unwillingness to face the issue of HIV status leads to ironic situations where nondisclosure is the only way that sex can be obtained. One informant says, "Most people in the community these days are willing to have unprotected sex with somebody whose status they ignore, but they're not willing to have protected sex with somebody who tells them they're positive."

If the recovering person adopts honesty as a way of life, nondisclosure of HIV status becomes less of an option. One of my informants went into detail about the need to disclose his status to potential partners:

> I'm HIV positive and I can tell you that I've always known in my head that it's best to disclose my status immediately before having sex with anybody. It's not just that I know in my head, it's even empirical evidence of what happened in the past when I disclosed immediately, always good things happen from it; sometimes not so good things, but very rarely. . . . Because [this program] opens up this issue of honesty and once you have sex with somebody and you don't tell them you're positive, it's almost like you can't see them again. It's too painful.

Disclosure of HIV status to a potential partner may lead to adoption of safer-sex practices, such as use of condoms for anal intercourse (Zea et al. 2003). Such rigorous honesty might also lead to having fewer partners, if it is true that young men would rather not know the HIV status of their partners. I examine reported changes in sexual behavior below.

Facing Reality

The next two elements I discuss are based especially on Step Four ("Made a searching and fearless moral inventory of ourselves") and Step Five ("Admitted to God, to ourselves, and to another human being the exact nature of our wrongs"). Before recovery, program participants report that they had lived in a fantasy world sustained by drinking and drugs, and that they had avoided rather than confronted their problems. While the new program member can make a choice to disregard safer sex, he or she cannot ignore the reality of HIV, as he or she may have been able to do while drinking and using. This knowledge may be overwhelming, but there is another slogan that states that "the Higher Power never gives us more than we can handle." One participant commented:

> It's pretty much, I won't say submitting, but surrendering to things that happen on a daily basis and trust in God. Because we act out, when things happen we . . . look, I used to run for the drugs and the alcohol. I need a drink, you know, let me take a hit because something's going on.

Facing the reality of one's HIV status has inspired some members to return to school and/or make other positive changes in their lives. One man said he was nine years sober, tested HIV positive two years ago (it is unknown when he was infected), and had since obtained his GED and was now in trade school. It should be emphasized that not everyone turns his or her life around, and for those who do, the process is often slow and discouraging. But the members seem unanimous that they could not embark on these changes without being clean and sober.

Inventory

In the original writings of AA, a great emphasis was placed on Step Four, "Made a searching and fearless moral inventory of ourselves." This inventory metaphor from business implied taking stock of one's life, identifying faults and assets. The founders of AA were convinced that without this inventory, the AA member would drink again, since this process, they believed, identified the character defects that led to drinking. This part of the program is underplayed in CMA. It is a new program, and very few members have "reached" the Steps Four and Five yet. Of course, this does not mean they will not tackle these steps in the future. One participant noted that, for him,

> morality . . . is more important than spirituality. Do I think I'll go to hell for the things that I do? Not necessarily, in a kind of religious sense. But if I can't wake up and feel good about myself about something I've done, I guess it kind of jeopardizes my morality. That plays a big role in my behavior.

Those who take this inventory step, and tell their inventory to someone else in Step Five, report that it frees them from the guilt and shame surrounding their past behavior, while ideally also identifying good traits that can form the basis of self-esteem. The relevant slogan in this context is: "You're only as sick as your secrets." As with the concept of honesty, telling one's secrets to another program member may be a prelude to being able to disclose status in a sexual situation.

One Day at a Time

The best-known slogan from AA, adopted by CMA as well, is the notion of "one day at a time." This phrase speaks to the difficulty of becoming abstinent from a substance forever, especially a substance that has given you pleasure in the past. Instead of swearing off the substance forever, the program asks only that you do not use it today. These "todays" string together—into weeks, months, and years. Like the other concepts examined here, the slogan "one day at a time" has application in all areas of life. Members of the twelve-step program are encouraged not to worry about the future or dwell upon the past. They may have used alcohol and drugs to drown out these regrets and worries and must learn new ways to "let go" of the future and the past.

The notion of "one day at a time" could also be applied to sexual behavior, especially for those who are trying to attain a particular goal having to do with sex. One informant was attempting to stay celibate for religious reasons. This goal might seem overwhelming if he had said to himself that he was going to have no more sex for the rest of his life. On the other hand, not having sex just for today is more attainable.

Being in recovery often means relearning basic life skills that fell into abeyance while the addicted person was drinking and using. These tasks might be overwhelming if looked at in their entirety. Thus, the program encourages the addicted person to do them one day, one hour, one minute at a time, making the achievement of difficult goals possible. This "one day at a time" philosophy is quite the opposite of an "eat, drink, and be merry" philosophy in which desires are indulged and consequences disregarded. Instead, the idea behind "one day at a time" is that you can go against your urges and desires and do something challenging for short periods of time.

Fellowship

A further element of the program that may impact HIV risk behavior is the network of friendships and associations that arises through attendance at meetings, or what people in the program call "the fellowship," and, more generally, the changes in one's relationships that occur upon affiliation with these programs. Attending meetings together strengthens some of the bonds already existing among meth users, since meth use, like most other drug use, takes place in a social context. New users were initiated into use, and meth was bought and sold within a subculture of late-night clubs and Internet chat rooms. The same people with whom the newly recovered addict had used drugs can now be found in the meetings. In fact, buyers and their former dealers sit together in the CMA meetings in Washington, D.C.

The strength of this fellowship fosters an atmosphere where it is possible to talk about intimate issues. Here, the relevant slogan is that "drug addiction is a disease of isolation." Belonging to the twelve-step group brings other people into one's life again. These new associations may affect sexual behavior, in that one is more accountable to one's friends and less likely to seek anonymous sex, which is sometimes a way of battling loneliness. Another slogan states, "Let us love you until you can love yourself."[1] Many members who are coming back from a relapse report that isolation was a prelude to returning to using drugs and/or drinking.

Part of the admission of personal powerlessness, which is central to the twelve-step doctrine, is allowing oneself to be guided by the group, both through what is heard in meetings and through sponsors and other group members (Morgenstern et al. 1996). This guidance (in AA doctrine, this is an initial stage of developing a sense of a higher power) may paradoxically be related to increased self-efficacy, such as confidence that one can resist the drug (Morgenstern et al. 1997). Guidance from the group may spill over from abstaining from alcohol or drugs into other areas of life, such as an increased mindfulness in sexual situations if the member discusses these potential situations with other group members.

Spirituality

Does the program's emphasis on spirituality have a role to play in reducing sexual risk taking, as it seems to have in attaining successful sobriety (Denzin 1987; Emrick et al. 1993; Morgenstern et al. 1997)? The twelve steps are based in the belief in a higher power, and the spirituality of the program may be one basis for a change in sexual habits. The first three steps of the twelve-step creed involve coming to believe in a power greater than oneself and turning one's will over to the care of that power (Alcoholics Anonymous 2001). That power is identified with God in the literature, but participants are invited to conceptualize God however they wish. A slogan heard in AA is that "the program does not have a spiritual component or part—it's all spiritual."

Spirituality pervades the CMA literature (taken from AA and NA), and the spiritually based twelve steps are read at every meeting. But spirituality seems to be less emphasized in speaker comments. Nonetheless, the notion that spirituality is at the center of the program and should be at the center of participants' lives came out strongly during the interviews. This is how one informant put it:

> [The program] says that once we begin to start practicing the steps and attending the meetings and we learn to stay clean on a daily basis—a daily reprieve—we tend to replace use of drugs with something else. And in most cases it is sex. But what comes to pass is that the more

you get yourself into the program, the more you'll find that what fills the void of the drugs and alcohol is the spirituality which you really need to work on within yourself.

The "daily reprieve" from drug and alcohol use permits this spiritual growth and presumably a movement away from sex as a means of filling "the void." This informant did not seem opposed to sex per se, but to sex as a substitute for a spiritual life.

Twelve-step program members often report that their entire lives are transformed (Denzin 1987; Galanter 1993), which may include their sexual life as well as abstinence from substances. I asked participants if spirituality had an influence on their sexual lives. Four denied that it did, but the others spoke of the pervasiveness of spirituality in their lives. "I think the main thing that works is it recognizes that the recovery process is a spiritual process. It's based on . . . spiritual values such as honesty, willingness, and open-mindedness, and everything starts from there."

Changes in Attitudes toward Sex

To summarize, many informants described changes in their attitudes toward sex since entering the CMA program. One informant stated that he had the specific goal of celibacy within the program:

My sexual life is dictated by my spiritual beliefs. One of my goals in recovery is to remain celibate. I don't believe in sex outside of marriage. And I know that in the past it's been very compulsive, and one of the issues that I've dealt with is why it is so compulsive. So I would like to return to celibacy.

Another stated that he planned to "incorporate spirituality into my relationship with my next partner. I'm going to try to, if he's interested. I'm pretty sure I'm going to meet someone who's in recovery. I don't want a mere mortal [someone outside the program]."

However, two other informants had the opposite attitude. They sought more casual partners after affiliation with the program than before. The first informant, who is HIV positive, stated:

It seems right now I'm acting out a lot. So it's increased. But it's more healthier, more conscious, more aware of what I'm doing, how I'm doing it. I've been more honest about my encounters with people. I let them know what my status is; they let me know what theirs is; we use condoms.

A second informant, who is HIV negative, reported having "one-night stands":

I think that being in the program, going to two meetings a day, not being in the bar scene, working a lot—I don't really have time to meet people. When I have met people, I shy away from spending a lot of time with them because I don't want to date anyone. You shouldn't, I was advised, in your first year of sobriety. So that . . . contributes to the one-night-stand occurrence in my sex life.

How were these changes in attitudes reflected in reported behavior? In response to specific questions on numbers of sex partners in the month prior and subsequent to entry into the program, most newly recovering meth addicts reported significantly fewer sexual encounters in recovery as compared to when they were using the drug. After entering the program, four men (20 percent) had had no sex at all. Six men (30 percent) had had sex with just one other man; in two cases this was a primary partner. The remaining ten subjects ranged from having three to ten partners in the months since they entered the program. When compared with the number of partners per month prior to entering the program, this represents a decline in sex partners per month for thirteen informants (65 percent), an increase for five informants (25 percent), and approximately the same per month before and after for two informants (one informant had zero partners before and after). It remains to be seen whether this marks a long-term change. One longitudinal study found a 70 percent decline in partners per month one year after treatment (Reback et al. 2004).

Condom use did not change in the same way. Four men (20 percent) on at least one occasion had anal sex without condoms after joining the program. These four stated that because they are HIV positive, they have not insisted on condoms when they are the receptive partner in anal sex, particularly with a lover or frequent sex partner. "I used condoms for insertive [sex], rarely used them—because I'm HIV positive—for receptive [sex], and never [for] oral [sex]." But two of the four recognized that they were risking reinfection with a different strain of the virus: "And two times it was unprotected. He's HIV too, and I'm HIV. We didn't use condoms, but we should have, you know, because you can get reinfected." Another stated, "But as far as when I would be [the receptive partner]? No, I didn't make anyone wear a condom if they didn't want to. It was totally up to them. Being that I already have HIV, I already have everything so what is it they're going to give me? Later to find out a bigger strain, or supervirus, or who knows what I've got now?" These statements may reflect the impact of recent prevention efforts to reach those already HIV positive with information about the dangers of reinfection.

Beyond a numerical count of reported sexual encounters, I also asked each informant to describe how his sexual life had changed as a result of coming into the program. As noted above, four men reported having no sex at all since they came into the program. In part, a diminished sex drive seems to be a by-product of recovery from crystal meth addiction. As one informant put it, "CMA encourages sex. You pray [sex] will start again because [your] sex life is gone." In part, the diminished sex drive may be due to lack of interest in other men who are not using: "And the thought of having sex with my partner, it just, it diminished. It was much more exciting having sex with these people who were on drugs with me and promiscuous."

Others decreased their sexual encounters, but reported that they continued to have sexual problems in early recovery. One informant reported that his sexual life is "probably nonexistent," but then stated that when he needed to reach out to his sponsor or to other CMA members, it was usually around sexual issues. Another informant has stayed completely celibate while in recovery, except for one occasion, but stated that when he relapsed, it was due to his sexual desire.

Two informants stated that sex was less exciting in recovery. A third found it more enjoyable without substances, stating, "Now it's like I enjoy it more. I'm more aware of what's going on. I don't feel as bad. I'm more cautious." Three of the men stated that sober sex was about intimacy, being in love, or being monogamous with a partner. As one informant said, he was "looking for Mr. Right."

I asked the men whether the AA or CMA program had an "attitude" or "policy" about sex in early sobriety. Five of the men stated that the policy was to discourage sex in early sobriety, but the remainder disagreed. As one stated, "Sex is fine as long as it doesn't get in the way of sobriety." Another stated, "No one says it's bad to have sex." A third informant said that while relationships are discouraged in the first year, the program encourages sex because that is a sign of recovery. Since the program discourages relationships and/or dating (as opposed to sex) in the first year of sobriety, this may account for the number of "one-night stands" increasing upon entry into the program for two of the men: they had sex but without any kind of emotional ties, since the latter would violate an unwritten rule of the program.

It is worthwhile to put twelve-step programs in the context of other kinds of interventions, such as harm reduction and educational interventions. While the program requires strict abstinence with respect to alcohol and drugs, it is looser and more forgiving about other behaviors, including, perhaps, sexual behavior. A form of what may be called harm reduction is promoted. The AA literature says, "We are not saints. The point is we are willing to grow along spiritual lines" (Alcoholics Anonymous 2001: 53; cf. Kurtz and Ketcham 1992).

Creating Meaning within the Program

These twelve-step programs are clearly a kind of "subculture" that is created by participants, and, as in other subcultures, events and symbols are invested with meaning. Within the twelve-step program, one of the most central events requiring interpretation is relapse. Going back to drinking and drug using, and then returning to meetings, means that one has to start one's "sobriety day count" over again and be essentially reborn as a newcomer, having to suffer all of the cravings and confusions of early sobriety all over again. Crystal meth users are highly prone to starting the drug again. One of my informants linked the frequency of relapse with the imperfection of God:

> It's like, cut people a break; they're going to relapse over and over again. . . . I got really picked on when I quoted that story of Cain and Abel. I hold that God actually isn't perfect. That's one of the few stories where God indirectly admits that he made a mistake. If God can admit that, then perhaps we shouldn't be so hard on people.

The notion that one's sobriety must come first entails the view that relapses or slips are the worst possible thing that can happen to someone. Yet in CMA especially, many participants seem able to use the drug and come quickly back to the meetings. Often they have apparently lost little in terms of material goods or health. When the meeting chairman asks, "Who here has under thirty (or sixty or ninety) days clean?" more than half of those at the meeting will raise their hands. Hence, the notion of the relapse as the horror that destroys lives may have a different resonance in CMA. At the same time, since those who start using the drug again and do not come back to the meetings are obviously not present to give their stories, we may be seeing the minority who are able to pick up and put down the drug with few consequences.[2]

There is another important way in which statements in meetings are invested with particular meaning: this is the notion that one's past is one's greatest asset. Telling one's story helps others. The speaker can convert the suffering, loneliness, and desperation of his or her past into something valuable, a narrative that can serve as an inspiration for others and also a reinterpretation of his or her own life for himself or herself. According to program lore, this narrative should be as simple as possible: the speaker needs merely to say "what it was like, what happened, and what it's like now." But the stories told go much deeper than that and are as various in style and content as there are recovering addicts to tell them. Many speakers include the circumstances under which they tested HIV positive. Although a statement read at the beginning of every CMA meeting states that speakers should "avoid glorifying drug taking and drug driven sex," many speakers discuss their sexual history in general terms. In this way, new members who cannot easily deal with their own HIV status and past behavior can silently identify with the speaker—what the literature on group therapy calls the "aha" experience (Yalom 1970).[3]

Conclusion

The concepts explored here—honesty, facing reality, taking inventory, "one day at a time," fellowship, and spirituality—are general enough to encompass not only the desire for abstinence from drugs and alcohol but other life goals as well. Other program components such as sponsorship are also important, but cannot be developed here. While CMA is closely modeled after AA, it has its own character, mainly because of the relative newness of members and of the program itself, because of the centrality of unsafe sex and HIV infection to the experience of so many gay and bisexual crystal meth addicts, and because of the high rate of "slipping" and returning to the program. We currently have no way, however, to quantify the relative rates of slipping for users of different kinds of drugs.

I have argued in this chapter that CMA program participants apply the principles of the program to their sexual risk taking, and this partly accounts for the changes in behavior reported by most of those interviewed. Most reduced the number of their sex partners and used condoms for anal sex. Two, however, increased their number of "one-night stands," partly in response to the program's discouragement of dating and relationships in the first year (one of the most controversial of the program's informal tenets). Hence, different formal and informal "teachings" of the program may have contradictory effects on sexual behavior.

It is too early to tell whether CMA will put a "dent" into the current epidemic of meth abuse. Amphetamine in its various forms has surpassed cocaine and is second only to marijuana as the world's most commonly used illicit drug (UNODC 2003). Demand shows no sign of abating. Do those who attend CMA meetings but who periodically return to drug using for short periods of time eventually attain the goal of long-term abstinence? Is this goal even desirable, or is some form of harm reduction more realistic? In terms of sex, is the diminished or vanishing sex drive experienced by many participants shortly after cessation of meth use a reflection of a long-term change? How will the CMA program itself grow and develop? My colleagues and I are currently beginning a longitudinal, qualitative study of meth addicts in recovery in Chicago, which may help to answer some of these questions.

Acknowledgments

I want to thank Joan Koss-Chioino and Keith Bletzer for many helpful comments.

Notes

1. Note, however, that one respondent said that being in recovery is lonely because you no longer hang out with the people you used to know, so the transition to this new social network may not always be easy.

2. This self-selection problem is endemic in studies of the efficacy of mutual help groups. My colleagues and I are currently beginning work on a longitudinal study that will address these concerns.

3. Yalom (1970) theorized that a key element of group therapy is that listening to others' problems can give one indirect insight into one's own problems.

References

Alcoholics Anonymous. 2001. *Alcoholics Anonymous.* 4th ed. New York: Alcoholics Anonymous World Services, 2001.

Bloomfield, K. A. 1990. Community in recovery: A study of social support, spirituality, and voluntarism among gay and lesbian members of Alcoholics Anonymous. D.P.H. thesis, University of California, Berkeley.

Cain, C. 1991. Personal stories: Identity acquisition and self-understanding in Alcoholics Anonymous. *Ethos* 19: 210–53.

Christo, G., and S. Sutton. 1994. Anxiety and self-esteem as a function of abstinence time among recovering addicts attending Narcotics Anonymous. *British Journal of Clinical Psychology* 33: 198–200.

Clatts, M. C., L. Goldsamt, A. Neaigus, and D. L. Welle. 2003. The social course of drug injection and sexual activity among YMSM and other high-risk youth: An agenda for future research. *Journal of Urban Health* 80(4): 26–39.

Clatts, M. C., and J. L. Sotheran, 2000. Challenges in research on drug and sexual risk practices of men who have sex with men: Applications of ethnography in HIV epidemiology and prevention. *AIDS and Behavior* 4(2): 169–79.

Clatts, M. C., D. L. Welle, and L. A. Goldsamt. 2001. Reconceptualizing the interaction of drug and sexual risk among MSM speed users: Notes toward an ethno-epidemiology. *AIDS and Behavior* 5(2): 115–30.

Cohen, S., and T. A. Wills. 1985. Stress, social support and the buffering hypothesis. *Psychological Bulletin* 98: 310–57.

Crystal Meth Anonymous (CMA). 2005. Homepage at http://www.crystalmeth.org.

Denzin, N. K. 1987. *The Recovering Alcoholic*. Newbury Park, Calif.: Sage.

Emrick, C. D., J. S. Tonigan, H. Montgomery, and L. Little. 1993. Alcoholics Anonymous: What is currently known? In *Research on Alcoholics Anonymous: Opportunities and Alternatives*, ed. B. S. McCrady and W. R. Miller, 41–76. New Brunswick, N.J.: Rutgers Center of Alcohol Studies.

Galanter, M. 1993. *Network Therapy for Drug and Alcohol Abuse*. New York: Basic Books.

Gorbach, P. M., and K. K. Holmes. 2003. Transmission of STDs/HIV at the partnership level: Beyond individual-level analyses. *Journal of Urban Health* 80(4): 15–26.

Gorman, E. M., B. Barr, A. Hansen, B. Robertson, and C. Green. 1997. Speed, sex, gay men, and HIV: Ecological and community perspectives. *Medical Anthropology Quarterly* 11(4): 505–15.

Gottheil, E., A. Lundy, S. P. Weinstein, and R. C. Sterling. 1998. Does intensive outpatient cocaine treatment reduce AIDS risky behaviors? *Journal of Addictive Diseases* 17(4): 61–69.

Gottlieb, B. H. 1988. Marshalling social support: The state of the art in research and practice. In: *Marshaling Social Support: Formats, Processes, and Effects*, ed. B. H. Gottlieb, 11–51. Beverly Hills, Calif.: Sage.

Halkitis, P. N., J. T. Parsons, and M. J. Stirratt. 2001. A double epidemic: Crystal methamphetamine drug use in relation to HIV transmission among gay men. *Journal of Homosexuality* 41(2): 17–35.

Israelstam, S. 1986. Alcohol and drug problems of gay males and lesbians: Therapy, counseling, and prevention issues. *Journal of Drug Issues* 16(3): 443–61.

Jensen, G. H. 2000. *Storytelling in Alcoholics Anonymous: A Rhetorical Analysis*. Carbondale: Southern Illinois University Press.

Klitzman, R. L., H. G. Pope, and J. I. Hudson, 2000. MDMA ("Ecstasy") abuse and high-risk sexual behaviors among 169 gay and bisexual men. *American Journal of Psychiatry* 157: 1162–164.

Kurtz, E., and K. Ketcham. 1992. *The Spirituality of Imperfection: Modern Wisdom from Classic Stories.* New York: Bantam Books.

Magura, S., A. Rosenblum, and E. M. Rodriguez. 1998. Changes in HIV risk behavior among cocaine-using methadone patients. *Journal of Addictive Diseases* 17(4): 71–90.

McCrady, B. S., and W. R. Miller, eds. 1993. *Research on Alcoholics Anonymous: Opportunities and Alternatives.* New Brunswick, N.J.: Rutgers Center of Alcohol Studies.

Montgomery, H. A., W. R. Miller, and J. S. Tonigan. 1995. Does Alcoholics Anonymous involvement predict treatment outcome? *Journal of Substance Abuse Treatment* 12(4): 241–46.

Morgenstern, J., C. W. Kahler, R. M. Frey, and E. Labouvie. 1996. Modeling therapeutic response to 12-step treatment: Optimal responders, non-responders, and partial responders. *Journal of Substance Abuse* 8(1): 45–59.

Morgenstern, J., E. Labouvie, B. S. McCrady, C. W. Kahler, and R. M. Frey. 1997. Affiliation with Alcoholics Anonymous after treatment: A study of the therapeutic effects and mechanisms of action. *Journal of Counseling and Clinical Psychology* 65(5): 768–77.

Paul, J. P., R. Stall, and F. Davis. 1993. Sexual risk for HIV transmission among gay/bisexual men in substance abuse treatment. *AIDS Education and Prevention* 5: 11–24.

Rappaport, J. 1994. Narrative studies, personal stories, and identity transformation in the mutual help context. In *Understanding the Self-Help Organization: Frameworks and Findings*, ed. T. Powell, 115–35. Thousand Oaks, Calif.: Sage.

Reback C. J., S. Larkins, and S. Shoptaw. 2004. Change in the meaning of sexual risk behaviors among MSM methamphetamine abusers before and after drug treatment. *AIDS and Behavior* 8(1): 87–97.

Rodin, M. B. 1986. Getting on the program: A biocultural analysis of Alcoholics Anonymous. In *The American Experience with Alcohol: Contrasting Cultural Perspectives*, ed. L. A. Bennett and G. M. Ames, 41–58. New York: Plenum Press.

Semple, S. J., T. L. Patterson, and I. Grant. 2002. Motivations associated with methamphetamine use among HIV+ men who have sex with men. *Journal of Substance Abuse Treatment* 22(3): 149–56.

Shoptaw, S., and D. Frosch. 2000. Substance abuse treatment as HIV prevention for men who have sex with men. *AIDS and Behavior* 4(2): 193–203.

Shoptaw, S., C. J. Reback, and T. E. Freese. 2002. Patient characteristics, HIV serostatus, and risk behaviors among gay and bisexual males seeking treatment for methamphetamine abuse and dependence in Los Angeles. *Journal of Addictive Diseases* 21(1): 91–105.

Shoptaw, S., C. J. Reback, D. L. Frosch, and R. A. Rawson. 1998. Stimulant abuse treatment as HIV prevention. *Journal of Addictive Diseases* 17(4): 19–32.

Simon, W., and J. H. Gagnon. 1987. A sexual scripts approach. In *Theories of Human Sexuality*, ed. J. H. Geert and W. T. O'Donohue, 363–84. New York: Plenum.

Stall, R., J. D. Paul, D. C. Barrett, G. M. Crosby, and E. Bein. 1999. An outcome evaluation to measure changes in sexual risk-taking among gay men undergoing substance use disorder treatment. *Journal of Studies on Alcohol* 60: 837–45.

Stall, R., and D. W. Purcell. 2000. Intertwining epidemics: a review of research on substance use among men who have sex with men and its connection to the AIDS epidemic. *AIDS and Behavior* 4(2): 188–92.

Steffen, V. 1997. Life stories and shared experience. *Social Science and Medicine* 45(1): 99–111.

Timko, C., R. H. Moos, J. W. Finney, B. S. Moos, and M. S. Kablowitz. 1999. Long-term treatment careers and outcomes of previously untreated alcoholics. *Journal of Studies on Alcohol* 60: 437–47.

United Nations Office on Drugs and Crime (UNODC). 2003. Ecstasy and amphetamines global survey. http://www.unodc.org/unodc/publications/report_ats_2003-09-23_1.html.

Wittmer, D. F. 1997. Communication and recovery: Structuration as an ontological approach to organizational culture. *Communication Monographs* 64: 324–49.

Yalom, I. 1970. *Theory and Practice of Group Psychotherapy*. New York: Basic Books.

Zea, M. C., C. A. Reisen, P. J. Poppen, and R. M. Díaz. 2003. Asking and telling: Communication about HIV status among Latino gay men. *AIDS and Behavior* 7(2): 143–52.

Zehner, M. A., and J. Lewis. 1983. Homosexuality and alcoholism: Social and developmental perspectives. *Journal of Social Work and Human Sexuality* (2–3): 75–89.

8

HIV Status, Risk, and Prevention Needs among Latino and Non-Latino Men Who Have Sex with Men in Connecticut

SCOTT CLAIR AND MERRILL SINGER

Earlier in the HIV epidemic, Singer and Marxuach-Rodriguez (1996) called attention to the need for a culturally appropriate HIV prevention intervention for Latino men who have sex with men (MSM). Part of their rationale was based on epidemiologic data showing that Latino MSM were at higher risk of HIV than their white counterparts; despite this, the heterogeneous Latino MSM population was very poorly understood (Burgos and Perez 1986). Looking at the situation eight years later, we can see that we still have a lot of work to do. The current chapter updates this information by examining the HIV risk behaviors of "at-risk" Latino MSM compared to African American and white MSM in a statewide sample in Connecticut. These risk behaviors are viewed from within the cultural context in which they occur. We also examine the relative exposure of Latino MSM to HIV prevention information. Finally, we outline a new antihomophobia social-marketing campaign targeted specifically to Latinos that was created and designed by the Hispanic Health Council based on extensive feedback from the community.

The Epidemiology

Recent estimates show that MSM in the United States have HIV prevalence rates rivaling those of adults in sub-Saharan Africa. Despite progress in HIV prevention over the last twenty years, there are more newly diagnosed HIV cases in the United States among MSM than any other group (CDC 1999a, 1999c). Specific subpopulations of MSM seem to be at a heightened risk of HIV, including those who heavily use drugs, African American and Latino men, and men with lower socioeconomic status (Catania et al. 2001; Diaz and Ayala 2001; Diaz et al. 1993; Singer et al. 1990). In 1998, there was an important turning point in the AIDS epidemic among MSM. This marked the first year in which a majority of the newly diagnosed AIDS cases were among ethnic minority men (CDC 2000). A recent study of young MSM conducted in seven U.S. cities found that 30 percent of young African American men and 15 percent of young Latino men were infected with HIV (Valleroy et al. 2000). Other studies have estimated that the prevalence of HIV among Latino MSM is over 20 percent (Diaz et al. 2000). In addition to high prevalence rates, recent studies show that HIV sexual risk behavior within this population may be increasing (CDC 1999b; Mansergh et al. 2002; Singer 2004), which suggests a potential increase in HIV incidence in the near future.

The epidemic in Connecticut has closely mirrored the epidemiologic patterns at the national level (Baer et al. 2004). Since 1981, when Connecticut began reporting AIDS cases, MSM have been the second largest at-risk group after injection drug users (IDUs). MSM represented 23 percent of the reported AIDS cases in Connecticut through 2000. Reviewing AIDS cases among MSM generally in the state, one notable shift is that the percentage of cases that are Latino has been rising, from 11 percent for the interval from 1990 to 1995 to 16 percent for the interval from 1996 to 2000, and there has been a corresponding decrease among white MSM (from 70 percent to 64 percent, respectively), while the rates for African American MSM have remained stable (Connecticut Department of Public Health 2001).

Recent data also suggest that rates of sexually transmitted infections (STIs) are increasing among MSM. Early findings from Seattle show increases in gonorrhea, syphilis, and chlamydia infection in the late 1990s (CDC 1999c; Williams et al. 1999). Looking at national data, Fox and colleagues (2001) found that MSM accounted for 4.5 percent of reported gonorrhea cases in 1992, a rate that had almost tripled to 13.2 percent by 1999. In addition, a seven-city surveillance study found that 11 percent of the MSM tested had hepatitis B (MacKellar et al. 2001). In Connecticut, the Department of Public Health reports that there was a 133 percent increase in the diagnosis of primary and secondary syphilis in the state from 2001 to 2002. Among those diagnosed with syphilis in 2002, 36 percent had HIV, as compared to 25 percent the previous year. While Connecticut does not report specific rates for MSM, Latino men moved up steadily from accounting for 8 percent of syphilis cases identified in Connecticut in 1998, to 12.5 percent in 1999, to 13.3 percent in 2000, and to 14.3 percent in 2002 (Connecticut Department of Public Health 2002).

Current research on MSM risk behavior has been limited by the following five methodological issues: many of the studies have an overrepresentation of white MSM, and there are rarely comparisons made across racial and ethnic groups of MSM; most studies of Latino MSM focus on Mexican or Mexican American men in the Southwest; most of the studies are conducted exclusively in the large urban cities in the United States; most studies have been limited to larger survey designs with limited use of in-depth qualitative methods that are known to help clarify the context and social and behavioral connections among research variables; and most of the research focuses on one problem in isolation and/or does not assess the social conditions that exacerbate the social problems occurring (Carballo-Diéguez 1995, 1997; Singer and Clair 2003).

Wolitski and colleagues (2001) suggest the proper "lens" through which to view this epidemiologic data. The key is to "recognize that HIV risk occurs within a broader context of physical and mental health problems, including psychological distress, substance use, violence and sexual assault and other STDs other than HIV. These factors, which are often interrelated, may have a common basis in the considerable prejudice, homophobia, and stigmatization that MSM in the United States continue to experience" (Wolitski et al. 2001: 885). The co-occurrence of multiple epidemics that are exacerbated by adverse social conditions is called a syndemic (Singer and Clair 2003).

The Survey

Given the troubling risk and prevalence trends among MSM, HIV prevention providers are looking for ways to maximize the effectiveness of their programs during times of diminishing fiscal resources (Kelly 1999). Toward this end, the Hispanic Health Council, a community-based health research, service, and advocacy institute, was subcontracted by a local AIDS service organization to conduct a service utilization and needs assessment survey of "at-risk" MSMs in Connecticut (Loue et al. 2000). For the purposes of this project, being "at-risk" was defined as the status of any individual who had visited gay bars, dance clubs, adult bookstores, or identified MSM cruising areas more than once in the last six months. MSMs were defined as any male or transgendered individual who reported having sex with men and/or self-identified as gay, bisexual, or "other" (that is, not heterosexual).

The Hispanic Health Council identified seven outreach interviewers from across the state to assist in the recruitment of the target population:

two were based in Hartford, one was based in Bridgeport, two were based in New Haven, and the other two were split across areas, one between Waterbury and New Haven and the other between Hartford and New Haven. Of the seven interviewers, six were providing HIV prevention services to MSM through their respective agencies and, as a result, were able to make appropriate referrals as needed. The survey was translated into Spanish, and three of the interviewers were bilingual. All study respondents were paid $10 for their participation in the interviews.

One of the key intervention questions motivating the survey was how to better target HIV prevention programs and messages to "at-risk" MSM. To answer this question, the project goals were to interview a large, heterogeneous sample of MSM distributed across the state, to use this information to create profiles of the primary MSM subgroups in need of HIV/AIDS prevention, and to develop outreach and prevention approaches and messages appropriate to each identified subgroup. Toward these ends, an eight-page survey was designed based on the study questions, prior research by the Hispanic Health Council, and the HIV/AIDS literature on risk among MSM and Latinos. The intent was to cover the necessary material while trying to keep the length of time required to complete the interview manageable.

The recruitment and referral plan proved to be quite successful, and ultimately 331 survey participants who met the inclusion criteria of the project were interviewed, forming what is likely the largest survey of the MSM population conducted to date in Connecticut. Of these 331 participants, 97.5 percent were males, and 2.5 percent were transgendered. Forty-five percent were white, 26 percent African American, 22 percent Latino, and 7 percent "other." Among the Latinos, the population of specific concern for this chapter, 76 percent were Puerto Rican, and 24 percent were from other Latino populations, including Mexicans, Cubans, Guatemalans, Argentineans, Brazilians, Columbians, Dominicans, Salvadorians, Peruvians, and Spanish. Thirteen percent of the sample stated that their primary language was Spanish, while the other 87 percent were primary English speakers. The average age for the sample was thirty-three years old, with a range from eighteen to fifty-eight years. The income distribution was also very diverse, with 36 percent of the sample stating that they had earned less than $1,000 in the past thirty days, while 12 percent of the sample said they had earned over $4,000 in the past thirty days. In terms of sexual orientation, 84 percent self-identified as gay or "homosexual," and another 14 percent identified as bisexual.

The survey was intended to be statewide, and participants came from thirty-nine different towns and cities in Connecticut. (It should be noted that all of Connecticut is assigned as part of one or another of the 169 towns and cities in the state; there are no unincorporated areas). There were 157 participants from Hartford, 64 from New Haven, 17 from Hamden, 12 from New Britain, 10 from East Hartford, 7 from Bridgeport, and 7 from Waterbury. The remaining thirty-two towns and cities represented in the study had 5 or fewer participants.

Eighty-one percent of the sample reported attending a gay bar or club more than once in the six months prior to being interviewed, 64 percent had visited pornographic bookstores more than once, and 60 percent had gone to gay cruising areas more than once in the last six months. In addition to potential sexual risk, 6 percent of the sample reported injecting drugs in the last six months. Finally, 22 percent of the sample self-reported that they were HIV positive. Many studies conducted with MSM have been critiqued for not being sufficiently diverse (Carballo-Diéguez 1997). With the possible exception of location, the present study appears to have more than adequately addressed this concern by identifying and recruiting a more representative selection of the "at-risk" MSM population. We believe that a large contributor to the diversity of the current sample was the careful selection of a similarly diverse cadre of outreach workers from the target population.

The Social Context: Social Stressors and Health

As pointed out by Wolitski and colleagues (2001) and by syndemic theory more generally (Singer 1996), in order to properly understand epidemics and the risk behaviors that provide their immediate impetus, we have to look closely at the wider social contexts in which they occur. For the current chapter, this requires looking at the influential features of the social contexts inhabited by "at-risk" MSM, particularly Latino MSM. Evans and colleagues (1997) noted the existence of an association between severe life stress and early disease progression among individuals with HIV disease.

Stress, a common consequence of poverty, discrimination, and other forms of structural violence, appears to be a primary route through which oppressive social conditions find expression as clinical symptoms and as causal factors in behavior. MSM in the United States are known to be regular targets of social stigmatization, prejudice, and violence. Each of these factors has been identified as a significant social stressor that can have an effect on an individual's physical and mental health (Herek et al. 1999; Meyer 1995; Rosario et al. 1996). Research looking directly at the issue of sexual orientation has found that social stigmatization is a risk factor for psychological distress, particularly depression and possibly anxiety (Cochran 2001; Kessler et al. 1999; Meyer 1995; Otis and Skinner 1996).

Many Latino MSM do not identify as gay (Morales 1990; Reitmeijer et al. 1998). Some have argued that this is "because they feel that this designation negates their racial and ethnic heritage" (Valdiserri 1989: 101). Others have suggested that this may partially be attributed to internalized homophobia (Reitmeijer et al. 1998). More generally, it is recognized that there is severe stigmatization of same-sex sexuality within the Latino culture (Diaz 1998; Marin 1988). As one of Diaz's (1998: 64) research participants commented, "*no hombres hombres*," (same-sex persons are not true men). Antigay stigma has been enhanced by AIDS stigma (just as AIDS stigma was enhanced by the early association of the disease with gay men), and, as a result, MSM are labeled not only as different and deviant but also as deadly.

According to Link and Phelan (2001: 365), stigma exists when the following interrelated components converge. In the first component, people distinguish and label human differences. In the second, dominant cultural beliefs link labeled persons to undesirable characteristics—to negative stereotypes. In the third, labeled persons are placed in distinct categories so as to accomplish some degree of separation of "us" from "them." In the fourth, labeled persons experience status loss and discrimination that lead to unequal outcomes. Finally, stigmatization is entirely contingent on access to social, economic, and political power that allows the identification of being different, the construction of stereotypes, the separation of labeled persons into distinct categories, and the full execution of disapproval, rejection, exclusion, and discrimination.

AIDS stigma, the social devaluing of infected individuals, involves both their labeling for avoidance (as they are perceived as being dangerous) and their targeting for painful discrimination and overt physical abuse as punishment for the behaviors that led them to getting the disease. AIDS stigma may result in individuals who identify as gay, alienating their families, friends, neighbors, and coworkers, and, as an alternative, individuals leading double lives and publicly identifying as bisexual or even heterosexual (de la Vega 1990). For Latino MSM, there are at least two additional forms of structural violence to which they commonly are subjected on a daily basis that white MSM are not: racism and classism. In addition to being stigmatized within Latino culture for being gay or bisexual, they are further stigmatized within the larger culture for being a gay Latino, and, if they are a Latino living in poverty, then they face additional discrimination as well.

Prior research suggests that populations that suffer multiple stigmatization (for example, Latino MSM) are at especially heightened levels of HIV risk (Friedman et al. 1997). In a series of focus groups conducted with Latino gay men, those participants who reported the highest levels of HIV risk behavior were more likely to talk about issues related to race and class (Diaz and Ayala 2001). In their study of Latino gay men, Diaz and Ayala found that men in the "high risk" group reported more experiences of racism, homophobia, and poverty as compared to those men in the "low risk" group. There are also certain factors that have been found to be associated with greater resiliency among MSM facing social stigmatization, including family acceptance and having gay role models (Diaz and Ayala 2001). The effects of multiple social stigmatization may make it difficult for Latino MSM to advocate on their own behalf. However, access to networks of social support and the development of coping strategies can be important factors in diminishing the deleterious effects of social stigmatization, and certainly many Latino MSM have become active in the public fight against AIDS discrimination.

In sum then, the critical context for Latino MSM in the AIDS epidemic is formed by the conflicted forces of stigmatization and structural violence, on the one hand, and social support and resiliency, on the other. On the stage formed by this dynamic tension, Latino MSM have encountered the once strange, but now all too familiar foe known as HIV.

Survey Findings

Identity and Survival Economics

With regard to sexual orientation, consistent with other studies, a significantly larger percentage of Latino MSM identified as bisexual (23.9 percent) compared to African American MSM (11.3 percent) and white MSM (8.6 percent). Also, Latinos reported significantly lower incomes in the past thirty days compared to the African Americans and whites in the sample.

Specifically, almost half of the Latino MSM (48.4 percent) reported earning less than $500 in the past thirty days compared to 16.6 percent of the African American MSM and 10.3 percent of the white MSM.

Latinos reported the highest rates of selling sex compared to the other groups. Overall, 19.1 percent of Latinos, 9.7 percent of African Americans, and 9.4 percent of whites in the target sample reported exchanging sex for money or drugs in the past six months. This is most likely related to the lower relative economic status of the Latinos in the sample. Various researchers have mentioned that a common reason given for engaging in commercial sex work is to help finance a drug habit (Reitmeijer et al. 1998). This would also seem to be a viable explanation in the current study because Latinos also reported the highest rates of injection drug use, with 10.3 percent of Latinos, 6.2 percent of whites, and 4.0 percent of African Americans reporting that they had injected drugs in the last six months. Past studies have also found a high rate of selling sex among Latino MSM (Singer and Marxuach-Rodriguez 1996).

Perception of Risk

Before addressing the behaviors the participants engaged in, we assessed how risky they perceived various behaviors to be. Participants were asked to rate a set of behaviors on a four-point scale, with 1 indicating "No Risk," 2 indicating "Low Risk," 3 indicating "Medium Risk," and 4 indicating "High Risk." The first statement to be rated was, "I believe unprotected oral sex between two men has X amount of risk." For this item, Latinos and whites both reported a 3.2, while African Americans rated it a 3.5, indicating that African Americans perceived this behavior as somewhat more risky than the other two groups. Similarly, for protected oral sex between two men, Latinos and whites rated this an average of 2.2, while African Americans reported a 2.5. For unprotected anal intercourse, Latinos and African Americans rated it as a 3.8, and whites rated it as a 3.9. Finally, for protected anal intercourse, Latinos rated it a 2.5, whites a 2.6, and African Americans a 3.1. The pattern that emerged across the four behaviors is that in each instance, Latinos reported the behaviors as less risky compared with African Americans, and in all but one case African Americans rated the behavior as having the greater risk. The differences across ethnic groups were statistically significant.

Condom Usage

Four different questions asked about the participant's condom use. Specifically, these looked at how often the participant used a condom when giving oral sex, receiving oral sex, giving anal sex (as a "top"), and receiving anal sex (as a "bottom"). Participants rated each of the items on a four-point scale with 1 indicating "Never," 2 indicating "Rarely," 3 indicating "Often," and 4 indicating "Always"; consequently, higher scores indicate higher levels of reported condom usage. For giving oral sex, Latinos averaged 2.0, whites 2.1, and African Americans 2.5. For receiving oral sex, Latinos averaged 1.9, whites 2.0, and African Americans 2.6. For giving anal sex, Latinos averaged 2.8, whites 3.0, and African Americans 3.2. Finally, for receiving anal sex, Latinos averaged 2.8, and whites and African Americans averaged 3.2. This pattern of results indicates that across all four behaviors, Latinos were the least likely to report using condoms, and African Americans were the most likely to report using condoms. However, only in situations involving oral sex were the differences statistically significant (for comparative data from New York City, see Carballo-Diéguez and Dolezal 1996). Again, these behaviors must be viewed within a specific context. For many Latinos regardless of sexual orientation, there is a cultural taboo against using condoms. Also, for the current sample, a larger percentage are involved in selling sex where sex workers are frequently paid more for performing sex acts without a condom.

HIV and Communication

Our survey assessed how often HIV communication occurred with three different items: asking about your partner's HIV status, telling your partner your HIV status, and talking about HIV in general with your partner. These items were rated on the same four-point scale as the condom usage questions, with 1 indicating "Never," 2 indicating "Rarely," 3 indicating "Often," and 4 indicating "Always." Higher scores indicate more frequent communication about HIV. Regarding asking about their partners' status, Latinos averaged 2.1, whites 2.6, and African Americans 2.7. Concerning how often they told their partner their HIV status, Latinos averaged 2.2, and whites and African Americans averaged 2.6. For talking about HIV in general with their partner, Latinos averaged a 2.1, whites 2.5, and African Americans 2.6. For each of the three items, Latinos were least likely to report communicating with their sexual partners about HIV, and all of these differences were statistically significant. These averages suggest that Latino MSM rarely talk about HIV with their sexual partners, while white and African American MSM fall between rarely and often talking about HIV with their partners.

We also asked a question about the participant's HIV status. Among white MSM, 16.1 percent reported being HIV positive, 20.5 percent of African

American MSM were HIV positive, while the rate of HIV infection among Latino MSM was 36.8 percent. It should again be emphasized that the current study recruited "at-risk" MSM and thus these self-reported infection rates should not be interpreted as prevalence estimates for the Latino or any other MSM population. However, the fact that over a third of the Latinos and over a fifth of the African Americans reported being HIV positive is still a very sobering finding and is consistent with other studies that have found that the rates of HIV among these groups in particular have been rising in recent years.

Looking at the social context that may play a role in HIV communication, Latinos have been found to be less likely to talk openly with their partners about sexual topics. In addition, as noted above, for the current sample, Latinos had the highest rates of HIV. Clearly the meaning and implication of "telling your partner your HIV status" are very different for an HIV-positive and an HIV-negative individual. Discussing HIV more generally or asking a partner's status opens the door to the possibility that an individual will also disclose his own status because of the pressure for reciprocity. Under these circumstances, individuals who are already HIV positive may be less likely to communicate with their partners about HIV for fear of rejection or worse.

HIV Prevention

Two general questions were asked that queried the participant's access and/ or knowledge about HIV prevention. First, we asked if the individual had ever attended an HIV prevention session. Sixty-three percent of the Latino MSM, 72 percent of the whites, and 77 percent of the African Americans in the study reported that they had not attended an HIV prevention session. Second, we asked if they could name an agency that provided HIV prevention in their area. Forty-eight percent of Latino MSM, 51 percent of whites, and 59 percent of African Americans could not name any agency that provided HIV prevention.

The next general question to be answered is: why are all participants not attending available HIV prevention sessions? All participants were asked, "Which of the following are some of the reasons you haven't attended these sessions?" This was followed by a series of eight choices, including an "other" option where participants could state whatever they wanted. Participants could give multiple responses to this question. One of the most common reasons listed was that participants simply did not know about a program (31 percent). Other responses included that they already knew the information (32 percent), that they thought that there was nothing new to learn (10 percent), and that they were already practicing safer sex (8 percent). This cluster of responses suggests that participants perceive that there is no new information that they can gain from attending HIV education sessions and that perhaps the prevention sessions are seen as focused exclusively on practicing safer sex. Two percent reported that they did not attend because they were already HIV positive. While HIV prevention efforts targeted to HIV-positive persons have been undertaken only relatively recently, more information should be provided to those who are HIV positive on the benefits prevention sessions can offer.

Another dynamic that was observed is that 8 percent of participants stated that they were tired of hearing about HIV, and another 8 percent did not want to know the information. This will most likely be the hardest portion of the population to recruit into prevention sessions. Being tired of hearing too much about AIDS and not wanting to know anything about the disease form two ends of a circular pathway, neither of which is open to prevention education. One potential solution to this dilemma, as some providers have learned, is not to focus exclusively on HIV in the sessions but on a variety of issues in which HIV is just one of the topics. Finally, 18 percent of our sample reported that they did not attend because they were already in a committed relationship. This option was added after feedback from a pilot test of the survey because a number of respondents believed that this should be included. The assumption seems to be that because the individual is in a committed relationship, he does not need to worry about HIV prevention, a perspective that is likely to be fairly common among heterosexuals as well.

A Community-Level Intervention

In light of our research findings, and given the mounting epidemiologic evidence showing that HIV among Latino MSM is spreading rapidly, as well as the existence of a known link between HIV risk behaviors and public discrimination, the Hispanic Health Council decided to try a new type of intervention for the community. In speaking with Latino gay, lesbian, bisexual, and transgendered (GLBT) participants in our service programs for the last several years, it has become painfully apparent that homophobia has had an enormously negative impact on their lives. Therefore, we decided to design an antihomophobia campaign targeted to Latinos in Hartford, Connecticut.

Many people have argued that you cannot do HIV prevention work without looking at the effects of homophobia. Project Orgullo, our continuing HIV prevention program for Latino MSM, which was first described by Singer and Marxuach-Rodriguez (1996), has had this topic included in its prevention curriculum since 1991, but the emphasis has always been on how homophobia affects the individual rather than on finding ways to reduce homophobia in the community. We see the social-marketing campaign being implemented by the Hispanic Health Council as an important next step in the prevention process because it shifts the focus from the level of individual change achieved through one-on-one intervention to a focus on community-level change. Others have stated that "HIV prevention must include strategies to counter racism, poverty, sexism, homophobia, and AIDS stigma in full awareness that reducing their impact on individuals will most likely result in a dramatic reduction of HIV incidence" (Diaz and Ayala 2001:vii). More generally, with a growing sense that much of what can be achieved in risk reduction at the individual level of change has already been achieved, there is a mounting interest in community and structural interventions in the AIDS epidemic (Sumartojo and Laga 2000).

The Hispanic Health Council has successfully employed a social-marketing model in the promotion of a healthy diet in the Latino community over the last several years. The program, which has been carefully evaluated, demonstrates that focused, intensive dissemination of positive, culturally sensitive messages and images about healthy eating can effectively penetrate community awareness and influence community dietary patterns. Our project is designed to adapt this same approach to address homophobia in the Latino community in a culturally informed and sensitive manner with the explicit goal of lowering misinformation, discriminatory attitudes, and hostile behaviors aimed at the GLBT population. The ultimate objective of this project is to lower various forms of risk in the Latino GLBT population, including HIV/AIDS risk, by reducing one of the social pressures that promotes risk behavior.

The social-marketing campaign is coordinated by the arts and communication director at the Hispanic Health Council and includes feedback from the community regarding the specifics of the message. The first six months of the program were spent developing the messages with the input of the community, and the remaining time is being spent getting the selected messages out to the community, through radio and television public service announcements, street and bus billboards, and bus stop shelter posters.

Message and image development are carried out in five phases: creating focus groups with Latino GLBT individuals to generate ideas, images, and messages for the social-marketing campaign, including identification of inappropriate messages; computer and graphics development of candidate materials and messages (for example, designs for posters or billboards, text for public service announcements); follow-up focus groups with Latino GLBT individuals to garner feedback on the social-marketing materials; revision of materials in light of focus group feedback; and saturation marketing of the materials with the intention of achieving "message reinforcement" (that is, having individuals in the community receive overlapping antihomophobia messages from two or more sources during the same period of time).

The Hispanic Health Council's antihomophobia social-marketing campaign was initially proposed as part of a state-funded HIV prevention program. However, given the limited funds available to the state for HIV prevention, the state was not able to fund this particular project. We were determined that the project needed to go forward regardless and that funds would be identified; after discussions with various other potential collaborators, the local GLBT health center agreed to help pay for the project through marketing funds that they had obtained.

During the first phase of development, the staff involved conducted a nationwide search via the Internet and contacting LLEGO, a national Latino GLBT organization, about other antihomophobia campaigns that had been targeted to the Latino community. We were surprised to learn that no one was aware of any other such programs and that we were apparently the first to attempt this. The arts and communication director determined that there were at least two core elements of Latino culture that needed to be incorporated: religion and the family (*familia*). As a result, it was decided early on that most, if not all, of the images would focus on gays and lesbians as family members being accepted by other relatives. It was also decided that in order to be credible, we would not use paid actors. Instead, we have recruited volunteers from the community who were willing to be part of the campaign.

Mockups of the various slogans were presented to the community for feedback using stock photography. Based on this feedback, a subset of the messages presented was developed with pictures of recruited models replacing the stock photography used in the earlier mockups. The campaign is still ongoing, and the initial response from the Latino GLBT community has been positive.

Conclusion

Over the last eight years, numerous studies have shown that the HIV rates among Latino and African American MSM have only gotten worse since our team's first article on the topic was written. In the current chapter, findings from a survey conducted with "at-risk" MSM found that Latinos, when compared to whites and African Americans, perceived various behaviors as less risky; Latinos were less likely to use condoms; and Latinos were less likely to communicate with their partners about HIV. Finally, over a third of the Latino MSM in our sample reported that they were HIV positive.

In order to properly understand these behaviors, we must also examine the social context surrounding them. For Latino MSM, in the current study almost half reported earning less than $500 in the past thirty days. Clearly, poverty is a factor in many of their lives as is the likely discrimination that goes along with it in the United States. Latinos were found to be twice as likely to report selling sex in the last thirty days as whites and African Americans. Living in poverty and selling sex, of course, are not unrelated. As Diaz (1998: 151) stresses, "sociocultural factors, rather than personal intentions, are the major regulators of sexual behavior."

Poverty can be a powerful force shaping decision making and the risks that develop from it. When someone is selling sex on the streets in order to survive, they may not have the luxury of asking someone to use a condom. This can result in a reduced likelihood of using condoms and, perhaps as a defense mechanism, to perceiving these behaviors as involving less risk. Latinos were twice as likely as African Americans and two and a half times as likely as whites to report being "bisexual," which some have argued may be a proxy for internalized homophobia and/or a sign of the extreme stigma directed at gay men within Latino culture, suggesting that both external and internalized homophobia may influence their actions.

At present, the need for effective HIV intervention for Latino MSM could not be greater. Since 1991, the Hispanic Health Council and other community and public agencies have provided culturally tailored HIV prevention programs for Latino MSM. Homophobia, racism, and poverty, and the ways they affect individual health and risk patterns, have been a part of the Hispanic Health Council's prevention curriculum. However, we believe that it is past time to take the next step. To draw an analogy, when working with the issue of domestic abuse, it is important to work with the survivor and help him or her cope with his or her situation. However, it is also necessary to intervene with the individual who perpetrated the domestic abuse in the first place.

To date, most if not all of the HIV prevention efforts targeted to Latino MSM have focused on how they can better cope with their situation, including the challenges of poverty, racism, and homophobia. The next step, and the one currently being implemented by the Hispanic Health Council through its social-marketing antihomophobia campaign, is a focus on changing the social conditions that at-risk Latino MSM are exposed to on a daily basis. By including both pieces of the puzzle—the individual characteristics as well as the underlying social conditions that influence risk patterns—we can more effectively provide HIV prevention. Only such a two-sided approach allows prevention to address the range of factors that contribute to HIV risk and transmission.

References

Baer, H., M. Singer, and I. Susser, I. 2004. *Medical Anthropology and the World System.* 2nd ed. Westport, Conn.: Greenwood.

Burgos, N., and V. Perez. 1986. An exploration of human sexuality in the Puerto Rican culture. *Journal of Social Work and Human Sexuality* 15(6): 343–55.

Carballo-Diéguez, A. 1995. The sexual identity and behavior of Puerto Rican men who have sex with men. In *AIDS, Identity and Community: The HIV Epidemic and Lesbians and Gay Men, Psychological Perspectives on Lesbian and Gay Issues*, ed. G. Herek and B. Greene, 105–14. Thousand Oaks, Calif.: Sage.

———. 1997. Sexual research with Latino men who have sex with men: Methodological issues. In *Researching Sexual Behavior: Methodological Issues*, ed. J. Bancroft, 134–44. Bloomington: Indiana University Press.

Carballo-Diéguez, A., and C. Dolezal. 1996. HIV risk behaviors and obstacles to condom use among Puerto Rican men in New York City who have sex with men. *American Journal of Public Health* 86(11): 1619–622.

Catania, J. A., D. Osmond, R. D. Stall, L. Pollack, J. P. Paul, S. Blower, D. Binson, J. A. Canchola, T. C. Mills, L. Fisher, K. Choi, T. Porco, C. Turner, J. Blair, J. Henne, L. L. Bye, and T. J. Coates. 2001. The continuing HIV epidemic among men who have sex with men. *American Journal of Public Health* 91: 907–14.

Centers for Disease Control and Prevention (CDC). 1999a. Increase in unsafe sex and rectal gonorrhea among men who have sex with men—San Francisco, California, 1994–1997. *Morbidity and Mortality Weekly Review* 48: 45–58.

———. 1999b. *1998 HIV/AIDS Surveillance Report.* Atlanta: Centers for Disease Control and Prevention.

———. 1999c. Resurgent bacterial sexually transmitted disease among men who have sex with men—King County, Washington, 1997–1999. *Morbidity and Mortality Weekly Review* 48: 773–77.

———. 2000. *1999 HIV/AIDS Surveillance Report*. Atlanta: Centers for Disease Control and Prevention.

Cochran, S. D. 2001. Emerging issues in research on lesbians' and gay men's mental health: Does sexual orientation really matter? *American Psychologist* 56(11): 931–47.

Connecticut Department of Public Health. 2001. *Epidemiological Profile of HIV and AIDS, December 2001*. Hartford: Connecticut Department of Public Health.

———. 2002. *Sexually Transmitted Diseases 1998–2002*. Hartford, Conn.: Sexually Transmitted Diseases Control Program.

de la Vega, E. 1990. Considerations for reaching the Latino population with sexuality and HIV/AIDS information and education. *SIECUS Report* 18(3): 1–18.

Diaz, R. M. 1998. *Latino Gay Men and HIV Culture, Sexuality, and Risk Behavior*. New York: Routledge.

Diaz, R. M., and G. Ayala, G. 2001. Social discrimination and health: The case of Latino gay men and HIV risk. Publication of the Policy Institute of the National Gay and Lesbian Task Force. www.ngltf.org.

Diaz, R. M., G. Ayala, and B. V. Marin. 2000. Latino gay men and HIV: Risk behavior as a sign of oppression. *Focus: A Guide to AIDS Research and Counseling* 15(7): 1–4.

Diaz, R. M., J. Buehler, K. Castro, and J. Ward. 1993. AIDS research trends among Hispanics in the United States. *American Journal of Public Health* 93: 504–9.

Evans, D., J. Leserman, D. Perkins, R. Stern, C. Murphy, B. Zheng, D. Gettes, J. Longmate, S. Silva, C. Vanderhorst, C. Hall, J. Folds, R. Golden, and J. Petitto. 1997. Severe life stress as a predictor of early disease progression in HIV infection. *American Journal of Psychiatry* 154(5): 630–34.

Fox, K. K., C. del Rio, K. K. Holmes, E. W. Hook, F. N. Judson, J. S. Knapp, G. W. Procop, S. A. Wang, W. L. H. Whittington, and W. C. Levine. 2001. Gonorrhea in the HIV era: A reversal in trends among men who have sex with men. *American Journal of Public Health* 91: 959–64.

Friedman, S., B. Jose, B. Stepherson, A. Neaigus, M. Goldstein, P. Mota, R. Curtis, and G. Ildefonso. 1997. Multiple racial/ethnic subordination and HIV among drug injectors. In *The Political Economy of AIDS*, ed. Merrill Singer, 105–28. Amityville, N.Y.: Baywood.

Herek, G. M., J. R. Gillis, and J. C. Cogan. 1999. Psychological sequelae of hate-crime victimization among lesbian, gay, and bisexual adults. *Journal of Consulting and Clinical Psychology* 67: 945–51.

Kelly, J. 1999. Community-level interventions are needed to prevent new HIV infections. *American Journal of Public Health* 89: 299–301.

Kessler, R. C., K. D. Mickelson, and D. R. Williams. 1999. The prevalence, distribution and mental health correlates of perceived discrimination in the United States. *Journal of Health and Social Behavior* 40: 208–30.

Link B., and J. Phelan. 2001. Conceptualizing stigma. *Annual Review of Sociology* 27: 363–85

Loue, S., M. Faust, and D. O'Shea. 2000. Determining needs and setting priorities for HIV-affected and HIV-infected persons: Northeast Ohio and San Diego. *Journal of Health Care for the Poor and Underserved* 11(1): 77–86.

MacKellar, D. A., L. A. Valleroy, G. M. Secura, W. McFarland, D. Shehan, W. Ford, M. LaLota, D. D. Celentano, B. A. Koblin, L. V. Torian, H. Theide, and R. S. Janssen. 2001. Two decades after vaccine license: Hepatitis B immunization and infection among young men who have sex with men. *American Journal of Public Health* 91: 965–71.

Mansergh, G., G. Marks, G. Colfax, R. Guzman, M. Rader, and S. Buchbinder. 2002. "Barebacking" in a diverse sample of men who have sex with men. *AIDS* 16: 653–59.

Marin, G. 1988. AIDS prevention issues among Hispanics. Paper presented at the meeting of the American Psychological Association, Atlanta.

Meyer, I. 1995. Minority stress and mental health in gay men. *Journal of Health and Social Behavior* 36: 38–56.

Morales, E. 1990. HIV infection and Hispanic gay and bisexual men. *Hispanic Journal of the Behavioral Sciences* 12: 212–22.

Otis, M. D., and W. F. Skinner. 1996. The prevalence of victimization and its effect on mental well-being among lesbian and gay people. *Journal of Homosexuality* 30: 93–121.

Reitmeijer, C. A., R. J. Wolitski, M. Fishbein, N. H. Corby, and D. L. Cohn. 1998. Sex hustling, injection drug use, and non-gay identification by men who have sex with men: Associations with high-risk sexual behaviors and condom use. *Sexually Transmitted Diseases* 25(7): 353–60.

Rosario, M., M. J. Rotheram-Borus, and H. Reid, H. 1996. Gay-related stress and its correlates among gay and bisexual male adolescents of predominantly black and Hispanic background. *Journal of Community Psychology* 24: 136–59.

Singer, M. 1996. A dose of drugs, a touch of violence, a case of AIDS: Conceptualizing the SAVA syndemic. *Free Inquiry in Creative Sociology* 24(2): 99–110.

———. 2004. Latinos and HIV/AIDS. In *The Encyclopedia of Latinos and Latinas in the United States.* Oxford: Oxford University Press.

Singer, M., and S. Clair 2003. Syndemics and public health: Reconceptualizing disease in bio-social context. *Medical Anthropology Quarterly* 17(4): 423–41.

Singer, M., M. Flores, L. Davison, G. Burke, Z. Castillo, K. Scanlon, and M. Rivera. 1990. SIDA: The sociocultural and socioeconomic context of AIDS among Latinos. *Medical Anthropology Quarterly* 4: 72–114.

Singer, M., and L. Marxuach-Rodriquez. 1996. Applying anthropology to the prevention of AIDS: The Latino Gay Men's Health Project. *Human Organization* 55(2): 141–48.

Sumartojo, E., and M. Laga. 2000. Structural factors in HIV prevention. *AIDS* 14 (Suppl. 1): 1–72.

Valdiserri, R. 1989. *Preventing AIDS: The Design of Effective Programs.* New Brunswick, N.J.: Rutgers University Press.

Valleroy, L., D. MacKellar, J. Karon, D. Rosen, W. McFarland, D. Shehan, S. Stoyanoff, M. LaLota, D. Celentano, B. Koblin, H. Thiede, M. Katz, L. Torian, and R. Janssen. 2000. HIV prevalence and associated risks in young men who have sex with men. *Journal of the American Medical Association* 284(2): 198–204.

Williams, L. A., J. D. Klausner, W. L. H. Whittington, H. H. Handsfield, C. Celum, and K. K. Holmes. 1999. Elimination and reintroduction of primary and secondary syphilis. *American Journal of Public Health* 79: 501–3.

Wolitski, R. J., R. O. Valdiserri, P. H. Denning, and W. C. Levine. 2001. Are we headed for a resurgence of the HIV epidemic among men who have sex with men? *American Journal of Public Health* 91: 883–88.

9

Ethnographic Fieldwork on Sexual Behavior

Developing Ethical Guidelines for Native Researchers

MARCELO MONTES PENHA, MICHELE G. SHEDLIN, CAROL A. REISEN,
PAUL J. POPPEN, FERNANDA T. BIANCHI, CARLOS U. DECENA,
AND MARIA CECILIA ZEA

In conducting ethnographic research, it is important that fieldworkers have ethical guidelines to provide direction concerning ethical standards, professional conduct, and methods of obtaining high-quality data. This chapter addresses issues that we faced in developing guidelines for ethnographic fieldwork on sexual behavior among Latino men who have sex with men (MSM). Ethnographic observations were conducted as part of a larger study concerning contextual influences on sexual risk among Brazilian, Colombian, and Dominican MSM in the New York metropolitan area. Gay-identified Latino fieldworkers carried out participant observation in venues where Latino men went to socialize and to find sex partners. Existing guidelines from professional organizations did not adequately address the unique and special conditions that these fieldworkers faced. Therefore, we set out to create our own.

The Need for Ethical Guidelines

Davidson and Layder (1994: 55–56) define ethics as "an abstract set of standards and principles which social researchers can refer to in order to decide what is appropriate and acceptable conduct." Ethics concern the responsibility of the researchers to everyone involved in the research, "including sponsors, the general public and most importantly, the subjects of the research" (Davidson and Layder 1994: 55–56). Thus, we viewed ethical conduct of research as encompassing mandates to protect the well-being, integrity, and privacy of human subjects and fieldworkers, as well as to uphold scientific rigor and accuracy. We wanted to generate ethical guidelines that would allow flexibility within ethical boundaries, so that fieldworkers would have reference points for professional conduct in the varied, complex, and unpredictable situations they might encounter in the field.

The ethical guidelines were developed in a multistage process that began with reference to existing professional codes of ethics. Members of the research team discussed possible or anticipated situations that could pose ethical dilemmas and generated ideas about appropriate ways of handling them. A preliminary version of the guidelines was created. Initial visits to the field enabled fieldworkers to identify other issues that needed to be addressed. The guidelines were augmented and modified to accommodate these additional issues. Over the course of the ethnographic data collection, we continued a dialogue about ethical concerns and revised the guidelines as necessary.

Three issues emerging from the project made the creation of ethical guidelines challenging. First, the research team was comprised of psychologists, anthropologists, and community members—groups having different perspectives on the criteria for the determination of appropriate and ethical behavior in research settings. Second, fieldworkers were participant observers within their own community and therefore were in situations in which they held multiple roles. Third, fieldworkers were observing in venues where partnering for sex was expected. In addition, the research topic was sex, one frequently treated differently from other types of behavioral interactions. In the sections below, we discuss how these three characteristics of the study affected the development of our ethical guidelines.

Professional Codes and Guidelines

Because the research team included psychologists and anthropologists, we turned initially to the codes of ethics provided by our respective professional organizations: the American Psychological Association (APA) and the American Anthropological Association (AAA). Both organizations hold ethical standards requiring professionals to safeguard the well-being of individuals with whom they work, to protect the safety and privacy of individuals with whom they work, and to promote accuracy and honesty in the field. There were, however, notable differences between the organizations in the specific approaches to accomplishing these principles.

The field of psychology generally tends toward a positivist approach, with a frequent goal of describing general laws or principles governing behavior. Objective observation is seen as critically important. In contrast, a frequent goal in anthropology is the description of subjective experience and the explanation of underlying meanings of specific behaviors. Relativity is emphasized, and increased challenges to objectivity are recognized as fieldwork extends over time.

These philosophical differences are reflected in the professional codes of ethics produced by the two organizations. The APA code lays out regulations concerning appropriate behavior, although it acknowledges that the application of regulations depends to some extent on the situation:

> The Ethical Standards set forth enforceable rules for conduct as psychologists in varied roles, although the application of an Ethical Standard may vary depending on the context. The Ethical Standards are not exhaustive. The fact that a given conduct is not specially addressed by an Ethical Standard does not mean that it is necessarily either ethical or unethical. (APA 2002)

In contrast, the AAA code of ethics provides less-structured guidelines in the form of general principles, and explicitly recognizes complexities inherent in various professional relationships:

> In a field of such complex involvements and obligations, it is inevitable that misunderstandings, conflicts, and the need to make choices among apparently incompatible values will arise. Anthropologists are responsible for grappling with such difficulties and struggling to resolve them in ways compatible with the principles stated here. (AAA 1998)

Because our project used insiders as observers in their own community, we recognized their potential involvement in multiple roles, including researcher, friend, potential friend, former sex partner, potential sex partner, or colleague. The two disciplines display different approaches to the issue of multiple roles. The APA code discourages professionals from simultaneously being in a professional role and another role with the same person, stating that a

> psychologist refrains from entering into a multiple relationship if the multiple relationship could reasonably be expected to impair the psychologist's objectivity, competence, or effectiveness in performing his or her functions as a psychologist, or otherwise risks exploitation or harm to the person with whom the professional relationship exists. (APA 2002)

Thus, multiple roles are seen as a potential threat to the well-being of a client or research participant. In the clinical context, there is typically an assumption that the professional distance between a therapist and client enables the therapeutic process to occur and that additional types of relationships would hinder that process. Moreover, in the research context, multiple roles are typically viewed as an impediment to objectivity.

Anthropology, on the other hand, builds upon the multiple relationships inherent in the research process, typically when anthropologists live and work over time within the community they are studying. The ethical issues, which can arise as a result of close, personal relationships and multiple roles, are acknowledged in the AAA code. Researchers are told to "adhere to the obligations of openness and informed consent, while carefully and respectfully negotiating the limits of the relationship" (AAA 1998).

In developing ethical guidelines for this project, the professional codes of ethics of the APA and AAA provided broad principles applicable across a range of situations. These codes, however, did not adequately address the specific situations and needs of our project. We thus saw the need to provide our fieldworkers with ethical guidelines that were less restrictive than those given in the APA code, but more specific than those described in the AAA code.

Multiple Roles of Fieldworkers

The fact that fieldworkers in our study were members of the community being studied had many advantages as well as presenting a second challenging issue to be addressed. However, the distinction between insider and outsider is not static because "the loci along which we are aligned with or set apart from those whom we study are multiple and in flux" (Narayan 1993). Narayan also identified education, class, and race among factors that can vary in their prominence at different times, thus changing one's perceived status as an insider or outsider. The role of researcher and the fieldworker's level of education set them apart and created a sense of being an outsider even in a context where they were "natives." To some degree, we sought to strike a balance between the "etic" (the observer's perspective; the outsider's view) approach with an "emic" (the subject's perspective; the insider's view) approach.

The insider status of our fieldworkers provided the study with substantial knowledge concerning Latino gay life in the New York City area, including access to organizations, publications, sites, events, and social networks. On some occasions they carried out fieldwork in settings frequented in their personal lives. However, despite the advantages, insider status also raised concerns about how best to maintain confidentiality, high standards of scientific rigor, and the safeguarding of the well-being and integrity of participants and fieldworkers. We recognized, as noted by Adler and Adler (1987), that although insiders doing research have access to and familiarity with the population, they need to develop a different relationship to the population in their role as researchers.

Insider researchers "must look at the setting through a fresh perspective, to develop relationships with people they did not associate with previously, to change the nature of their pre-existing relationships, and to become involved with the setting more broadly. This can be difficult, awkward, and heighten the sense of unnaturalness that invariably surrounds the research enterprise" (Adler and Adler 1987: 69–70). Because our fieldworkers were members of the Latino gay community and shared sexual orientation, gender, language, national or cultural background, and racial/ethnic background with many individuals within the target research sample, they experienced the awkwardness described by Adler and Adler.

We emphasized the primacy of the role of researcher during ethnographic observation. Information obtained during fieldwork activities was strictly confidential. Moreover, fieldworkers always identified themselves as researchers to individuals with whom they interacted in settings where ethnographic observation was being carried out. We established clear boundaries on certain behaviors in order to make the research role more prominent and the personal role less so. For instance, our guidelines prohibited the offer, acceptance, or consumption of alcoholic beverages, or the engagement in any sexual activity or romantic behavior. Also, our guidelines directed fieldworkers not to engage in data collection with individuals or in situations where physical attraction or an existing relationship might threaten the integrity of the research. After completion of observations in a given site, the researchers left; they did not stay in the site to socialize in their nonresearcher role.

The guidelines drew a temporal separation between personal and professional roles. Fieldworkers returned to the site on other occasions for personal purposes. However, they were encouraged to act with integrity and respect for others, and to consider possible consequences of their behavior on their work, their colleagues, the study, and the institutions supporting the study.

Personal Networks

Fieldworkers often encountered their friends and acquaintances during work time. They reported that friends could be both a help and a hindrance to their work, typically expecting and pressuring them to socialize with the group. Because the consumption of alcohol is a normative expectation in these environments, fieldworkers alerted members of their network about their work activities, thus avoiding friends' expectations of socialization during work time. On the other hand, friends frequently contributed to the research as key informants, providing information on different venues and suggesting sites for additional ethnographic observation. Moreover, friends supported the research by describing in detail their adventures in sex clubs, bars, and sex parties, including the physical space, people in attendance, and people's behaviors.

The guidelines also acknowledged that the fieldworkers' personal knowledge and experiences, both historical and current, would provide valuable information to the study. Fieldworkers could note information or data acquired during their own personal time, if appropriate and relevant to the study and clearly specified as such. In this way, we benefited from the richness of their experiences.

Sex as a Research Topic

Another issue that represented a challenge to the research team was sex as a research topic. The gay male researcher, despite his professional credentials, training, and personal integrity, will often be seen as a sexually driven being. As Carrier has pointed out, the "ethics of a gay man conducting participant observation studies of male homosexuality is generally given special scrutiny and viewed with suspicion" (Carrier 1999: 208). He notes that there is the assumption that a gay male researcher's behavior is determined by uncontrollable sexual urges and that research participants may be sexually pursued or victimized by the researcher. Awareness of this homophobic belief outside of the gay community was yet another impetus for the development of guidelines for the field staff. We found ourselves having to reconcile the conviction that gay researchers are not different from heterosexual researchers investigating their chosen communities with the sense that gay researchers need protection from the suspicion and scrutiny that may surround their conduct in the field.

Because of their membership in the study population, sexual partners of fieldworkers might come from the study population. Both the AAA and the APA codes of ethics address exploitive sexual relationships and sexual harassment and the potential for exploitation and conflict of interest that can arise from sex between participants and researchers. The AAA, in fact, at the time of this writing is considering the development of specific guidelines concerning sexual relationships between anthropologists and their research subjects. The AAA Committee on Ethics had posted on its Web site and made available for comment a briefing paper concerning this issue (Watkins 2004). The position paper notes the importance of real or perceived power differences between researchers and members of the study population in determining the potential for exploitation.

Moreover, it states that decisions about sexual relationships with members of the study population must take into account ways in which sex is culturally defined and displayed, as well as the meaning, gender implications, and economic consequences of sexual relations. In this position paper, Watkins notes that sexual relations between researchers and study participants have the potential to affect scientific integrity: "While a sexual relationship carried out between the researcher and a member of the population being studied may be totally acceptable, consensual, and between adults, it is important that the researcher recognize that such a relationship might impact the objectivity of the anthropological study" (Watkins 2004: 12).

Anthropologists themselves have also addressed the issue of sexual relationships between fieldworkers and research subjects. Kulick, for example, noted "a kind of unwritten, unspoken, and, for the most part, unquestioned rule about the ethics of sex in the field that all anthropology students somehow absorb during their graduate education. That rule can be summarized in one word: *Don't*" (Kulick 1995: 10).

Anthropologists have not universally accepted that rule. Dubish questioned the assumption that a sexual relationship was qualitatively different from other types of intimate social contact:

> We do almost everything else with our "informants": share their lives, eat with them, attend their rituals, become part of their families, even become close friends, and sometimes establish life-long relationships. . . . Could a sexual relationship be any more intimate, committing, or exploitive than our normal relations with the "natives"? (Dubish 1995: 31)

Feminist and gay anthropologists have called for the inclusion in professional contexts of discussions about erotic subjectivity or experience of researchers (Newton 1996). Just as personal characteristics of the researcher, such as gender, class, or race, can influence perception and interpretation of observed people and events, so, too, can the researcher's sexuality and sexual orientation.

Some gay anthropologists have included discussions of their own sexuality in their writing about gay research populations. Bolton (1995) and Carrier (1999) noted that their participation in sexual relationships provided entrance and acceptance into the research population and resulted in a more informed ethnography. Both researchers established principles for themselves that governed their conduct in sexual relationships with men from the study population. Also, Carrier (1999) described the need to revise the ethical guidelines he had created as he faced new situations in the field. For example, his initial guidelines for his study of MSM in Guadalajara required that his personal sex partners be completely separate from his study participants. He found, however, that his partner introduced him to many people who provided valuable information. Thus, despite his original plan to keep professional and personal contacts distinct, it became clear that his private sex life contributed greatly to the study.

In establishing the ethical guidelines for our study, we reflected upon these various sources and opinions about sexual relationships between researchers and individuals from the study population. Unlike Bolton and Carrier, our fieldworkers were members of the ethnic community that they were observing. Therefore, they did not need to have sex with participants to obtain entrance into the community. Furthermore, a proscription against sexual relationships with individuals from the study population would have been unreasonable. However, we considered the implications of such relationships and created guidelines that protected research participants, fieldworkers, and the data.

Conclusion

The final version of the ethical guidelines is presented in the chapter's appendix. We do not see these guidelines as rigid rules, but rather as principles that could be adjusted and applied to other studies. Our goal in this chapter was to explore the ethical issues we faced and to describe our thinking about appropriate approaches to those issues.

The challenges of working in the field for this project helped the team identify, discuss, and strategize how to negotiate the thin line that separates recruitment from flirting, watching peoples' behavior from voyeurism, and participant-observation from having fun. Although sex could have been a problem for the team while conducting fieldwork, incorporating ethical concerns into the thinking that informed fieldwork activities helped the fieldworkers gain confidence in their role as researchers. Furthermore, the role of researchers helped these community members see familiar environments in an unfamiliar way, thus gaining insights into their own social reality in ways that enriched the data obtained for this study.

Acknowledgments

The research described in this chapter was funded by RO1 HD046258 (Zea, P.I.). The authors would like to thank Mark Padilla, Ralph Bolton, and Joseph Carrier for feedback on preliminary versions of the ethical guidelines.

Appendix: Guidelines for Ethnographic Fieldwork of Sexual Risk Among Latino MSM

The guidelines listed below were created based on the following general principles: to protect the well-being, safety, and privacy of participants; to protect the well-being and safety of fieldworkers; to improve the accuracy and quality of the data; to represent the profession well; and to maintain good relationships with the community. Although it is impossible to anticipate every situation that can occur in the field, these principles can be applied to guide behavior in order to achieve transparency, respect, and integrity while carrying out research.

I. Guidelines to Protect the Well-being, Safety, and Privacy of Participants

A. CONFIDENTIALITY AND TRANSPARENCY

1. The fieldworker protects the privacy of participants in the research. Information obtained is confidential and is not linked to anything that might identify the participant.
2. The fieldworker informs participants of the limits of confidentiality, specifically that child abuse and expressed suicidal or homicidal intent are exceptions to the principle of confidentiality and could be reported, as mandated by the state.
3. The fieldworker identifies himself as a researcher to potential participants, explains the study and participants' rights, and shows professional identification if requested.[1]

B. BOUNDARIES OF COMPETENCE

1. If emotional upset and distress emerge during conversations/interviews and focus groups, the fieldworker does not attempt to provide psychological counseling. He acknowledges the feelings expressed and provides a referral for appropriate services if necessary.
2. The fieldworker does not get involved in participants' legal or financial concerns, but makes referrals to appropriate professionals or agencies that provide aid. Similarly, he does not intervene or try to resolve conflicts of persons who are not involved in the study.

II. Guidelines to Protect the Integrity of the Research

A. PRIORITY OF THE RESEARCH ROLE

1. While conducting fieldwork in sexual venues (e.g., bars, darkrooms, saunas, sex clubs, sex parties, porn theaters), the fieldworker does not engage in any sexual activity.
2. When approached for sex by anyone during fieldwork, the fieldworker explains that his role in the study prohibits him from engaging in any sexual or romantic behaviors.
3. The fieldworker dresses according to the norms of the environment in which he is conducting observations. He also avoids displaying symbols that may identify him as a member of a specific group or as having a behavioral/sexual orientation.
4. The fieldworker does not consume alcoholic drinks while conducting observations. He neither accepts nor offers alcoholic beverages.
5. When mutual attraction or current relationships might interfere with the integrity of the fieldwork, the fieldworker does not recruit that individual as an informant, interviewee, or focus group participant.

B. BOUNDARIES BETWEEN PERSONAL AND PROFESSIONAL ROLES

1. The fieldworker does not take advantage of his role as a researcher to obtain personal, financial, or sexual benefits.
2. During his personal time at sites that are also used for observation, the fieldworker maintains an awareness that he may return to the same site for fieldwork. He acts with integrity and respect for others. The fieldworker considers how his social engagements during

his leisure time may affect his work, the study, his colleagues, the institutions involved in the project, and the profession.

3. The potential for friendship or a sexual relationship may result from contact between fieldworkers and participants. The fieldworker is clear about the need to maintain boundaries between his work and personal life.

4. After completing observations in a specific site, the fieldworker leaves. He goes to another site if he wants to socialize with friends whom he happened to meet during fieldwork at the original site.

Notes

An earlier version of this chapter was presented at the annual meeting of the American Public Health Association, Washington, D.C., November 2004.

1. Because all researchers and subjects were male, we use the male gender throughout.

References

Adler, Patricia A., and Peter Adler. 1987. *Membership Roles in Field Research*. Qualitative Research Methods Series No. 6. A Sage University Paper.

American Anthropological Association (AAA). 1998. *Code of Ethics of American Anthropological Association*. www.aaanet.org/committees/ethics/ethcode.htm, accessed January 12, 2005.

American Psychological Association (APA). 2002. *Ethical Principles of Psychologists and Code of Conduct*. 2005. www.apa.org/ethics/code2002.html, accessed January 12, 2005.

Bolton, R. 1995. Tricks, friends, and lovers: Erotic encounters in the field. In *Taboo: Sex, Identity, and Erotic Subjectivity in Anthropological Fieldwork*, ed. D. Kulick and M. Willson, 140–67. New York: Routledge.

Carrier, Joseph. 1999. Reflections on ethical problems encountered in field research on Mexican male homosexuality: 1968 to present. *Culture, Health and Sexuality* 1: 207–21.

Davidson, J. O., and D. Layder. 1994. *Methods, Sex and Madness*. Florence, Ky.: Taylor and Frances/Routledge.

Dubish, J. 1995. Lovers in the field: Sex, dominance, and the female anthropologist. In *Taboo: Sex, Identity, and Erotic Subjectivity In Anthropological Fieldwork*, ed. D. Kulick and M. Willson, 29–50. New York: Routledge.

Kulick, D. 1995. The sexual life of anthropologists: Erotic subjectivity and ethnographic work. In *Taboo: Sex, Identity, and Erotic Subjectivity in Anthropological Fieldwork*, ed. D. Kulick and M. Willson, 1–28. New York: Routledge.

Narayan, Kirin. 1993. How Native Is a "Native Anthropologist"? *American Anthropologist* 95: 671–86.

Newton, Esther. 1996. My best informant's dress: The erotic equation in fieldwork. In *Out in the Field: Reflections of Lesbian and Gay Anthropologists*, ed. Ellen Lewin and William L. Leap, 212–35. Urbana: University of Illinois Press.

Watkins, J. 2004. Briefing paper for consideration of the ethical implications of sexual relationships between anthropologists and members of a study population. American Anthropological Association Committee on Ethics. http://www.aaanet.org/committees/ethics/bp6.htm, accessed September 22, 2004.

10

Bisexualities, Sexual Cultures, and HIV Prevention Programs for Latino Men in New York City

MIGUEL MUÑOZ-LABOY AND RICHARD PARKER

Bisexually active Latino men are typically lumped together with "homo-sexually" active men under the umbrella of HIV/STI (sexually transmitted infections) prevention for men who have sex with men (MSM).[1] Labeling individuals under one category leads to the misrepresentation of MSM as a homogeneous group in their sexual practices and issues relevant to their sexual lives. Recent reports have demonstrated the heterogeneity of sexual patterns among MSM (e.g., Bingham et al. 2003; Brooks et al. 2003) and even among bisexually active men (e.g., Muñoz-Laboy 2004).

HIV/STI prevention programs targeting Latino MSM typically fall within the following categories: HIV/STI risk awareness, behavioral change through increasing sexual negotiation skills, and changing norms about sexual risk, empowerment, and community building (e.g., Herek et al. 2001; Marin 2003; Ramirez-Valles and Brown 2003; Remien et al. 2002; Toro-Alfonso et al. 2002; Zea et al. 2003). Once individuals are recruited into the above types of interventions, the evidence seems to indicate that sexual risk is reduced, but the major determinant of their success or failure is whether the design and implementation of these interventions have taken the social context of participants into account (Elford and Hart 2003). This suggests the need to consider the social contexts and cultural meanings of sexual practices as an integral part of tailoring HIV/STI prevention programs.

The social context of sex could be defined in multiple ways. It may refer to the physical location where sex take places, the roles of social actors en-gaging in sexual practices, the meanings attached to a particular space, the socioeconomic conditions in which individuals are immersed, and/or the culture and traditions within specific settings. Because contexts are con-stantly shifting in the sexual lives of individuals, we consider the notion of an "erotic landscape" as a framework for understanding how social spaces serve as sexual venues, or sexualized spaces, during the sexual activities of individuals. We use the concept of erotic landscapes as a way of linking what might be described as "sexual geography" (the spatial organization of sexual experience) with "sexual culture" (the symbolic meanings and representations associated with sexual conduct in different social and cultural settings) (see Bell and Valentine 1995; Parker 1991, 1999).

The study of erotic landscapes among Latinos in the United States is very limited. However, erotic landscapes have been well documented by researchers working on sexuality in several Latin American societies. By turning our attention to this body of literature, we can better understand the erotic landscape of bisexually active Latino men living in the United States (see, e.g., Parker 1996, 1999; Parker and Tawil 1991).

It is safe to argue that most Latin American societies have experienced processes of structural oppression against same-sex sexuality because of the authority the Roman Catholic Church had within the government and society for more than five centuries (De Moya and Garcia 1996). Moreover, urbanization in Latin America has facilitated the development of new strategies for controlling what is viewed as "immoral behavior," while simultaneously providing new spaces for same-sex and bisexual experiences, reproducing, and resisting against structural oppression. This is exemplified in the anonymity of cities such as Rio de Janeiro, Brazil, where the development of public same-gender sexuality in urban settings has led the complex space of the city to become increasingly eroticized. This homoerotic undercurrent permeates Brazilian urban life, though in large part without organizing sharply defined gay ghettos along the lines found in many Anglo-European societies (Parker 1999).

The city provides an anonymous space in which the appropriation of the gaze of "the other" as an expression of desire enables men with homoerotic and bierotic desires to transform the otherwise hostile space of the dominant, heterosexual world into a field of erotic possibilities (Parker 1999). Under this paradigm, public spaces such as parks, beaches, public toilets, and movie theaters can become sites for sexual interactions. These could be interpreted as a reproduction of the oppression and domination of traditional sexual life, in which social interaction between MSM is expelled to the dangerous world of the street. Here, interactions must be carried out clandestinely and with the constant threat of physical or verbal violence on the part of offended onlookers, with the police or vigilante groups seeking to clean up society for "respectable" citizens.

Recently, Brazilian urban settings have gone through a process of constant appropriation through transgressions of what were traditionally conceived as "straight spaces" (Parker 1999), creating a world of homoerotic bodies and pleasures as ways of resistance in the face of strong sexual oppression. The homoerotic transformations of otherwise heterosexual spaces have been central to gay life in Brazil, both in relation to the development of sexual communities and also to the sustainability of a broader sexual subculture organized around a notion of sexual diversity (Parker 1999).

The findings of those who have studied same-sex and bisexual erotic landscapes in Brazil are similar to those for other parts of Latin America (e.g., De Moya [2003] in the Dominican Republic; Ramirez [1999] in Puerto Rico; Schifter [2000] in Costa Rica; Taylor [1978] and Carrillo [2002] in Mexico) where public space is the domain of men, where sexual interactions transcend the privacy of homes and penetrate into the streets and into public space more broadly, and where homoerotic spaces are carved out within predominantly normative heterosexual landscapes.

Locally, the study of bisexual erotic landscapes is recent (e.g., Hemmings 2002), and there is only very limited research on the sexual landscapes of Latino bisexuals. This is in part due to the structural barriers confronted by expressions of bisexuality in Latino cultures in the United States and elsewhere. For example, the impacts of hegemonic ideologies of heterosexuality have served to create a systemic pressure to silence expressions of alternative (nonheterosexual) sexualities, including bisexuality. This in turn creates complex psychosocial obstacles (for example, a culturally sanctioned understanding of sexual orientation, stereotypes, and socioculturally induced biphobia) in the development and evolution of the bisexual's diverse sexual identity, contributing to the continued marginalization of the bisexual population—a fact that is sometimes accentuated in ethnic minority populations (Guidry 1999; Rust-Rodriguez 2000).

Given the constant flux of ideas and people between Latin American countries and the United States, notions of sexuality, masculinity, and space get transported and reconfigured in the lives of Latinos in the United States. This is critical to the tailoring of HIV/STI prevention programs for bisexual Latino men.[2] Thus, the aim of this chapter is to explore the erotic landscape of bisexually active Latino men through the sexual history of one of our research participants, Angelito (a pseudonym).[3]

By examining Angelito's sexual life, we will try to highlight some of the erotic landscapes where sexual activity takes place on the part of bisexually active men. We recognize that Angelito does not represent all Latino bisexual men and that even in a small study there are vast numbers of kinds of sexual experiences, as well as ways in which individuals construct their sexual desire.[4]

Erotic Exploration

Angelito was in the first grade when he first realized his attraction to both "girls" and "boys." The first loves of his life were Martha and Joseph, "very pretty kids." In his mind, he made no distinction between boys and girls; he also remembers being very curious about the bodies of other kids, as well as his own body. His contact with girls at that time was "very little." However, with boys Angelito experienced more mutual contact through playing sports, wrestling, pushing, and simply touching.

Growing up in New York City made Angelito "very aware" of sexual diversity at an early age. He remembers hearing about "homosexuals" when he was only five. His older friends used to tell him that "*patos*" (literally "ducks," but a term used in some Latino communities to refer to same-sex persons) are "wrong and they dress like women." Angelito said that he had a completely "screwed up" perception of what a gay man was.

Although he does not remember the details of his first erection, Angelito remembers that it was around age eleven. His reaction was, "What the hell is going on [laughs] and doesn't this feel good?" Shortly after his first erection, he masturbated for the first time. It was in the bathroom of his house. The problem was that his parents could walk into any room. He remembered that these types of experiences always took place in the bathroom because it was the one room where he could lock the door.

In terms of HIV/STI transmission, Angelito's exploratory practices involved no significant risk. What stands out in his account, however, is how in the context of an urban space like New York City, the notion of same-sex sexuality can be perceived at an early age. This may be especially important to take into account in seeking to design programs and policies aimed at more proactively promoting egalitarian views on sexual and gender expressions, or to counteract norms that stigmatize sexual difference.

Sexual Initiation

When Angelito was around fifteen years old, he had his first sexual contact with another person. Angelito was often involved in sports during high school. He used to go to basketball courts on public playgrounds in New York City, and he remembers frequently seeing older guys going into the woods in the park. He was curious about that. He wanted to know "what's going on there." One day he decided to "check it out." He went into the woods on his own, and it did not take very long before somebody "responded" to him. A white non-Latino man approached Angelito. The man was fully aroused (Angelito could see it through his pants). They walked together to a spot. The man kissed him on his mouth. It was Angelito's first kiss on the mouth with another man. He did not enjoy it because this man was a "bad kisser." Angelito took his shirt off, and the man pulled his pants down. Then he put the man's penis in his mouth and performed oral sex. The man grabbed Angelito's head and guided him through the sex act.

This was the first time that Angelito performed fellatio on someone, and no one had ever performed it on him. The man ejaculated outside Angelito's mouth. The man then invited him to go to his house if Angelito "wanted to do more." They did go to his house and went straight to the man's bedroom and disrobed fully. Then the man put his penis into Angelito's anus and penetrated him without a condom and ejaculated outside his anus.

> Everything was new to me, so I told him afterwards that his was my first time and he told me I should've told him that, but I think he knew all along because he could tell from my [looks] I was very young. I had mixed feelings about it. I didn't particularly like it, so then I thought, oh, I'm not gay because if I liked it, I would feel different. So I thought, well good, it was just a phase. . . . It made me even more sexually curious. I wanted to have sex with women, right away. I also felt a little ashamed, because I barely knew him. I immediately threw away his phone number even though he wanted to stay in touch with me but I figured if I had no contact it would be easier for me to forget. Well, that wasn't the case. About six to eight months later I was aroused again. I was horny again. And I was trying to find him. I remember riding my bike through his neighborhood trying to find his building and couldn't remember which one it was 'cause they all looked the same to me. So, I just never saw him again. And, so this time I figured I have to find someone else. And so I became almost like a predator, looking, seeing if I could find any kind of sign in somebody that they'd be interested.

Angelito never knew the name of the man, and he estimates that the man was around twenty-five years old. He looked around for people to have sex with in his high school, but he was extremely afraid of being caught having sex with his male classmates. He went back to the "woods" several times. He said that it was not hard to find men who were interested in him. He met several men in the field whose names he never knew (names were not important for Angelito). But all these experiences were limited to performing or receiving fellatio and mutual masturbation.

At that time, Angelito also wanted to have intercourse and other sexual experiences with women. He "got together" with his female classmates in parties, but never in emotional relationships. Most of them never let him touch their genitals, and they never touched his genitals, so his heterosexual experiences were limited to kissing, fondling breasts, and hugging until two years later when he met Kathy.

Angelito (who was then seventeen years old) met her (an eighteen-year-old Latina) while working after school in a small company. She was very significant in his life. She was beautiful and a "wild sexual partner." For him, she was "wild" because

> well, we did every position imaginable. She let me have sex with her without a condom, without protection. She gave me a blow job and swallowed, stuff like that. Those were all firsts for me, so that's why I thought she was very wild, and she also did something I never expected a woman to ever do. She licked my rectum, which was strange, because I knew guys liked to do that. That's what some guys would do in the park or wherever, but I never experienced that with a girl, except for her.

Kathy taught him most of what he now knows sexually. She was "uninhibited" and "so much fun to be with." They had anal intercourse frequently. By this time he also had other sexual experiences, including penetrating other male partners, which allowed him to make comparisons:

> It was, like, very tight and it actually made me feel extremely hot and horny. Like wow, I'm doing something extremely taboo and dirty. It's different only . . . because I felt I had to coax her more. The guys I've been with, I had no problem getting them to do that. It felt like I'm doing something, like accomplishing something much more difficult to do, you know. And I know she hadn't had much experience there because she was very tight. So that kind of like turned me on; that I was doing something that most people haven't done with her anyway.

Kathy and Angelito had sexual relations in diverse settings: in the privacy of their homes, but also in more public settings such as the workplace, the hallways of their buildings, benches in the park, and movie theaters. Indeed, one of the things that was most striking about his relations with her, and that reinforced his notion of her as sexually "wild," was precisely their mutually constructed erotic landscape, which was characterized by sexual relations in contexts that would be publicly forbidden and prohibited. It was this quality that most clearly intensified the "hot" and "horny," "taboo" and "dirty" perception of their sexual relations.

After a month of having sex with Kathy, while Angelito was sucking her breast, breast milk came out. (It is common that breast milk is present at early stages of pregnancy. It is different from the type of milk produced right after the birth.) He knew that she had other sexual experiences prior to him, but at that moment he thought that he was going to be a father. He was "surprised," "relieved," but also "insulted" when she revealed to him that he was not the father. The father was a male she was dating just before him. She aborted her pregnancy.

Angelito recalled that the thing he liked most about her was her freedom, her free spirit. She knew how to have fun. He was very strict, and she made him feel more liberated. He thinks that, otherwise, he would probably be a different person today. The relationship lasted for two years, but he then left her. She became obsessed with him, and he eventually grew tired of her "craziness." He discovered she was "cheating" on him, and then did not believe a word she said after that.

Angelito's history of sexual initiation exemplifies a type of compartmentalized experience where sex with male partners was typically initiated in specific spaces such as highly impersonal public venues, while sexual contacts with female partners would be much more likely to be initiated in more normative social spaces such as school, parties, or work—but in which what were perceived to be especially sensual, hot, or erotic interactions with female partners, like those with males, were often associated with prohibited spatial settings. Not all bisexually active Latino men experience sexual initiation (let alone ongoing interaction) in the same way (e.g., Muñoz-Laboy 2004). Thus, Angelito's sexual initiation and sexual history must not be interpreted as an example of a developmental stage of bisexuality. Rather, the aim here is to illustrate the diverse contextual venues available for initiation among individuals with bisexual desire.

Programs on HIV/STI prevention at sexual initiation, for cases such as Angelito's, should focus on tailoring messages outside the context of dating (for example, most of his sexual experiences with female partners can be considered casual sex or as part of an initial sexual affair in the workplace). Furthermore, public spaces also play an important role in creating access to homoerotic interactions where sexual negotiation skills are not necessarily the same as those that apply in private contexts or similar to those used with female partners. Therefore, exploring what set of sexual negotiation skills are needed in one context and how these can be transferred or reconfigured in others is an ongoing challenge of the sexual health promotion practitioner.

Dating, Intimacy, and Sex

In college, Angelito met Marcos (Latino ancestry) who became very significant in his life:

> He is the one who taught me I could have relationships with men. It didn't just have to be sex. Before that, I just thought the only purpose of another man besides friendship or companionship, is just sex with them and that's it. I didn't want anything. I would never marry a man. I would never. That's why I said before, names weren't even important to me. So long as I can get off safely, I knew I wasn't doing anything risky. I didn't care who they were. But he taught me that it didn't have to be that way. Men could be loving, compassionate, just as much of a companion as a woman could be.

Angelito and Marcos met in their first year of college. He immediately thought that Marcos was a very "good looking" man. They became good friends who occasionally changed clothes in front of each other, and Angelito used to "take a peak" at his roommate. During their first year of college, on several occasions, they would wrestle to get things out of each other's hands, such as a bottle of cologne. During one of these playful wrestling, Marcos grabbed Angelito's testicles. His thoughts were: "I just couldn't believe, do I have his hand on my balls? The protective nature came over me again. If somebody walked in right now they'd get the wrong idea. So he moved his hand and then, things kind of cooled."

By his sophomore year, Angelito wanted very much to see Marcos's nude body. One day Angelito accidentally saw Marcos in the shower, and he noticed that Marcos had a long, big penis, although it was flaccid. Later that year Marcos subtly suggested that they engage in mutual masturbation, but it did not occur. That same year they again wrestled playfully, and this continued to happen more and more frequently. During one of these events, they both were in their underwear. In the middle of wrestling Angelito told Marcos:

I think you want me to fuck you, you know, whatever. If you want that I'm going to do that to you. So I start humping him with my clothes on, but he didn't stop me. So I kept doing it, and then the protective nature again would take over and said to him: "You are enjoying this too much." He hesitated, and he let go, and that was the end of that.

By their junior year of college, they began to argue about "silly stuff." One night, after a discussion, Marcos was ready to break off the friendship. Angelito told him that he did not want him to leave:

I was basically telling him, I don't know what I could do to save this friendship anymore. He just turned the lights out, gave me a hug and wouldn't let go. So I hugged him back and then he kissed me on the cheek, and then I said, "Do you want to stay here tonight?" He just kind of nodded "yes," and we slept in the same bed together. And that's how things started up. That was like heaven for me because here was my best friend, and now I have a man in my own room. And a man I wanted for a long time and totally turned on by. It was like heaven for me that year. I got the best grades ever [he laughs]. I was happy every day.

That night they masturbated and had oral sex, but did not have anal sex because Marcos was "too big" for Angelito. Marcos also did not want to be penetrated. Sexually, Angelito then did something that he had never done before:

The thing that was a new thing for me, which I had never done before and have never done since, was I would allow him to come in my mouth and I would swallow it. And the only reason why I did that was 'cause I felt safe with him. I knew him as opposed to the other men who I didn't even know at all, and I knew he had no other relations with other guys. So I felt comfortable with him. That's the only person I've ever done that with.

The relationship between the two of them ended when Marcos transferred to another college. They never saw each other again. During those years in college, Angelito also had several sexual relationships with both women and men. During his second year of college, as a result of "getting crabs," he was tested for HIV and other STIs for the first time, and the results were negative. Since then, he has remained HIV negative.

After college, Angelito fell "profoundly in love" and almost got married to Sandra, but the engagement did not last when she became aware of his sexual affairs with men. Shortly after the break-up, he experienced a process that he referred to as "coming out":

> I came out of the closet and I decided that I'm going to explore this around the age of twenty-three and twenty-four, and it was perfect for me because I was a young attractive man in New York City. I was also going to give women time to get to know me. But in my early twenties, I thought, I didn't want to have a child right away. This is the perfect time to date guys exclusively, so at that time I would have defined my-self more as gay. But, at all times, I'm bisexual deep down. It doesn't matter what I'm calling myself.

During his twenties, he did not have many sexual relationships with women. From his perspective, it was because it was hard for them to accept the fact that he also liked to have sex with men. He also had his first and only experience as a sex worker. When someone gave Angelito money for having sex, he was twenty-two. A man in New York's Greenwich Village offered him money to have sex, which he accepted. He never accepted money again for sex.

He recalls that when he was twenty-five years old he wanted to have sex with a female "prostitute." He found one in the phone book. He also invited a male bisexual friend of his, and the three of them had sex that night.

In the past twelve months, he has had sex with only three people. One of them was a one-night stand with a man he met in a gay bar. Six months prior to the interview, Angelito had a sexual affair with Natalia, a white non-Latina woman in her midtwenties who was the girlfriend of a friend. The three of them used to go out together. He thinks that she was always attracted to him, but his best friend was very attracted to her. At the time they met, more than a year ago, he used to drink a lot and was very socially active, and he thinks that those things made him attractive to her. He said that she liked "bad boys" like him. They met for the first time on a trip to the beach. They were attracted to each other immediately, and they began "flirting right away." To him, she was very sexual in everything that she did. Natalia was the mother of two children. He wanted to be friends with her. She was bisexual herself. That made him feel more comfortable with her: "Here I am finding another person who's just like me but female. . . . I was intrigued by her. I wanted her around me."

One night they went to a lesbian nightclub. Angelito's male friend got very drunk and was about to pass out. While Natalia and Angelito were dancing very closely, they began kissing outside the view of their friend. They went to the ladies room together, where they continued kissing and began fondling each other's genitals. He sucked her breasts. She had a mini-skirt on. She took his hand and put it underneath her underwear. She was "very excited" and was wrapping her legs around him. She undid his pants and put his penis inside her vagina. She thrusted up and down for a short while, but then they stopped. They were afraid that they were going to be discovered by their friend, and they did not have much time. Neither of them reached orgasm. They did not use condoms on that occasion. They adjusted and straightened out their clothing, not saying a word to each other as they left the restroom.

Weeks later, he went to her home. Her children were not there. They took a shower together. In the shower they both kissed, and he massaged and licked her body all over. He performed cunnilingus on her, and she masturbated him. They both reached orgasms this time. After that time, she dated his friend again. He was financially more stable than Angelito. In addition, from his perspective, Natalia only wanted a sexual affair with Angelito, and she became bored with him.

Angelito is currently dating David, "his perfect man." Only a few people know about their relationship. To him, David looks perfect—tall, with a model's body, and "too good to be true." They met at a gay event a few months ago and were attracted to each other immediately. Both also had a long history of sexual relationships with women. He describes David as "very charming, down to earth, good natured, a wonderful human being." They have had sex on numerous occasions, but are extremely careful since David is HIV positive. Angelito's ideal sexual life involves being with men and women. But recently he has been seriously thinking of becoming a father. He hopes that Natalia will agree to help him with that goal.

Bierotic Landscape

When dating and intimacy (that is, the development of emotional ties) enter into the formulation of the sexual lives of bisexually active Latino men like Angelito, their erotic landscape becomes more complex and intertwined. To help in the process of unpacking the bierotic landscape of Angelito and other men in our study, we proposed conceptualizing this erotic landscape as the interactions among three factors: sexual venues, the residential/socialization context, and the desired gender of partners that produce specific sexualized spaces where sexual practices take place.

Under our conceptual model, sexual venues refer to spaces where potential sexual partners can meet, including public spaces such as parks, street corners, and restrooms; occupational spaces such as school or work; close social spaces of networks such as those comprised of friends and/or relatives; commercial spaces such as bars, nightclubs, sex clubs, and escort services; or digital-cyberspaces such as Internet chat rooms or dating services. Although the above venues can be observed across most residential settings in cities like New York, depending on whether bisexually active Latino men live in mostly heteronormative environments or gay neighborhoods (such as New York's Chelsea, the West Village, or Park Slope), they will remain in or visit spaces outside their residential context in order to find their desired partner or partners.

The following brief descriptions of the current sexual lives of some of our research informants illustrate examples of these interactions:

1. Antonio lives in a predominantly heterosexual non-Latino neighborhood. His current boyfriend and his female sexual partners in the past two years have been people whom he has met in his neighborhood and through his personal-familial networks.

2. Carlos is married and a father of two children. Some days after work he goes to the park to look for men to have sex with them. He lives in a mostly Latino and heteronormative neighborhood. He currently has a boyfriend whom he sees during the weekends.

3. Lucas lives in a mostly heterosexual environment. He has been dating women off and on most of his life. He meets his female sexual partners through personal networks and social activities. He also regularly visits gay nightclubs, usually once a week, sometimes twice a week.

4. Esteban, an unmarried young man, met his current boyfriend through an Internet chat room. He enjoys masturbating while watching heterosexual, gay, and bisexual pornography. Esteban has also met women through chat rooms.

5. Norbert is a middle-age man who lives near Greenwich Village ("the Village"), a gay neighborhood in Manhattan. Most of his social life occurs there. He meets his same-gender sexual partners either by socializing and cruising in the Village or in chat rooms. In the past year, Norbert has dated and had sex with several women. However, most of his female-centered sexual desire is satisfied through chat rooms.

6. Gamaliel lives in Chelsea, another gay section of Manhattan. All his social and sexual life is there. He meets women through his personal and kin networks. He is unmarried and lives with his boyfriend. Occasionally, he has secret sexual affairs with his female friends, coworkers, and friends whom he meets in heteronormative environments.

The above patterns are not static throughout the lives of the men in our study. They reflect the plurality of the multiple configurations of bierotic landscapes across a sample of individuals at a given time. This specific focusing on the sexual venues, gender of partners, and context of residence/socialization allows us to examine how sexual spaces and erotic landscapes are produced as integral elements of the bierotic landscape.

HIV/STI Prevention Implications

By understanding the bierotic landscape, we can clearly identify three implications for HIV/STI prevention programming:

1. *Access to information.* Because of the large-scale social mobilization of gay and lesbian movements in cities like New York, HIV/STI testing and treatment have been widely open in gay geographical communities such as Chelsea and the West Village, but also in new Latino gay communities such as Jackson Heights in the borough of Queens. As discussed earlier, gay geographical communities, as well as gay economies, are sometimes (but not always) part of the erotic landscape of bisexually active Latino men. Depending on bisexual men's level of involvement in gay or community spaces, messages promoting safe sex can be accessed through participation in mainstream gay culture. However, it is also crucial to design campaigns to reach bisexually active Latino men who are isolated or who construct their erotic landscapes outside the realm of gay culture. To achieve this, we need to assure the quality and appropriateness of the information provided.

2. *Quality of information.* Generic messages on sexual health promotion (such as using a condom or "be safe") might be ineffective if they do not address the specific needs of bisexually active Latino men. Messages need to be tailored to specific contexts and at the same time capture the nuances of the erotic landscape of individuals. Furthermore, the quality of the information would also depend

on the ability to move beyond common misconceptions about bisexuality. For example, in this study we had individuals who live
what can be considered gay lifestyles but who are actively involved
in sex with women, while the messages in their environments focus
exclusively on same-sex practices. Assumptions about the sexual
practices or the types of locations where bisexually active men can
be found (for example, men who cruise in parks or public toilets for
sex) may sometimes be partially true but often fail to capture what
are actually far more complex erotic landscapes. Such assumptions
can thus become barriers to the development of more comprehensive prevention programs for this population.

3. *Participation in sexual health programs.* Beyond a level of awareness
of HIV/STI risk, behavioral change, empowerment, and change in
sexual risk-related norms are modes of prevention that have been
effective across several groups to reduce their risk of HIV/STI infections. In spite of the fact that many interventions operate under the assumption that the target population must participate in
sexual health promotion programs, a prerequisite for these types
of programs is identifying with the program, a process of group
formation. This is a difficult task with bisexually active individuals
whose identities may or may not be linked to their practices. By
reflecting on the erotic landscape of our target population, sexual
health promoters could develop not only an adequate curriculum
but also conceptual mapping that would guide efforts of recruitment to meet the specific needs for HIV/STI prevention among
bisexually active Latino men.

This case study of bisexually active Latino men in New York City demonstrates the relevance of examining social erotic landscapes for the development of HIV/STI prevention programs. Through a fuller understanding
of the complex ways in which bisexually active Latino men navigate within
their often highly diverse erotic landscapes, sexual health promotion practitioners need to tailor the content of messages and interventions to have the
adequate specificity to be effective in reducing HIV/STI risk in the target
population.

Acknowledgments

This study was made possible through support provided by the HIV Center for Clinical and Behavioral Studies, with funds from the National Institute of Mental Health (dissertation minority supplement through grant P50-MH43520 and postdoctoral fellowship grant T-32 MH19139) and the Center for Gender, Sexuality and Health in the Department of Sociomedical Sciences at the Mailman School of Public Health, Columbia University, with funds provided by the Ford Foundation (grant #1020-1481).

Notes

1. The term "bisexually active" is used to refer to a person who has a history of bisexual experiences and is currently engaging in any sexual encounter with a man and a woman at least once with each during the twenty-four months prior to the entry into the study. The concept of "Latino" refers to people of Latin American ancestry, in other words, people whose birthplace, or the birthplace of their parents or grandparents, is in any territory of Latin America regardless of whether the respondents are Spanish/Portuguese speakers. Under this definition, several subgroups of individuals are classified as one category, Latinos, even though they may vary in terms of their country of origin (for example, Peru, Cuba, or Mexico) and ethnic background (for example, Otomis, Nahualt, or Mestizo). The heterogeneity—consisting of the cultural, political, economic, and historical differences—behind the Latino identity makes it difficult and almost conceptually impossible to make generalizations about all Latinos. Then, what is the rationale for using the Latino category at all? In this study, the intention was to employ the notion of Latino to capture the bisexual experiences of men of Latin American ancestry whose major commonality is their socio-legal-political relationship with U.S. politics: a minority status, as classified within the dominant or hegemonic cultural system constructing ethnicity in the United States.

2. Public health researchers became interested in sexuality and landscapes mostly after the onset of the AIDS epidemic. Understandings of space were limited to physical locations, and little attention was given to the relationship between space and sexuality. This resulted in a general stigmatization of public sex by promoting the myth that sexual risk taking was particularly likely to occur during sexual encounters in public spaces. Early AIDS prevention strategies, aimed at reducing public sex, used this myth to aggressively prosecute anyone found to be involved in public sexual activities, to close the baths, and to increase policing of the parks. Leap (1998: 4) argues that it should not be assumed that "public sex and sexual risk taking are inseparable components of gay culture." Instead, they propose to examine the connections between risk taking and male same-sex desire within the context of "particular locations, and to draw conclusions about gay-related sexual practices and AIDS prevention strategies in equally situated terms."

3. All the names used in this chapter are pseudonyms to protect the identity of research participants. To protect informants' privacy and human rights, approval from the Columbia University Department of Psychiatry and the New York State Psychiatric Institute Institutional Review Board (IRB No. 3905) and a Federal Certificate of Confidentiality (No. MH-00-07) were obtained for this study.

4. For more information on this and the methods used in the study, see Munoz-Laboy (2004).

References

Bell, D., and G. Valentine. 1995. *Mapping Desire: Geographies of Sexualities*. London: Routledge.

Bingham, T., N. Harawa, D. Johnson, G. Secura, D. MacKellar, and L. Valleroy. 2003. The effect of partner characteristics on HIV infection among African American men who have sex with men in the Young Men's Survey, Los Angeles, 1999–2000. *AIDS Education and Prevention* 15 (Suppl. 1): 39–52.

Brooks, R., M. J. Rotheram-Borus, E. Bing, G. Ayala, and C. Henry. 2003. HIV and AIDS among men of color who have sex with men and men of color who have sex with men and women: An epidemiological profile. *AIDS Education and Prevention* 15 (Suppl. A): 1–6.

Carrillo, H. 2002. *The Night Is Young: Sexuality in Mexico in the Time of AIDS*. Chicago: University of Chicago Press.

De Moya, A. 2003. Power games and totalitarian masculinity in the Dominican Republic. In *Caribbean Masculinities: Working Papers*, ed. R. Ramírez, V. García-Toro, and I. Cunningham, 105–46. San Juan: University of Puerto Rico.

De Moya, A., and A. Garcia. 1996. AIDS and the enigma of bisexuality in Dominican Republic. In *Bisexualities and AIDS: International Perspectives*, ed. P. Aggleton, 121–35. Bristol, Pa.: Taylor and Francis.

Elford, J., and G. Hart. 2003. If HIV prevention works, why are rates of high-risk sexual behavior increasing among MSM? *AIDS Education and Prevention* 15(4): 294–308.

Guidry, L. 1999. Clinical intervention with bisexuals: A contextualized understanding. *Professional Psychology: Research and Practice* 30(1): 22–26.

Hemmings, C. 2002. *Bisexual Spaces: A Geography of Sexuality and Gender*. New York: Routledge.

Herek, G., M. Gonzalez-Rivera, F. Fead, and D. Welton. 2001. AIDS educational videos for gay and bisexual men: A content analysis. *Journal of the Gay and Lesbian Medical Association* 5(4): 145–53.

Leap, W. 1998. Introduction. In *Public Space/Gay Space*, ed. W. Leap, 1–22. New York: Columbia University Press.

Marin, B. 2003. HIV prevention in the Hispanic community. *Journal of Transcultural Nursing* 14(3): 186–92.

Muñoz-Laboy, M. 2004. Beyond "MSM": Sexual desire among bisexually active Latino men in New York City. *Sexualities* 7(1): 55–80.

Parker, R. G. 1991. *Bodies, Pleasures and Passions: Sexual Culture in Contemporary Brazil.* Boston: Beacon Press.

———. 1996. Behavior in Latin American men: Implications for HIV/AIDS interventions. *International Journal of STD and AIDS* 7 (Suppl. 2): 62–65.

———. 1999. *Beneath the Equator: Cultures of Desire, Male Homosexuality and Emerging Gay Communities in Brazil.* New York: Routledge.

Parker, R. G., and O. Tawil. 1991. Bisexual behavior and HIV transmission in Latin America. In *Bisexuality and HIV/AIDS*, ed. R. A. P. Tielman, M. Carballo, and A. C. Hendriks, 59–63. Buffalo, N.Y.: Prometheus Press.

Ramirez, R. 1999. *Dime Capitan: What It Means to Be a Man—Reflections on Puerto Rican Masculinity.* Trans. Rosa E. Casier. New Brunswick, N.J.: Rutgers University Press.

Ramirez-Valles, J., and A. Brown. 2003. Latinos' community involvement in HIV/AIDS: Organizational and individual perspectives on volunteering. *AIDS Education and Prevention* 15 (Suppl. 1): 90–104.

Remien, R., G. Wagner, C. Dolezal, and A. Carballo-Dieguez. 2002. Factor associated with HIV sexual risk behavior in male couples of mixed HIV status. *Journal of Psychology and Human Sexuality* 13(2): 31–48.

Rust-Rodríguez, P. 2000. Review of statistical findings about bisexual behavior, feelings and identities. In *Bisexuality in the United States: A Social Science Reader*, ed. P. Rodríguez-Rust, 129–84. New York: Columbia University Press.

Schifter, J. 2000. *Public Sex in a Latin Society.* New York: Haworth Hispanic/Latino Press.

Taylor, C. 1978. El Ambiente: Male Homosexual Social Life in Mexico City. Ph.D. diss., University of California, Berkeley.

Toro-Alfonso, J., N. Varas-Diaz, and I. Andujar. 2002. Evaluation of an HIV/AIDS prevention intervention targeting Latino gay men and men who have sex with men in Puerto Rico. *AIDS Education and Prevention* 14(6): 445–56.

Zea, C. M., C. Reisen, and R. Diaz. 2003. Methodological issues in research on sexual behavior with Latino gay and bisexual men. *American Journal of Community Psychology* 31(3–4): 281–91.

11

Developing HIV Behavioral Interventions for Men Who Have Sex with Men

Comparing Experiences from the United States and Australia

MARY SPINK NEUMANN, JEFFREY H. HERBST,
AND CAROLYN A. GUENTHER-GREY

The histories of the AIDS epidemic in the United States and Australia started similarly, with HIV infections concentrated among men who have sex with men (MSM). Gay communities in both countries reacted by mounting their own "grassroots" education, service, and advocacy programs, and both countries' governments reacted by funding medical and epidemiologic research (Counter 1996). Behavioral prevention efforts followed closely thereafter. In the following decades, the United States has seen HIV spread to injection drug users and heterosexuals (CDC 2003), while in Australia the epidemic continues to be predominately among MSM (Commonwealth Department of Health and Aged Care 2000).

The HIV/AIDS epidemic is changing in other ways. For HIV-infected persons, anti-retroviral treatments extend survivorship but provide a longer period of infectivity and may contribute indirectly to decreases in safer sex. Infection continues to spread to younger MSM. Rates of sexually transmitted diseases among MSM in the United States have increased (Ciesielski 2003), as have rates of unprotected anal intercourse among Australian MSM (Van de Ven, Rawstorne, et al. 2002). In light of these recent changes, it behooves us to expand our information sources and intervention techniques.

The purpose of this chapter is to review the HIV/AIDS behavioral literature focusing on MSM from both countries to better understand and learn how to develop HIV behavioral interventions from the combined experience of HIV prevention researchers from Australia and the United States. We compare the two countries' HIV/AIDS prevention approaches and the specific types of information used to inform the development of interventions. This comparison seeks to identify which data seem to be the most useful for designing interventions that are acceptable to MSM and have been effective in changing risk behavior. Based on our review, we make recommendations on what data to collect about MSM and the context of their behaviors and choices. To put the approaches of the United States and Australia in context, we begin with a brief overview of the two countries' response to the AIDS epidemic among MSM.

Background

Highlights of the Response to AIDS among MSM in the United States

In the United States, the first AIDS cases were diagnosed in 1981 among five MSM (CDC 1981), and gay political action groups began educating MSM soon after (Gay Men's Health Crisis 2003). The first Multicenter AIDS Cohort Study (MACS) of HIV-infected MSM (Kaslow et al. 1987) and the San Francisco Young Men's Health Survey (Winkelstein et al. 1987), both funded by the National Institutes of Health, were conducted in 1984. The first group-level behavioral intervention research trial for MSM, the AIDS Prevention Project, was conducted in 1986 (Valdiserri et al. 1989). The "America Responds to AIDS" mass media campaign, which targeted the general public, began in 1987 (Gluck and Rosenthal 1996). Federal HIV prevention funds were extended to community-based organizations in 1988, which also was the year that the first community-level intervention research trial for MSM was undertaken (Kelly et al. 1992).

From 1994 through 2000, the CDC-funded Young Men's Survey examined behavioral risks for HIV infection among young MSM in seven cities (Gallagher et al. 2003; Valleroy et al. 2000). In 1999, the CDC published a compendium of effective behavioral interventions, which identified five such interventions for MSM (CDC 1999). In 2003, the CDC announced a national system for HIV behavioral surveillance that would target at-risk groups and be used for planning and evaluating HIV prevention activities (Gallagher et al. 2003). Among other things, this surveillance system collects information on MSM's patterns of HIV risk behaviors, HIV testing patterns, and use of HIV prevention services. This brief history does not include all local surveys, grassroots activities, or interventions for MSM done in the United States.

Currently, the HIV/AIDS epidemic in the United States is addressed by the government, researchers, and nongovernmental organizations (NGOs). In the United States, many behavioral scientists conduct various types of

research to identify the prevalence of HIV, AIDS, or other sexually transmitted diseases and associated risk behaviors, or to develop and test their
own interventions (Gluck and Rosenthal 1996). Most interventions target
individuals or small groups, and intervention effects are usually measured
from three to twelve months after the end of the intervention, except in
the case of interventions targeting entire communities. NGOs may conduct
literature searches or consult with other NGOs to find and use information
from the researchers' publications on interventions and prevalences of behavioral risks. These NGOs, informed by research findings or not, develop
their own interventions but seldom evaluate them.

Highlights of the Australian Response to AIDS among MSM

In Australia, the first case of AIDS was diagnosed in 1982. In 1983, the
country mounted a coordinated response and divided prevention efforts
among three entities: the Commonwealth of Australia, the Australian state
governments, and NGOs (Dowsett 1996). According to Dowsett (1996), the
Commonwealth was in charge of policy, guidance, funds, research, and national education using AIDS awareness and health promotion mass media
campaigns that were intended to reach MSM who are less attached to the
gay community. The states were initially responsible for their own prevention programs and later also for health services, school programs, and coordination of the NGOs. The NGOs, which were mainly gay AIDS service
organizations, educated affected gay communities. This partnership continues as part of the national strategy (Commonwealth Department of Health
and Aged Care 2000). Same-sex behavior was decriminalized in New South
Wales in 1984 (Altman 1986) but remained a crime in all but two other
states. In 1986, two important surveys were conducted: the first behavioral
survey of MSM in Sydney and parts of New South Wales, titled "Social Aspects of the Prevention of AIDS" (SAPA) (Dowsett 1996; Kippax, Connell,
et al. 1993), and the national geographically stratified survey of HIV-related
risk behaviors (Ross 1988a). In 1987, the Commonwealth launched the
"Grim Reaper" mass media campaign targeting the general public (Morlet
et al. 1988). In 1988, community attachment strategies for MSM were used
to generate peer education and outreach, such as hotlines and educational
materials (Dowsett 1996).

In 1989 and 1991, the second and third behavioral surveys of MSM were
performed: the "Class, Homosexuality and AIDS Prevention" (CHAPS) in
New South Wales and the "Sustaining Safer Sex" (Triple S) in New South
Wales and Tasmania, respectively. The first national preventive education

campaigns by the government targeting MSM occurred in 1991 (Dowsett 1996). In 1994, a fourth survey of MSM was conducted, the national "Project Male-Call" (Dowsett 1996; Kippax et al. 1994). The first individual-level behavioral intervention trial for MSM was conducted in 1994 (Gold and Rosenthal 1995). In 1996, the Commonwealth undertook the explicit, community-based "Do . . . Choose . . . Enjoy" social-marketing campaign (Meese 1997). Periodic gay community surveys commenced in Sydney in 1996 and were expanded to other major cities, such as the 2002 survey in Queensland (Hull et al. 2002). In 1997, research to identify and promote existing protective strategies among MSM identified negotiated safety as a common risk reduction technique (Kippax et al. 1997). The Australian Federation of AIDS Organisations' (AFAOs') Internet-based Gay/HIV Education Survey (Australian Federation of AIDS Organisations 1999) started in 1998. This summary does not include all community educational campaigns and surveys for MSM done in Australia.

In the current Australian approach to HIV/AIDS prevention, behavioral scientists usually conduct research at the request of NGOs, which develop and implement all HIV prevention interventions (Kippax and Kinder 2002). Researchers identify community-level trends, such as existing protective practices; NGOs implement social marketing to change community norms and promote the soundest practices; and researchers evaluate the overall results. Often, trends in HIV/AIDS incidence (Dowsett 1996) or serial surveys of behaviors (Ross et al. 1989) are used as evidence of the social-marketing's effects. Researchers consider long-term trends in practices or HIV incidence to be the most meaningful measures of health promotion effects (Van de Ven and Aggleton 1999). Implementation of the national strategy also includes professional contributions to health promotion, training, research, treatment and care, and policy development and implementation by national centers in HIV research (Commonwealth Department of Health and Aged Care 2000).

This brief review of the HIV prevention efforts for MSM in the United States and Australia suggests that both nations have been working to change the AIDS-related knowledge, attitudes, and risk behaviors of MSM, but use somewhat different approaches to achieve this goal. The approach in the United States has focused chiefly on research that seeks to determine what influences MSM to engage in risk behaviors and to change those behaviors that place individuals at risk, and on NGOs that intervene locally with interventions of their own design. The Australian research approach seeks to understand the contexts, norms, and cultures or social forces that influence

MSM's risk behavior (Van de Ven personal communication, 2004), while the government of the Commonwealth conducts mass media campaigns, and NGOs implement AIDS education locally. These approaches need not be mutually exclusive. Much can be learned from both approaches to achieve HIV risk reduction among MSM.

Methods

We conducted an extensive literature review to identify which data seem to be the most useful in the United States and Australia for designing interventions. For this chapter, we are defining an intervention to be a specific strategy intended to change risky sexual behavior. We categorized studies as "formative" if they reported on qualitative or quantitative data collected, or literature reviewed, in preparation for an intervention study, or to provide recommendations for future interventions, or if an intervention study cited the "formative study" as a basis for the intervention. Surveys of behaviors or behavioral correlates included: citations that presented quantitative data on the prevalence of HIV-related risk behaviors; cognitive, interpersonal, or contextual factors associated with these behaviors; or both.

Our main source of citations was the CDC's HIV/AIDS Prevention Research Synthesis (PRS) database. As part of the PRS project, a database system was developed to accumulate the HIV/AIDS and sexually transmitted disease (STD) prevention literature from 1988 and onward (Crepaz et al. 2003). The PRS project database was updated through July 2003 for a recent review of HIV behavioral interventions targeting MSM (Herbst et al. 2003). To accomplish this update, a comprehensive search strategy was employed that included searching electronic bibliographic databases (AIDSLINE, MEDLINE, PsycINFO, EMBASE, SocioFile, ERIC, the Science Citation, and Social Sciences Citation indexes for publications from 1988 through 2002); international registries, including the Cochrane Controlled Trials Register and the Current Controlled Trials Register; and reference lists of relevant articles. In addition, researchers were contacted to identify current and ongoing MSM research, and a hand search of over forty relevant journals was conducted to update the literature up to July 2003.

The following strategy was used to identify citations in the PRS database that report HIV prevention investigations for MSM in the United States. First, we identified all citations that were coded as having an HIV, AIDS, or STD behavioral prevention focus—that is, citation reports that focused on any aspect of HIV, AIDS, or STD prevention and that concerned assessing or modifying behaviors that could affect disease transmission.[1] Next, we refined the search by searching for the following phrases and keywords: "men who have sex with men," "MSM," "gay," "bisexual," or "homosexual." This search strategy yielded 1,235 citations, of which 638 citations were linked to studies that were conducted in the United States and focused on MSM as a target population. Among these 638 citations, 72 were formative studies, 328 were surveys of behaviors or behavioral correlates, and 74 were HIV prevention behavioral or social intervention reports representing 27 unique studies. The remaining 164 citations covered other AIDS-related issues, including research methods, disease incidence, history, reviews, commentaries, medical studies, and information from HIV prevention activities that were not part of a study. Publication dates for research on interventions for MSM range from 1989 to 2003.

Our search for behavior-related Australian research in the PRS database used the same key words, with the addition of "Australia," "Brisbane," "Canberra," "Gold Coast," "Melbourne," "New South Wales," "Perth," "Queensland," "Sunshine Coast," and "Sydney," and found seventy-eight citations. Searches of international registries and databases—such as EMBASE—assisted in identifying additional Australian research studies. We also consulted the reference lists of available articles and book chapters, contacted leading Australian HIV researchers, and searched several Australian Web sites, including www.afao.org.au, www.aids.net.au, www.ancahrd.org, www.latrobe.edu.au, www.med.unsw.edu.au/nchecr (National Centre in HIV Epidemiology and Clinical Research), and www.arts.unsw.edu.au (National Centre in HIV Social Research), to find additional citations. Many of the Australian NGO Web sites contained materials to be used in local educational campaigns but did not report the type of information on which these materials were based, so we excluded these materials from our compilation. Some resources for educators, such as that by Murphy and Spina (2002), reported risk behavior survey data and a consultative process as the bases for their recommendations but did not describe a particular intervention, and so these resources for educators were excluded from our consideration.

Searching the reference lists of journal articles and book chapters and the Web sites of Australian NGOs and universities and contacting researchers identified an additional 61 citations, for a total of 139 unique citations focusing on MSM in Australia. Of these 139 citations, 20 were formative studies, 58 were surveys of behaviors or behavioral correlates, 5 were HIV prevention behavioral or social interventions representing four unique studies, and 56 covered other AIDS-related issues, including research methods, book reviews, policy discussions, program evaluations, commentaries, and history. Publication dates for intervention research on MSM range from 1988 to 2003.

While reading the intervention studies, we noted the types of information on which the researchers reported basing their intervention designs. The following were the most commonly reported bases: the stated underlying theory; background HIV, AIDS, or STD disease prevalence; the study population's behavioral risks; reported gaps in existing intervention research; and findings from formative research conducted by the intervention's designer or someone else. We also collected information on the study population's risk behavioral determinants, social and environmental contexts for their risk behaviors, and any intervention components suggested by the researcher. Our notations cover those types of information that were collected during the intervention trial and reported in the article or report. We assume that similar formative data, or similar theory, informed the intervention design methods.

In addition, we noted the rigor of the study's design and whether the intervention was effective. Our rigor criteria were: prospective design with a comparison group, randomized controlled trial (RCT) or an unbiased method of assignment, greater than or equal to a three-month follow-up for intervention and comparison groups, and a participant retention rate of at least 70 percent for individual or group-level interventions having follow-up periods ranging from three months to less than twelve months, or at least 60 percent retention for follow-ups greater than or equal to twelve months (Herbst et al. 2003). We considered the intervention to be effective if the study reported at least one statistically significant positive effect in changing a risk behavior and no statistically negative or harmful effects.

For each intervention study, we noted only information that was reported in publications about the study. If in our search we identified more than one publication about a given study, we reviewed all of the publications to assess whether they included these types of information. However, because of space constraints we have listed only the primary publication for each study in our tables and list of references. We consider the primary publication to be the publication that presented outcome data, or for studies that have not yet published outcome data, the baseline data or description of the study.

We also reviewed all citations that were designated as formative research and made note of three topics. First, we noted the research methods used—qualitative, quantitative, literature review, content analysis, or statistical models. The second topic involved the focus of the formative research—

utility of a theory, principle, or method; determinants or precursors of risk behaviors; factors facilitating or inhibiting risk behaviors; and delivery of services. The third topic concerned whether the citation provided specific recommendations regarding intervention components.

Results

Intervention Studies

Among the twenty-seven behavioral and social intervention studies for MSM in the United States, the majority (67 percent) of the interventions were delivered to groups (see table 11.1). Three-quarters were evaluated using a randomized controlled trial, and 74 percent reportedly were theory-based interventions. The most frequently used theories among all of the intervention studies were diffusion of innovations (22 percent), social cognitive or social learning theory (22 percent), and model of relapse prevention (19 percent) (see table 11.2). A gap in intervention research informed the development of 74 percent of the interventions, and the most commonly cited gap was lack of intervention research for persons of a particular ethnicity or culture (22 percent). Five of the intervention studies were conducted within the first decade of the AIDS epidemic and twenty-two in the second. A total of fifteen (56 percent) interventions were developed from earlier formative research, most often attributed to behavioral surveillance (30 percent).

Disease prevalence was reported to be the basis for nearly half (48 percent) of the interventions; the prevalence cited most often (48 percent) was HIV or AIDS. Risk behavior data was reported for 44 percent of the interventions; the most commonly reported was sexual risk behavior (41 percent), including unprotected sex and number of sex partners. Of the nine rigorously designed and evaluated interventions for MSM, seven (78 percent) had statistically significant positive effects in changing sexual risk behaviors. Two studies, whose interventions are named "Community Intervention Trial for Youth" (CITY) and "Project EXPLORE," had not reported formal outcome evaluations at the time of our literature search.

As shown in table 11.1, 11 percent of the twenty-seven U.S. interventions were informed by one type of information, 30 percent were developed with two types, 27 percent had three types, 26 percent relied on four types, and 11 percent had five types. Most of the studies published in 1994 or earlier included an identified gap in intervention research as a basis for their intervention design (78 percent), followed by formative research (56 percent) or

Table 11.1. HIV prevention interventions for men who have sex with men in the United States and Australia and their bases

Study Intervention Name	Intervention Type	Basis for Intervention				
		Theory	Disease Prevalence	Risk Behavior Data	Gap in Intervention Research	Formative Research
UNITED STATES (N = 27)						
Stress Reduction Training for HIV-positive MSM Coates et al. 1989	Group RCT				X	
Structured Group Intervention for AIDS Patients Fawzy et al. 1989	Group				X	X
Project ARIES (AIDS Risk Intervention Series) Kelly et al. 1989	Group RCT	X	X	X	X	
AIDS Prevention Project[a] Valdiserri et al. 1989	Group RCT				X	
Skills-Training Intervention (ARIES Replication) Kelly et al. 1990	Group	X		X	X	X
Popular Opinion Leader (POL)[a] Kelly et al. 1991	Community RCT	X			X	X
Milwaukee AIDS Project Kelly et al. 1993	Group RCT	X				X
University of Minnesota Youth and AIDS Project Remafedi 1994	Group				X	
Intensive HIV Intervention Program (HIP) Rotherum-Borus et al. 1994	Group		X	X		
Keep It Up! Miller 1995	Group	X	X		X	

Study	Design					
Asian Pacific Islander Living Well Project[a] Choi et al. 1996	Group RCT	X	X		X	X
Mpowerment Project[a] Kegeles et al. 1996	Community RCT	X	X		X	X
African American MSM Intervention Peterson et al. 1996	Group RCT	X	X	X	X	X
Popular Opinion Leader (POL) Replication[a] Kelly et al. 1997	Community RCT	X	X			X
Project Aries Roffman et al. 1997	Group RCT	X	X		X	X
Hustler Project Miller et al. 1998	Group	X			X	X
Cognitive/Behavioral Group Counseling Roffman et al. 1998	Group	X	X	X	X	
AIDS Community Demo Project/Shiftin' Gears[a] Goldbaum et al. 1999	Community	X	X		X	X
Intervention for Substance-Using MSM Stall et al. 1999	Group	X	X		X	X
Post-Exposure Prevention (PEP) Waldo et al. 2000	Community		X		X	X
Community Intervention Trial for Youth (CITY)[b] Peterson et al. 2001	Community RCT		X		X	X
Telephone-Based Motivational Enhancement Picciano et al. 2001	Individual RCT	X	X			
Counseling Intervention for Repeat Testers[a] Dilley et al. 2002	Individual RCT	X			X	X
Mpowerment Project Replication Kegeles et al. 2002	Community	X			X	X
Minnesota 500 Men's Study Rosser et al. 2002	Group RCT	X			X	X

continued

Table 11.1.—*Continued*

Study		Basis for Intervention				
Intervention Name	Intervention Type	Theory	Disease Prevalence	Risk Behavior Data	Gap in Intervention Research	Formative Research
Intervention for Latino MSM in Puerto Rico Toro-Alfonso et al. 2002	Group	X	X	X	X	X
Project EXPLORE[b] Chesney et al. 2003	Group RCT	X	X	X	X	
United States Totals		20	13	12	20	15
AUSTRALIA (N = 4)						
Counseling and Testing Ross 1988b	Individual					X
Grim Reaper Campaign Morlet et al. 1988	Mass media	X				X
Rosser 1991		X				
Examining Self-Justifications Gold and Rosenthal 1995	Individual	X				X
Examining Self-Justifications—Replication Gold and Rosenthal 1998	Individual		X			X
Australia Totals		3	1	0	0	4

Note: Demo=demonstration; MSM=men who have sex with men; RCT=randomized control trial.

[a]Rigorous studies reporting at least one positive effect in changing risk behavior.

[b]New studies that have not yet reported findings.

Table 11.2. Bases used to inform the development of interventions targeting men who have sex with men

General Basis	Specific Basis	Used to Inform Interventions in the United States (N = 27)[a]	Used to Inform Interventions in Australia (N = 4)
Theory	AIDS Risk Reduction Model (ARRM)	2	0
	Diffusion of Innovations	6	0
	Fear Arousal	0	1
	Health Belief Model	4	0
	Health promotion principles	0	1
	Information-Motivation-Behavior (IMB)	1	0
	Model of Relapse Prevention	5	0
	Social Cognitive Theory/Social Learning Theory	6	0
	Theory of Reasoned Action	3	0
	Transtheoretical Mode of Behavior Change	1	0
	Other Cognitive/Behavioral principles/theory	6	0
Disease Prevalence	HIV/AIDS	13	1
	Sexually transmitted diseases	3	0
	Hepatitis	1	0
Risk Behavior Data	Drugs/alcohol	5	0
	Sexual risk behavior (e.g., UAI, number of sex partners)	11	0
Gaps in Intervention Research	Evaluation of community programs	2	0
	Innovation in intervention delivery	4	0
	Ethnicity or culture	6	0
	Type of risk behavior	4	0
	Work done in the first decade of the epidemic	5	0
Formative Research	Behavioral surveillance research	8	1
	Ethnographic research	5	1
	Replication of previous intervention	5	1

Note: UAI = unprotected anal intercourse.

[a]Many of the interventions have more than one specific basis within a general basis data type.

theory (44 percent). One-third of the earlier interventions were based on both theory and formative research. After 1994, 89 percent of the studies' interventions were reported to be based on theory and at least one other data type, most commonly a gap in intervention research (72 percent), disease prevalence (61 percent), or formative research (56 percent). Over half (56 percent) of the later interventions were based on both theory and formative research.

Of the four behavioral and social intervention studies for MSM in Australia, three of the interventions were delivered to individuals, and three had interventions based on theory, either fear arousal or health promotion principles (see tables 11.1 and 11.2). All of the interventions were developed from earlier formative research—either ethnographic research, behavioral surveillance, or replication of a previous intervention. Disease prevalence (HIV/AIDS) was reported to be a basis for one of the interventions. Of the four studies, two had interventions informed by two types of information, and one was developed with three types of information. Four studies are insufficient for examining intervention research trends over time.

The results presented above are dominated by the United States' approach in which researchers develop and test HIV prevention behavioral interventions and publish the results. Consequently, more information on interventions from the United States is available than is available for Australian interventions. We explored other types of HIV-related studies to find additional information generated by the Australian approach. Since much of Australian researchers' work is done in support of the NGOs responsible for designing HIV prevention interventions, we also examined the twenty formative studies from Australia and the seventy-two formative studies from the United States to identify methods by which the formative data were collected and topics on which the research focused (see table 11.3).

Formative Studies

The majority of the twenty Australian formative research studies collected data using quantitative methods (50 percent) or qualitative methods (35 percent), including ethnography and case studies. Half of the Australian formative studies focused on the determinants or precursors of risk behaviors—such as attitudes of HIV-infected MSM (e.g., Gold and Ridge 2001), predictors of condom use (e.g., Kelaher et al. 1994; Ross et al. 1990), and use of stereotypes when selecting sex partners (e.g., Gold et al. 1999). A quarter focused on studying the utility of a theory, such as the theory of reasoned action (e.g., Gallois et al. 1994); a principle, such as pedagogy in HIV/AIDS

Table 11.3. Research methods, focus, and recommendations from formative studies on men who have sex with men

Methods, Focus, and Recommendations	Specific Types	Number of Studies in the United States (N = 72)	Number of Studies in Australia (N = 20)
Research Methods	Qualitative	14[a]	7[b]
	Quantitative	27	10
	Literature review	20	2
	Content analysis	6	1
	Statistical models	5	0
Focus of Formative Research	Utility of a theory, principle, or method	27	5
	Determinants or precursors of risk behaviors	13	11
	Factors facilitating or inhibiting risk behaviors	13	3
	Service delivery	11	1
	Multiple foci (more than one of the above)	8	0
Recommended Specific Intervention Components	No	28	10
	Yes	44	10

[a]Five of which were ethnographic.
[b]One of which was ethnographic.

education (e.g., Dowsett et al. 2001); or a method, such as modifying a scale to measure HIV/AIDS attitudes (e.g., Ross 1988a; Visser and Antoni 1994).

A few of the formative studies investigated factors that facilitate or inhibit risk behaviors—such as MSM's social class, use of the Internet to find sex partners, and sociocultural formation (e.g., Dowsett and McInnes 1996). The authors of half of the studies recommended specific intervention components, delivery methods, or both that would apply their formative findings—such as use of peer educators (e.g., Ross and McLaws 1992), uses of the Internet for health promotion (e.g., Hurley 2003), countering the practice of inferring a sex partner's HIV serostatus (e.g., Gold et al. 1999), fluid heuristic of sexual risk behaviors (Lowy and Ross 1994), and print materials appropriate for MSM of lower educational experience, working-class status, and less connection to the gay community (e.g., Dowsett et al. 1992).

The majority of the seventy-two formative studies by researchers in the United States collected data using quantitative methods (38 percent) or literature reviews (29 percent). The most common focus of their formative research (38 percent) was the utility of a theory—such as the health belief model (e.g., Montgomery et al. 1989), AIDS risk reduction model (e.g., Gillis et al. 1998), and theory of reasoned action (e.g., Fisher et al. 1995)—or method—such as psychoeducation in AIDS prevention (e.g., Fullilove et al. 1989), the sexological approach to HIV prevention (e.g., Robinson et al. 2002), and participant-observation ethnographic methods (e.g., Clatts and Sotheran 2000). The authors of 61 percent of the studies recommended specific intervention components or delivery methods from their findings that could be incorporated in intervention designs. Examples of such recommendations include community involvement in changing social norms (e.g., McKirnan et al. 1996), addressing immediate life concerns such as dating and intimacy (e.g., Seal et al. 2000), formal and informal outreach (e.g., Hoff et al. 1997; Ramirez-Valles 2002), skills building (e.g., Rye et al. 2001; Wulfert et al. 1996), interventions that could be specifically tailored for subpopulations of MSM (e.g., Doll and Beeker 1996; Rosser et al. 1993; Semple et al. 2000), and use of the Internet as a risk mediator and intervention route (Benotsch et al. 2002).

Many of the findings that inform intervention development in the United States are found in our formative category of studies. However, Australia evaluates and adjusts its interventions based on trends in individual and community practices, and many of these findings are found in the studies we categorize as surveys of behaviors or behavioral correlates. Although these surveys are not cited as formative bases for interventions in published sources, their authors sometimes suggest their findings' implications for health promotion. It is also possible that the surveys are used by NGOs in developing their unpublished interventions. Therefore, we examined the forty-nine Australian survey studies to identify variables on which data were collected.

Survey Studies

Of the fifty-eight Australian surveys of behaviors or behavioral correlates, 22 percent collected information on HIV/AIDS-related knowledge, attitudes, or perceptions; 22 percent explored correlates of risk behaviors; 16 percent investigated risk reduction strategies used by MSM; and 12 percent examined MSM's "connectedness" to the gay community and the effect that connectedness has on sexual practices. Range of sex practices, HIV testing, variables associated with high risk or with seroconversion, and the nature of interpersonal relationships were each covered by 10 percent or fewer surveys.

Based on our review of national approaches, intervention and formative prevention research for MSM in the United States and Australia, and Australian surveys, it appears that Australian researchers are more likely than researchers from the United States to specify how to apply their findings in the design of a prevention intervention. Australia has been conducting national behavioral surveys of MSM for planning and evaluation purposes much longer than has the United States. Researchers and NGOs in the United States seem more likely to develop interventions to follow the shifting epidemic and to fill gaps in existing intervention research than their Australian counterparts, perhaps because HIV/AIDS in Australia has always been concentrated among MSM. Researchers in both countries seem to use the theory and formative research types of information most often as the basis for their interventions for MSM. However, those in the United States draw on a broader range of theories. Researchers in the United States evaluate interventions and publish outcomes more often than do Australian researchers.

The United States and Australia also differ in their use of national mass media educational campaigns. The only such national campaign in the United States, "America Responds to AIDS," was conducted in five phases from October 1987 to December 1990 and was intended to increase awareness about AIDS among members of the general public. Message recall, amount of airtime (Gentry and Jorgensen 1991; Siska et al. 1992), and broadcast patterns for public service announcements (PSAs) were studied, but the campaign's effect on changing risk behaviors was not evaluated (Ratzan et al. 1994; Woods et al. 1991). The first Australian mass media campaign, "Grim Reaper," also started in 1987 and was designed to inform the nation about AIDS and increase perceived personal risk. While aimed at the general public, it was intended to affect persons at risk of infection. Its effects on demand for HIV testing (Morlet et al. 1988) and on sexual practices of MSM (Rosser 1991) were studied and found to be counterproductive in changing the behavior of at-risk persons.

Discussion

Lessons learned from the United States' approach to the AIDS epidemic make several useful contributions to designing interventions that are relevant and acceptable to MSM. First, effective interventions for MSM are found to be based on behavioral and social science theories, particularly social learning theory, diffusion of innovations, and model of relapse prevention. Theories can provide a framework for the intervention components, evaluation, and interpretation of outcomes (Bonell and Imrie 2001).

Second, rigorous outcome evaluation methods, including but not restricted to randomized control trials, can ascertain interventions' effectiveness. As effective interventions are identified, they can then be replicated with fidelity and packaged for dissemination and promoted nationally for use by NGOs (Neumann and Sogolow 2000). The CDC has recently developed a national-level strategy, the Diffusion of Effective Behavioral Interventions (DEBI) project, to provide high-quality training and ongoing technical assistance on selected effective HIV prevention interventions to state and community HIV service providers and NGOs (Collins et al. 2003).

Third are quantitative analyses of determinants, precursors, and facilitators of risk behaviors. This line of research seeks to identify and study the subpopulations of MSM who engage in various HIV risk behaviors and to determine what influences their decisions to engage in these behaviors. Once this information has been ascertained, it can be used to inform the development of behavioral interventions and other prevention programs.

Fourth, theory-driven formal and informal outreach can be more than information delivery and motivational messages; it can teach people the practical and interpersonal skills they need to act upon the information. Although the national mass media is not commonly used in the United States, it is informative and persuasive; however, it lacks group dynamics and interactive skills building and may be difficult to tailor for subpopulations.

The fifth contribution from the United States' approach involves the emerging utility of the Internet in intervention strategies. A study by Benotsch and colleagues (2002) found that the high prevalence of Internet use by MSM as a method of meeting sexual partners suggests that important sexual networks may be forming over the Internet. Thus, the Internet has the potential to provide opportunities for new HIV primary prevention interventions as a tool to mediate risk behavior.

The Australian approach also makes many important contributions to fighting the AIDS epidemic and in identifying data useful for designing relevant interventions. One contribution is considering the context in which risk behaviors take place (Bennett et al. 1989; Connell et al. 1990; Dowsett 1996; Gold and Rosenthal 1998; Kippax 2003; Prestage and Drielsma 1996). Context can include choice of venues for finding sex partners or for having sex, situational factors and self-justifications for unsafe sex, and the meanings of various sexual practices.

A second contribution is the concept of "connectedness" or "community attachment" (Dowsett 1990, 1996; Gold 1995; Prestage and Drielsma 1996; Van de Ven, Rawstorne, et al. 2002). Involvement in the gay community has been found to have protective effects for MSM, presumably through enhanced self-efficacy and exposure to safer sex norms, so many Australian interventions encourage MSM to become more involved in their local gay community.

A third contribution is taking MSM's existing effective risk reduction techniques identified through qualitative research and promoting them in interventions (Dowsett et al. 2001; Kippax and Race 2003). The use of negotiated safety is one example, although its campaign has not been evaluated (Crawford et al. 2001; Kippax, Crawford, et al. 1993; Kippax and Kinder 2002; Kippax et al. 1997). Negotiated safety is a strategy wherein steady HIV-negative partners agree that all sex they may have outside of their relationship will be safer. This strategy allows the couple to maintain their seronegativity and to have unprotected sex within their primary relationship. A strictly behavioral survey, which does not include contextual measures, possibly would incorrectly identify such a couple as being at high or moderate risk.

A fourth contribution is not a type of information but a useful method. "Critical reflexivity" is a two-way partnership process whereby community members and researchers gain an active awareness of issues in information assessment and a capacity to understand and interact with collections of personal practices. Community members assist with interpreting behavioral research findings (Hurley 2003; Kippax and Kinder 2002).

A fifth contribution is another method: periodic national and local behavioral surveys (Kippax 2003; Kippax et al. 1998; Ross et al. 1989; Van de Ven et al. 1997). These cohort and longitudinal cross-sectional surveys can explore the extent of and trends in risk behaviors and risk reduction strategies.

Our study is subject to several limitations. One limitation is that we relied solely on what researchers reported in their articles in order to determine the bases for their interventions. Whether researchers fully describe formative research, theory, or prevalence of disease or risk behaviors that have informed their intervention can be dependent on journal style and space constraints. For this reason, whenever possible, we reviewed more than one publication about a given study. A second limitation is that we had access to and included unpublished reports and evaluations from the United States, but we did not have direct access to unpublished Australian reports and evaluations. A third limitation is that relatively few studies from Australia were found in our search of the PRS database. This may be because the PRS project has greater access to published and unpublished studies from the United States, the database's inclusion criteria exclude nonbehavioral research, and Australia does not always appear in titles or keywords of Australian articles. A fourth limitation was that we could not obtain all of the Australian articles and book chapters we had identified through our search methods. We either could not include them in our study or relied on the information presented in the publication's abstract, if that was all that we had available.

We believe that, collectively, the contributions from the United States and Australia that we have identified indicate specific information to routinely collect about MSM and the context of their behaviors—data that can be used to inform interventions and to monitor behavioral and epidemiologic trends. We recommend that researchers collect information on MSM in nine major areas (see table 11.4). These areas were selected by combining the topics on the CDC HIV Behavioral Surveillance System (Gallagher et al. 2003) with the efforts targeting MSM in the Australian National Strategy (Commonwealth Department of Health and Aged Care 2000) and the most frequently noted topics among the United States' and Australia's intervention and formative studies and Australia's behavioral survey studies. Data on these areas can be collected using quantitative or qualitative methods.

Both countries have different approaches to HIV prevention among MSM. Combined, their various methods give breadth and depth of knowledge. The intent of this chapter is not to decide which country's approach is better but, rather, to suggest a new approach that will stimulate research using contributions from both countries for HIV prevention efforts among MSM.

Acknowledgments

The authors want to acknowledge Julia Britton DeLuca for performing the electronic searches of the HIV/AIDS Prevention Research Synthesis database for this chapter. The authors also are indebted to Paul Van de Ven of the National Centre for HIV Social Research at the University of New South Wales, Sydney, Australia; to B. R. Simon Rosser of the HIV/STI Intervention

Table 11.4. Recommended areas for routine data collection in HIV/AIDS behavioral surveillance, intervention, and formative research for men who have sex with men

Area	Examples
Attitudes[a, b]	Beliefs about transmission, condom use, treatment optimism, personal vulnerability, individualism or collectivism
HIV testing[a, b]	HIV testing history, whether or not respondents know their test results, test results
Correlates of risk behaviors[b]	Mood state, substance use, mental health, mobility and travel, degree of anonymity at the sexual venue, self-justifications for unsafe behaviors, use of pornography, internalized homophobia
Risk reduction strategies[b]	Risk reduction strategies in popular use, regardless of their effectiveness, and any problems experienced with the strategies. Examples of risk reduction strategies may include avoiding anal sex, exclusive sex with a regular partner, using condoms, strategic positioning (Van de Ven, Kippax, et al. 2002), partner selectivity, withdrawal before ejaculation, reliance on undetectable viral load
Risk behaviors[a]	Specific risk behaviors—such as anal intercourse, number of sex partners, number of sexual encounters, types of sex partners (including women)
Connectedness[b]	Involvement in the gay community, the nature and extent of that involvement
Range of sex practices[b]	Types of protected and unprotected sex, variations with regular and casual partners, receptive and insertive positioning, variations according to partners' HIV seroconcordance, discordance, or unknown status, esoteric sexual practices
Prevention services[a]	Exposure to and use of medical and behavioral prevention services
Treatment[a]	Enrollment of HIV-infected persons in treatment, level of treatment adherence, understanding of viral load and other clinical markers

[a]United States origin of recommendation.
[b]Australia origin of recommendation.

and Prevention Studies (HIPS) Center of the University of Minnesota; to Michael W. Ross of the WHO Center for Health Promotion and Prevention Research, School of Public Health, University of Texas, Houston; and to Nicole Crepaz, team leader of the Centers for Disease Control and Prevention's HIV/AIDS Prevention Research Synthesis project, for their insightful comments on this chapter.

Note

1. Citations excluded from our study are reports that focus on pregnancy prevention, sex education, sexual health promotion, vertical transmission, drug treatment trials, postexposure prophylaxis, vaccine trials, disease surveillance, surveys of knowledge or attitudes, genetic epidemiology, occupational exposure, exposure to blood products, and prevention research methods.

References

Note: References include only the publications cited. For a full list of Australian publications reviewed for this chapter, please contact Mary Spink Neumann at msnl@cdc.gov. For a full list of U.S. publications reviewed for this chapter, please contact Jeffrey H. Herbst at afo4@cdc.gov.

Altman, Dennis. 1986. *AIDS and the New Puritanism*. Sydney: Pluto Press.

Australian Federation of AIDS Organisations. 1999. Survey results. http://www.afao. org.au/indes_afa_771.asp?action+view_articleandid=125landsection=663, accessed September 27, 2003.

Bennett, Garrett, Simon Chapman, and Fiona Bray. 1989. Sexual practices and "beats": AIDS-related sexual practice in a sample of homosexual and bisexual men in the western area of Sydney. *Medical Journal of Australia* 151: 309–14.

Benotsch, Eric G., Seth Kalichman, and Maggi Cage. 2002. Men who have met sex partners via the Internet: Prevalence, predictors, and implications for HIV prevention. *Archives of Sexual Behavior* 31(2): 177–83.

Bonnell, Chris, and John Imrie. 2001. Behavioural interventions to prevent HIV infection: Rapid evolution, increasing rigour, moderate success. *British Medical Journal* 58: 155–70.

Centers for Disease Control and Prevention (CDC). 1981. Pneumocystis pneumonia—Los Angeles. *Morbidity and Mortality Weekly Report* 30: 250–52.

———. 1999. *Compendium of HIV Prevention Interventions with Evidence of Effectiveness.* Atlanta: Centers for Disease Control and Prevention. Also available at http://www.cdc.gov/hv/pubs/HIVcompendium/hivcompendium.htm.

———. 2003. *HIV/AIDS Surveillance Report, 2002,* 14: 1–48. Also available at http://www.cdc.gov/hiv/stats/hasrlink.htm.

Chesney, Margaret A., Beryl A. Koblin, Patrick J. Barresi, Marla J. Husnik, Connie L.

Celum, Grant Colfax, Kenneth Mayer, David McKirnan, Franklyn N. Judson, Yijian Huang, Thomas J. Coates, and the EXPLORE Study Team. 2003. An individually tailored intervention for HIV prevention: Baseline data from the EXPLORE study. *American Journal of Public Health* 93: 933–38.

Choi, Kyung-Hee, Steve Lew, Eric Vittinghoff, Joseph A. Catania, Donald C. Barrett, and Thomas J. Coates. 1996. The efficacy of brief group counseling in HIV risk reduction among homosexual Asian and Pacific Islander men. *AIDS* 10: 81–87.

Ciesielski, Carol A. 2003. Sexually transmitted diseases in men who have sex with men: An epidemiologic review. *Current Infectious Disease Reports* 5: 145–52.

Clatts, Michael C., and Jo L. Sotheran. 2000. Challenges in research on drug and sexual risk practices of men who have sex with men: Applications of ethnography in HIV epidemiology and prevention. *AIDS and Behavior* 4(2): 169–79.

Coates, Thomas J., Leon McKusick, Richard Kuno, and Daniel P. Stites. 1989. Stress reduction training changed number of sexual partners but not immune function in men with HIV. *American Journal of Public Health* 79: 885–87.

Collins, Charles B., Janet Cleveland, Camilla Harshbarger, and Richard Sawyer. 2003. Diffusion of effective behavioral interventions for HIV prevention through a public health prevention service delivery system. Paper presented at the 2003 National HIV Prevention Conference, Atlanta.

Commonwealth Department of Health and Aged Care. 2000. *Changes and Challenges: National HIV/AIDS Strategy 1999–2000 to 2003–2004.* Canberra: Department of Health and Aged Care.

Connell, R. W., June Crawford, Gary W. Dowsett, Susan Kippax, V. Sinnott, Pam Rodden, R. Berg, Don Baxter, and Lex Watson. 1990. Danger and context: Unsafe anal sexual practice among homosexual and bisexual men in the AIDS crisis. *Australian and New Zealand Journal of Sociology* 26: 187–208.

Counter, Mark. 1996. A history of the people living with HIV/AIDS (PLWHA) movement in Australia. *Social Alternatives* 15(4): 25–27.

Crawford, June M., Pam Rodden, Susan Kippax, and Paul Van de Ven. 2001. Negotiated safety and other agreements between men in relationships: Risk practice redefined. *International Journal of STD and AIDS* 12: 164–70.

Crepaz, Nicole, Cynthia M. Lyles, Jeffrey H. Herbst, Linda Kay, Julia Britton, and the HIV/AIDS Prevention Research Synthesis Team. 2003. Synthesis of HIV prevention research: Lessons learned from the CDC's HIV/AIDS Prevention Research Synthesis Project (PRS). Paper presented at the National HIV Prevention Conference, Atlanta.

Dilley, James W., Williams J. Woods, James Sabatino, Tania Lihatsh, Barbara Adler, Shannon Casey, Joanna Rinaldi, Richard Brand, and Willi McFarland. 2002. Changing sexual behavior among gay male repeat testers for HIV: A randomized, controlled trial of a single-session intervention. *Journal of Acquired Immune Deficiency Syndromes* 30: 177–86.

Doll, Lynda S., and Carolyn Beeker. 1996. Male bisexual behavior and HIV risk in the United States: Synthesis of research with implications for behavioral interventions. *AIDS Education and Prevention* 8: 205–25.

Dowsett, Gary W. 1990. Reaching men who have sex with men in Australia. An overview of AIDS education: Community intervention and community attachment strategies. *Australian Journal of Social Issues* 25(3): 186–98.

———. 1996. AIDS: A fact of life. In *Practicing Desire: Homosexual Sex in the Era of AIDS*, ed. Gary W. Dowsett, 60–89. Stanford, Calif.: Stanford University Press.

Dowsett, Gary W., Jonathan Bollen, David McInnes, Murray Couch, and Barry Edwards. 2001. HIV/AIDS and constructs of gay community: Researching educational practice within community-based health promotion for gay men. *International Journal of Social Research Methodology* 4: 205–23.

Dowsett, Gary W., M. D. Davis, and R. W. Connell. 1992. Working class homosexuality and HIV/AIDS prevention: Some recent research from Sydney, Australia. *Psychology and Health* 6: 313–24.

Dowsett, Gary W., and David McInnes. 1996. Gay community, AIDS agencies and the HIV epidemic in Adelaide: Theorising "Post AIDS." *Social Alternatives* 15: 29–32.

Fawzy, I., Sheila Namir, and Deane L. Wolcott. 1989. Structured group intervention model for AIDS patients. *Psychiatric Medicine* 7: 35–45.

Fisher, William A., Jeffrey D. Fisher, and Barbara J. Rye. 1995. Understanding and promoting AIDS-preventive behavior: Insights from the theory of reasoned action. *Health Psychology* 14(3): 255–64.

Fullilove, Mindy, Robert Fullilove III, and Edward Morales. 1989. Psychoeducation: A tool for AIDS prevention in minority communities. *Journal of Psychotherapy and the Family* 1(2): 143–60.

Gallagher, Kathleen M., Patrick S. Sullivan, and Ida Onorato. 2003. A national system for HIV behavioral surveillance in the United States. Paper presented at the 2003 National HIV Prevention Conference, Atlanta.

Gallois, Cynthia, Deborah Terry, Perri Timmins, Yoshihisa Kashima, and Malcolm McCamish. 1994. Safe sexual intentions and behavior among heterosexuals and homosexual men: Testing the Theory of Reasoned Action. *Psychology and Health* 10: 1–16.

Gay Men's Health Crisis. 2003. The Gay Men's Health Crisis HIV/AIDS timeline. http://www.gmhc.org///about/timeline.html, accessed June 6, 2004.

Gentry, Eileen M., and Cynthia M. Jorgensen. 1991. Monitoring the exposure of "American Responds to AIDS" PSA campaign. *Public Health Reports* 106: 651–55.

Gillis, J. Roy, Heino F. L. Meyer-Bahlburg, Theresa M. Exner, and Anke A. Ehrhardt. 1998. The predictive utility of an expanded AIDS Risk Reduction Model (AARM) among adult gay and bisexual men. *Canadian Journal of Human Sexuality* 7: 31–49.

Gluck, Michael, and Eric Rosenthal. 1996. Office of Technology assessment report: The effectiveness of AIDS prevention efforts. In *Office of Technology Assessment. The Effectiveness of AIDS Prevention Efforts: A State-of-the-Science Report*, 1–32. Washington, D.C.: American Psychological Association Office on AIDS.

Gold, Ron S. 1995. Why we need to rethink AIDS education for gay Men. *AIDS Care* 7 (Suppl. 1): 11–19.

Gold, Ron S., and D. T. Ridge. 2001. "I will start treatment when I think the time is right": HIV-positive gay men talk about their decision not to access antiretroviral therapy. *AIDS Care* 13: 693–708.

Gold, Ron S., and Doreen A. Rosenthal. 1995. Preventing unprotected anal intercourse in gay men: A comparison of two intervention techniques. *International Journal of STD and AIDS* 6: 89–94.

———. 1998. Examining self-justifications for unsafe sex as a technique of AIDS education: The importance of personal relevance. *International Journal of STD and AIDS* 9: 208–13.

Gold, Ron S., Michael J. Skinner, and John Hinchy. 1999. Gay men's stereotypes about who is HIV infected: A further study. *International Journal of STD and AIDS* 10: 600–605.

Goldbaum, Gary M., Wayne Johnson, Richard J. Wolitski, Cornelis Rietmeijer, Robert W. Wood, Danuta Kasprzyk, Daniel Montano, and the AIDS Community Demonstration Projects Research Group. 1999. Sexual behavior change among non-gay-identified men who have sex with men: Response to a community-level intervention. Unpublished manuscript. Contact Gary Goldbaum at ggoldbaum@shd.snohomish.wa.gov.

Herbst, Jeffrey H., R. Thomas Sherba, Lev Zohrabyan, Angela B. Hutchinson, Nicole Crepaz, and Ron Stall. 2003. A meta-analytic review of U.S. and international HIV prevention interventions on sexual risk behaviors for men who have sex with men (MSM). Paper presented at the 131st annual meeting of the American Public Health Association, San Francisco.

Hoff, Colleen C., Susan M. Kegeles, Michael Acree, Ronald Stall, Jay Paul, Michael Ekstrand, and Thomas J. Coates. 1997. Looking for men in all the wrong places . . . : HIV prevention small-group programs do not reach high-risk gay men. *AIDS* 11: 829–31.

Hull, Peter, Patrick Rawstorne, Paul Van de Ven, Garrett Prestage, Susan Kippax, Jodie Walton, Geoffrey Harrison, Fiona Tunley, and Gary Ferguson. 2002. *Gay Community Periodic Survey: Queensland 2002*. Sydney: National Centre in HIV Social Research.

Hurley, Michael. 2003. Electronic technologies, HIV education and health promotion targeting gay men and men who have sex with men. Report to Dermon Ryan, Manager ANET and Indigenous Projects.

Kaslow, R. A., D. G. Ostrow, R. Detels J. P. Phair, B. F. Polk, and C. R. Rinaldo. 1987. The multicenter AIDS cohort study: Rationale, organization, and selected characteristics of the participants. *American Journal of Epidemiology* 126(2): 310–18.

Kegeles, Susan M., Robert B. Hays, and Thomas J. Coates. 1996. The Mpowerment Project: A community-level HIV prevention intervention for young gay men. *American Journal of Public Health* 86: 1129–136.

Kegeles, Susan M., Robert B. Rebchook, Robert B. Hays, and Lance M. Pollack. 2002. Staving off increases in young gay/bisexual men's risk behavior in the HAART era. Paper presented at the Fourteenth International AIDS Conference, Barcelona.

Kelaher, Margaret, Robert B. Ross, Richard Rohrsheim, Michael Drury, and Andrew Clarkson. 1994. Dominant situational determinants of sexual risk behaviour in gay men. *AIDS* 8: 101–5.

Kelly, Jeffrey A., Debra A. Murphy, G. Richard Bahr, Seth C. Kalichman, Michael G. Morgan, L. Yvonne Stevenson, Jeffrey J. Koob, Ted L. Brasfield, and Barry M. Bernstein. 1993. Outcome of cognitive-behavioral and support group brief therapies for depressed, HIV-infected persons. *American Journal of Psychiatry* 150: 1679–686.

Kelly, Jeffrey A., Debra A. Murphy, Kathleen J. Sikkema, Timothy L. McAuliffe, Roger A. Roffman, Laura J. Solomon, Richard A. Winett, Seth C. Kalichman, and the Community HIV Prevention Research Collaborative. 1997. Randomised, controlled, community-level HIV-prevention intervention for sexual-risk behaviour among homosexual men in U.S. cities. *Lancet* 350: 1500–1505.

Kelly, Jeffrey A., Janet S. St. Lawrence, Ron Betts, Ted L. Brasfield, and Harold V. Hood. 1990. A skills-training group intervention model to assist persons in reducing risk behaviors for HIV infection. *AIDS Education and Prevention* 2: 24–35.

Kelly, Jeffrey A., Janet S. St. Lawrence, Yolanda E. Diaz, L. Yvonne Stevenson, Allan C. Hauth, Ted L. Brasfield, Seth C. Kalichman, Joseph E. Smith, and Michael E. Andrew. 1991. HIV risk behavior reduction following intervention with key opinion leaders of population: An experimental analysis. *American Journal of Public Health* 81: 168–71.

Kelly, Jeffrey A., Janet S. St. Lawrence, Harold V. Hood, and Ted L. Brasfield. 1989. Behavioral intervention to reduce AIDS risk activities. *Journal of Consulting and Clinical Psychology* 57: 60–67.

Kelly, Jeffrey A., Janet S. St. Lawrence, L. Yvonne Stevenson, Allan C. Hauth, Seth C. Kalichman, Yolanda E. Diaz, Ted L. Brasfield, Jeffrey J. Koob, and Michael G. Morgan. 1992. Community AIDS/HIV risk reduction: The effects of endorsements by popular people in three cities. *American Journal of Public Health* 82: 1483–489.

Kippax, Susan. 2003. Recommendations for multi-component risk reduction messages for MSM. Presentation at HIV Risk Communication Consultation, Centers for Disease Control and Prevention, Atlanta.

Kippax, Susan, Danielle Campbell, Paul Van de Ven, June Crawford, Garrett Prestage, Stephanie Knox, A. Culpin, John Kaldor, and Paul Kinder. 1998. Cultures of sexual adventurism as markers of HIV seroconversion: A case control study in a cohort of Sydney gay men. *AIDS Care* 10: 677–88.

Kippax, Susan, R. W. Connell, Gary W. D. Dowsett, and June Crawford. 1993. *Sustaining Safe Sex: Gay Communities Respond to AIDS*. London: Falmer.

Kippax, Susan, June Crawford, M. Davis, Pam Rodden, and Gary Dowsett. 1993. Sustaining safe sex: A longitudinal study of a sample of homosexual men. *AIDS* 7: 257–63.

Kippax, Susan, June Crawford, Pam Rodden, and K. Benton. 1994. *Report on Project Male-Call: National telephone survey of men who have sex with men*. Canberra: Australian Government Publishing Service.

Kippax, Susan, and Paul Kinder. 2002. Reflexive practice: The relationship between social research and health promotion in HIV prevention. *Sex Education* 2: 91–104.

Kippax, Susan, Jason Noble, Garrett Prestage, June M. Crawford, Danielle Campbell, Don Baxter, and David Cooper. 1997. Sexual negotiation in the "AIDS Era": Negotiated safety revisited. *AIDS* 11: 191–97.

Kippax, Susan, and Kane Race. 2003. Sustaining safe practice: Twenty years on. *Social Science and Medicine* 57: 1–12.

Lowy, Eva, and Michael W. Ross. 1994. "It'll never happen to me": Gay men's beliefs, perceptions and folk constructs of sexual risk. *AIDS Education and Prevention* 6: 467–82.

McKirnan, David J., David G. Ostrow, and B. Hope. 1996. Sex, drugs and escape: A psychological model of HIV-risk sexual behaviors. *AIDS Care* 8: 655–69.

Meese, Peter. 1997. Do . . . Choose . . . Enjoy: Contributions of a community based campaign. *Venereology* 10(2): 81–82.

Miller, Robin L. 1995. Assisting gay men to maintain safer sex: An evaluation of an AIDS service organization's safer sex maintenance program. *AIDS Education and Prevention* 7: 48–63.

Miller, Robin L., David Klotz, and Haftan M. Eckholdt. 1998. HIV prevention with male prostitutes and patrons of hustler bars: Replication of an HIV preventive intervention. *American Journal of Community Psychology* 26: 97–131.

Montgomery, Susanne B., Jill G. Joseph, Marshall H. Becker, David G. Ostrow, Ronald C. Kessler, and John P. Kirscht. 1989. The health belief model in understanding compliance with preventive recommendations for AIDS: How useful? *AIDS Education and Prevention* 1: 303–23.

Morlet, Andrew, James J. Guinan, Irwin Diefenthaler, and Julian Gold. 1988. The impact of the "Grim Reaper" national AIDS educational campaign on the Albion Street (AIDS) Centre and the AIDS hotline. *Medical Journal of Australia* 148: 282–86.

Murphy, Dean, and Aldo Spina. 2002. *All things considered: Gay men's education consultation.* Sydney: Australian Federation of AIDS Organisations.

Neumann, Mary S., and Ellen D. Sogolow. 2000. Replicating effective programs: HIV/ AIDS prevention technology transfer. *AIDS Education and Prevention* 12 (Suppl. A): 35–48.

Peterson, John L., Roger Bakeman, Joseph Stokes, and the Community Intervention Trial for Youth Study Team. 2001. Racial/ethnic patterns of HIV sexual risk behaviors among young men who have sex with men. *Journal of the Gay and Lesbian Medical Association* 5(4): 155–62.

Peterson, John L., Thomas J. Coates, Joseph Catania, Walter W. Hauck, Michael Acree, Dennis Daigle, Bobby Hillard, Lee Middleton, and Norman Hearst. 1996. Evaluation of an HIV risk reduction intervention among African-American homosexual and bisexual men. *AIDS* 10: 319–25.

Picciano, Joseph P., Roger A. Roffman, Seth C. Kalichman, Scott Rutledge, and James Berghuis. 2001. A telephone based brief intervention using motivational enhancement to facilitate HIV risk reduction among MSM: A pilot study. *AIDS and Behavior* 5(3): 251–62.

Prestage, Garrett, and Paul Drielsma. 1996. Indicators of male bisexual activity in semi-metropolitan New South Wales: Implications for HIV prevention strategies. *Australian and New Zealand Journal of Public Health* 20: 386–92.

Ramirez-Valles, J. 2002. The protective effects of community involvement for HIV risk behavior: A conceptual framework. *Health Education Research* 17: 389–403.

Ratzan, Scott C., J. Gregory Payne, and Holly A. Massett. 1994. Effective health message design: The America Responds to AIDS campaign. *American Behavioral Scientist* 38: 294–309.

Remafedi, Gary. 1994. Cognitive and behavioral adaptations to HIV/AIDS among gay and bisexual adolescents. *Journal of Adolescent Health* 15: 142–48.

Robinson, Beatrice "Bean" E., Walter O. Bockting, B. R. Simon Rosser, Michael Miner, and Eli Coleman. 2002. The sexual health model: Application of a sexological approach to HIV prevention. *Health Education Research* 17: 43–57.

Roffman, Roger A., Lois Downey, Blair Beadnell, Judith R. Gordon, Jay N. Craver, and Robert S. Stephens. 1998. Cognitive-behavioral group counseling to prevent HIV transmission in gay and bisexual men: Factors contributing to successful risk reduction. *Research on Social Work Practice* 7(2): 165–86.

Roffman, Roger A., Joseph F. Picciano, Rosemary Ryan, Blair Beadnell, Douglass Fisher, Lois Downey, and Seth C. Kalichman. 1997. HIV-prevention group counseling delivered by telephone: An efficacy trial with gay and bisexual men. *AIDS and Behavior* 1(2): 137–54.

Ross, Michael W. 1988a. Attitudes towards condoms as AIDS prophylaxis in homosexual men: Dimensions and measurement. *Psychology and Health* 2: 291–99.

———. 1988b. Relationship of combinations of AIDS counselling and testing to safer sex and condom use in homosexual men. *Community Health Studies* 12(3): 322–27.

Ross, Michael W., Brook Freedman, and Ralph Brew. 1989. Changes in sexual behavior between 1986 and 1988 in matched samples of homosexually active men. *Community Health Studies* 13(3): 276–80.

Ross, Michael W., and M. L. McLaws. 1992. Subjective norms about condoms are better predictors of use and intention to use than attitudes. *Health Education Research* 7: 335–39.

Ross, Michael W., K. Rigby, B. R. Simon Rosser, M. Brown, and P. Anagnoustou. 1990. The effect of a national campaign on attitudes towards AIDS. *AIDS Care* 2: 339–46.

Rosser, B. R. Simon. 1991. The effects of using fear in public AIDS education on the behaviour of homosexually active men. *Journal of Psychology and Human Sexuality* 4(3): 123–34.

Rosser, B. R. Simon, Walter O. Bockting, Deborah L. Rugg, Beatrice "Bean" E. Robinson, Michael W. Ross, Greta R. Bauer, and Eli Coleman. 2002. A randomized controlled intervention trial of a sexual health approach to long-term HIV risk reduction for men who have sex with men: Effects of the intervention on unsafe sexual behavior. *AIDS Education and Prevention* 14: 59–71.

Rosser, B. R. Simon, Eli Coleman, and Paul Ohmans. 1993. Safer sex maintenance and reduction of unsafe sex among homosexually active men: A new therapeutic approach. *Health Education Research* 8: 19–34.

Rotheram-Borus, Mary Jane, Helen Reid, and Margaret Rosario. 1994. Factors mediating changes in sexual HIV risk behaviors among gay and bisexual male adolescents. *American Journal of Public Health* 84: 1938–946.

Rye, Barbara J., William A. Fisher, and Jeffrey D. Fisher. 2001. The theory of planned behavior and safer sex behaviors of gay men. *AIDS and Behavior* 5(4): 307–17.

Seal, David W., Jeffrey A. Kelly, F. R. Bloom, L. Yvonne Stevenson, Brenda I. Coley, Lew A. Broyles, and the Medical College of Wisconsin CITY Project Research Team. 2000. HIV prevention with young men who have sex with men: What young men themselves say is needed. *AIDS Care* 12: 5–26.

Semple, Shirley J., Thomas L. Patterson, and Igor Grant. 2000. Partner type and sexual risk behavior among HIV positive gay and bisexual men: Social cognitive correlates. *AIDS Education and Prevention* 12: 340–56.

Siska, Michael, Janine Jason, Paul Murdoch, Wen Shan Yang, and Robert J. Donovan. 1992. Recall of AIDS public service announcements and their impact on the ranking of AIDS as a national problem. *American Journal of Public Health* 82: 1029–32.

Stall, Ronald D., Jay P. Paul, Donald C. Barrett, G. Michael Crosby, and Edward Bein. 1999. An outcome evaluation to measure changes in sexual risk-taking among gay men undergoing substance use disorder treatment. *Journal of Studies on Alcohol* 60: 837–45.

Toro-Alfonso, José, Nelson Varas-Díaz, and Iván Andújar-Bello. 2002. Evaluation of an HIV/AIDS prevention intervention targeting Latino gay men and men who have sex with men in Puerto Rico. *AIDS Education and Prevention* 14: 445–56.

Valdiserri, Ronald O., David W. Lyter, Laura C. Leviton, Catherine M. Callahan, Lawrence A. Kingsley, and Charles R. Rinaldo. 1989. AIDS prevention in homosexual and bisexual men: Results of a randomized trial evaluating two risk reduction interventions. *AIDS* 3: 21–26.

Valleroy, Linda A., Duncan A. MacKellar, John M. Karon, Daniel H. Rosen, William McFarland, Douglas A. Shehan, Susan R. Stoyanoff, Marlene LaLota, David D. Celentano, Beryl A. Koblin, Hanne Thiede, Mitchell H. Katz, Lucia V. Torian, Robert S. Janssen, and the Young Men's Survey Study Group. 2000. HIV prevalence and associated risks in young men who have sex with men. *Journal of the American Medical Association* 284(2): 198–204.

Van de Ven, Paul, and Peter Aggleton. 1999. What constitutes evidence in HIV/AIDS education? *Health Education Research* 14: 461–71.

Van de Ven, Paul, Danielle Campbell, Susan Kippax, Garrett Prestage, June Crawford, Don Baxter, and David Cooper. 1997. Factors associated with unprotected anal intercourse in gay men's casual partnerships in Sydney, Australia. *AIDS Care* 9: 637–49.

Van de Ven, Paul, Susan Kippax, June Crawford, Patrick Rawstorne, Garrett Prestage, Andrew Grulich, and Dean Murphy. 2002. In a minority of gay men, sexual risk practice indicates strategic positioning for perceived risk reduction rather than unbridled sex. *AIDS Care* 14: 471–80.

Van de Ven, Paul, Patrick Rawstorne, June Crawford, and Susan Kippax. 2002. Increasing proportions of Australian gay and homosexually active men engage in unprotected anal intercourse with regular and with casual partners. *AIDS Care* 14: 335–41.

Visser, Adriaan, and Michael Antoni. 1994. Current perspectives on AIDS/HIV education and counseling. *Patient Education and Counseling* 24: 191–98.

Waldo, Craig R., Ronald D. Stall, and Thomas J. Coates. 2000. Is offering post-exposure prevention for sexual exposures to HIV related to sexual risk behavior in gay men? *AIDS* 14: 1035–39.

Winkelstein, Warren, M. Samuel, N. S. Padian, J. A. Wiley, W. Lang, R. E. Anderson, and J. A. Levy. 1987. The San Francisco Men's Health Study: III. Reduction in human immunodeficiency virus transmission among homosexual/bisexual men, 1982–1986. *American Journal of Public Health* 76(9): 685–89.

Woods, Diana R., David Davis, and Boni J. Westover. 1991. "America Responds to AIDS": Its content, development process, and outcome. *Public Health Reports* 106: 616–22.

Wulfert, Edelgard, Choi K. Wan, and Cheryl A. Backus. 1996. Gay men's safer sex behavior: An integration of three models. *Journal of Behavioral Medicine* 19: 345–66.

12

Substance, Kinship, and the Meaning of Unprotected Sex among Gay Men in Australia

SEAN SLAVIN AND JEANNE ELLARD

That some gay men continue to have unprotected anal sex in the context of the HIV epidemic represents on ongoing challenge for HIV prevention efforts. In recent years, explanations have been more keenly sought than ever. In Australia, North America, and Europe, various studies have monitored increases in both unprotected sex and HIV incidence among gay men (Calzavara et al. 2002; Dukers et al. 2002; Elford et al. 2002; Hull et al. 2003; Katz et al. 2002; NCHSR 2003). One way this issue has developed in public discussion has been through the phenomenon of "barebacking," a practice that is invariably invoked as risky. *Poz Magazine*, a national U.S. periodical for HIV-positive people, first publicized the term in 1997 to describe unprotected sex between HIV-positive men (Gendin 1997). This article has since become notorious, not least for the breathless quality of its prose and the heated exchange of views it engendered in many Western gay media and communities.

Barebacking has since become a common term that extends from everyday use to some social research. Almost immediately, however, it shifted from its original, quite specific meaning to generally refer to all unprotected anal intercourse. In the United States, this has sometimes included discussions of "bug chasing" and "gift giving," two terms that describe the deliberate transmission of HIV from an infected to an uninfected person. Much of this discussion has failed to acknowledge that some men sometimes negotiate unprotected sex in ways that are relatively safe, and have been doing so right throughout the epidemic. These public discussions have a corollary in various social research projects, where investigators have sought to develop explanations for unprotected sex, usually relying on cognitive behavioral models that suggest men who engage in such practice are ipso facto irrational (e.g., Gold and Skinner 1992; Kalichman 1999; Kalichman et al. 2003). While such research invariably concludes that cognitive behavioral interventions are effective in changing behavior, they do little to improve an understanding of the meanings of unprotected sex to those who engage in it.

This chapter discusses cultural meanings of unprotected sex among gay men in relation to dominant ideals of romantic love and unity, embedded within and suffused through Western forms of relationships, including such kinship categories as marriage and the family. Sexual relationships are social and cultural relationships, which may give rise to the risk of HIV. The meaning of these relationships and the potential risk of HIV will be explored through an analysis that includes an understanding of larger cultural systems—in this case, kinship—and the bearing these have on individual lives. In doing so, the analysis challenges the view that the practice of unprotected sex arises from individual pathology.

Like heterosexual people in Western societies, gay men are deeply involved in cultural systems of kinship. Gay men both produce kinship relationships and are produced by them. In the first instance, they are sons and brothers. In the second, they are often sexual and/or relational partners and sometimes fathers. In recent years, there has been considerable debate about how gay relationships should be symbolized—for instance, the widespread interest in the Western Anglophone world in whether the institution of legal marriage should be extended to gay men and lesbians, the extent to which gay couples should be regarded as fit and proper parents, and more generally whether gay people can or should make families (Borneman and Hart 2004; Wakeling and Bradstock 1995; Weeks et al. 2001; Weston 1991). While this debate has largely centered on symbolic and legal rights, new relationships to technology and biology, such as offered by assisted reproductive technologies, continue to produce possibilities for different kinds of kinship and indeed different kinds of humans that may be progressive for a diverse range of people and relationships not culturally regarded as "normal" (Haraway 1991; Strathern 1992, 1997a).[1]

While much recent intellectual and political attention has been given to "alternative" family making, less attention has been devoted to the effects on gay men and their relationships from participating in a cultural system that arguably excludes them but from which they cannot entirely escape. How, for instance, do gay men's sexual practices intersect with dominant meanings of romantic love, unity, and relatedness embedded in Western expressions and understandings of kinship? It is our contention that gay men do engage these symbols, often in different forms, but not necessarily always with different meanings.

Our discussion draws on narratives collected in interviews with gay men living in three Australian cities: Sydney, Melbourne, and Perth. Some of these interviews involved one-to-one discussions with men who had recently acquired HIV infection and concerned the incident that they believed led to their infection and their sexual practices more generally. Other interviews explored meanings of unprotected sex among HIV-positive and HIV-negative men one-to-one and in focus groups. The vast majority of men in the sample stem from Anglo-Saxon or Anglo-Celtic backgrounds, as do all the men quoted. This necessarily places a caveat on the extent to which the discussion can be generalized to other ethnic or cultural traditions within Australia or other Western societies.[2]

The anthropologist David Schneider (1968) identified that in American culture, blood and law define American kinship.[3] Relations of blood, according to Schneider, are formulated in concrete, biogenetic terms, which are regarded as natural. Further, blood relations are not chosen; they are "facts of nature." Relations of law are established through practices such as marriage and adoption. They are chosen and legitimized through social and legal sanction (Schneider 1968).

Schneider argues that sexual intercourse is the preeminent figure on which the cultural system of American kinship turns. It defines family members as relatives, distinguishes the family as the fundamental kinship unit, and marks it as natural. Both relations of blood and law are symbolized, in the context of the family, by love of two kinds. Cognatic, or non-sexual, love characterizes blood relations between parents and children and among siblings. Conjugal, or erotic, love characterizes the law relation between husband and wife, for whom sexual intercourse is also "making love": "It is the symbol of love which links conjugal and cognatic love together and relates them both to and through the symbol of sexual intercourse. Love in the sense of sexual intercourse is a natural act with natural consequences according to its cultural definition. And love in the sense of sexual intercourse at the same time stands for unity" (Schneider 1968: 39).

Thus, sexual intercourse, in the context of marriage, invokes both blood and law. It occurs within a legally sanctioned relationship, and it leads to progeny. A key concept employed by Schneider to evoke the ambiguity and multiplicity of the connections between blood and law that are both material (for example, genes) and social (for example, nurture) is that of "substance."

"Substance" is an important term for Schneider and anthropologists interested in kinship who have followed him. Just as in everyday English, it

carries manifold meanings and associations and can be frustratingly ambiguous.[1] First, substance is material. It can indicate bodily substances such
as saliva, sweat, and sperm, or it can refer to genes. Common genetic material is what is meant in Western kinship by shared blood. As genes cannot
be seen with the naked eye and in any case were only discovered in the
nineteenth century, blood also carries a second meaning. It metaphorically
alludes to the fundamental "nature" of the family and its members, the underlying connection that constitutes the family (Carsten 2004). Thus, for
Schneider (1968), blood involves substance and implies a particular social
relationship or code for conduct. The last point to be made about substance
is that it alludes to what is fundamental about people. A person of substance
is one of integrity, not swayed by fashion or whim. This kind of substance
in people is believed to be deep and immutable, representing a core truth
about who they are. In this chapter, we use substance both as a concept and
a way of talking about material such as semen and DNA. Among the men
we interviewed and in Western culture generally, substance is both. Just as
bodily fluid cannot be separated from cultural meaning (Douglas 1966),
there is no conceptual substance that does not also invoke material bodies
and things.

The other key term in Western kinship identified by Schneider is "love."
This he characterizes as a kind of relationship within the context of the
family as "enduring, diffuse solidarity." It is "enduring" in the sense that
it is meant to last; a blood relationship cannot be terminated, and the law
relationship of marriage is supposed to "endure and preserve, until death
do us part." Love is "diffuse" in that it is not instrumental, not tied to any
specific goal. Further, love relations are based on solidarity because they are
"supportive, helpful, and cooperative" (Schneider 1968: 52).

This portrait of kinship is, for our purposes, an ideal type, not a description of empirical reality or, as Schneider would have it, an overarching system of symbolic meaning that more or less determines practice. We are not
arguing that gay men are simply a variation to heterosexuals or, as Schneider would argue, that forms of variance at the level of everyday practice
do not alter culture, that indeed culture "envelops and imposes its forms"
on gay and lesbian individuals (Schneider 1997: 273). We do not agree with
Schneider's view of culture as an abstract domain, distinct from practice and
history (Gutiérrez 1997; Yanagisako 1978; Yanagisako and Delaney 1995).

We are, however, interested in some of the cultural meanings of love,
family, and substance Schneider identifies and the way they influence the
relationship practices of gay men. We find them useful as a description of

some of the normative roles and hegemonic cultural symbols within Western kinship that, to a greater or lesser extent, influence the ways in which Western people understand themselves in the contexts of their significant relationships. This seems obvious enough when thinking about nuclear families based on heterosexual marriage and reproduction, but less obvious when thinking about gay men's sexual and emotional relationships. Schneider's model has a tendency to produce particular kinship forms as universal across Western culture, something we want to avoid, while also acknowledging their seeming ubiquity. While many gay men and lesbians do contest dominant kinship ideals, their practice—the everyday conduct of their lives and relationships—to some extent occurs in relation to these dominant discourses. This is explicit when gay men and lesbians attempt to create "alternative" families, or implicit in the narratives to be presented here that speak to issues of sex, love, HIV, and unprotected sex.[4]

According to Schneider (1968), (hetero)sexual intercourse symbolizes unity. The following comments from Luke (all names of informants are pseudonyms) both speak to an understanding of sexual intercourse as unity and reveal the inherent contradictions in a representation of sexual intercourse as symbolic of unity. In the following statements, he talks about the feeling of unprotected sex:

> I can close my eyes and imagine it's meant as much to them as it has to me, that the love was there. I wasn't just doing it for a fuck. That something was going on between the two of us, something special.

At one level, unity is an imaginative or intellectual act; at another, it is bodily. In Luke's case, it is not just sexual intercourse but sex without condoms that symbolizes unity. He goes on to make a distinction between sex without condoms and sex with condoms:

> If I'm in a relationship with someone and we've been together for six months or so then okay, we'll have unprotected anal sex. We won't have safe sex. I need to be sure that person knows who I am, that they've been faithful to me, and I suppose if I *really* like them I'll just do it.

For Luke, unprotected sex symbolizes commitment, monogamy, love, and desire for "endurance." Sex without condoms is understood and experienced by him as an expression of love as opposed to sex with condoms that is more guarded and, for him, lacks both the material and symbolic potential for unity. Love, he believes, is a spiritual act that transcends the material expression of sex and at the same time symbolizes unity. This unity works here in at least three ways. First, it is expressed as a discourse of romance that is not peculiar to gay men. Second, there are specific cultural meanings and practices that are particular to gay men and the ways they conduct relationships. And third, there are two bodies, in this instance both male. For Schneider, sexual intercourse is a practice and a symbol that works through all these levels: "As a symbol of unity, or oneness, love is the union of the flesh, of opposites, male and female, a man and a woman. The unity of opposites is not only affirmed in the embrace, but also in the outcome of that union, the unity of blood, the child. . . . Both love and sex turn on two distinct elements. One is the unification of opposites. The other is the separation of unities" (Schneider 1968: 39).[5]

This schema relies on the notion of complementary opposites joined in the union of marriage and love. Regardless of whether it is reasonable or accurate to describe men and women as opposite, this is a powerful metaphor of heterosexual love and attraction that alludes to figures of speech such as "opposites attract" and the couple as "two halves that make a whole." If this were so, it follows that sexual relations between men must be fundamentally different. Gay men negotiate difference in the context of their sexual relations insofar as they are discrete persons. Difference is not necessarily symbolized as an opposition based on gender. Some other explicit ways that gay men symbolize difference binomially include top-bottom, dominant-passive, boy-man, and master-slave, categories not commensurate with male and female (Bersani 1995; Butler 1990, 1997; Halperin 1995; Sedgwick 1994). Furthermore, to assume that male-to-male relations are based on sameness would be to crudely privilege a categorical notion of biological sex above a plethora of cultural symbols that render difference at individual and interpersonal levels.[6]

This fact calls into question the basis of Schneider's view of unity as preceded by gender opposition or difference. We suggest instead that the discreteness of persons is more fundamental to the desire for unity. This desire is a powerful figure of speech in many of our narratives, one that is played out at the levels of discourse, cultural practice, and bodies. In this regard, gay men are not substantially different from heterosexuals; rather, the effects are different. The normative pursuit of unity in heterosexual couples leads to marriage and conjugal relations involving the transmission of substance. This transmission then leads to the production of shared substance in the form of children. For gay men, striving at unity through substance potentially leads to HIV infection. The following informant makes this explicit:

> I feel that it's being part of you, having a part of them inside you, and you've got to work for it and you can have part of them inside you, then you can walk around all day with part of them inside you. It turns me on. I'll give you an example. When I was in a relationship with my boyfriend, we'd have sex in the morning and so he'd fuck me, okay, and he came inside me and all the rest of the day, I'd go off to work and do whatever I do, and one minute at work I'll just think, hey I've still got part of his semen inside me. I think, you know, there's a part of him inside me and that's, um, special and I think having a condom cheapens it. (Josh)

In this case, unprotected sex literally allows the transmission of substance. While in these circumstances sperm cannot produce shared substance in the form of progeny, it can nonetheless preserve this symbolic possibility. For Josh, semen is here symbolic of his partner, a part of his body, and his substance in the sense of his self. Substance is thus much more than an eroticized body fluid. It symbolizes the partner's self in both a biological and spiritual sense, that thing that melds in the unity-creating act of sex and is symbolized by love. The interviewer later asked him what he meant by the condom "cheapening" this experience, and he responded that it made the sex "mechanical" and "emotionless," thereby implying that sex without a condom is both emotional and possibly organic or natural. Paradoxically, sex with love is also regarded as work, echoing a distinction between the serious and arduous business of procreation and the frivolous nature of sex for pleasure. For this man, sexual love is profoundly linked to the sharing of substance, which is literally semen and is symbolically his partner.[7] The removal of condoms in this context looks like an example of "enduring, diffuse solidarity."

Similar ideas around substance, unity, love, and unprotected sex exist within many of the narratives that inform this chapter. The following quote comes from a man who is trying to make sense of why and how he became infected with HIV and explicitly refers to a gendered model of courtship and reproduction, rendering aspects of his own behavior as feminine and heterosexual:

> Most of my friends in Sydney have got it [HIV], and they're all ten years older than me. . . . And it's sort of like the young woman syndrome,

which wants to get pregnant to catch the man. That's sort of what it was like for me. It wasn't consciously wanting to try and capture him by getting positive, but looking back I was so much in love with him and still am. I want to, like, prove how much I loved him by pushing myself that little bit further and doing whatever he wanted, and if that meant not using a condom for my own health, that's what it took. The whole emotional side just overruled common sense. (Craig)

The explicit connection in this quote with normative heterosexual forms of substance sharing is striking. It evokes romantic love, penetration, and possession. Such a discourse can be read as deploying the cultural symbolics of blood-dependent kinship and the symbolic importance of sharing substance in order to create unity. Alluding again to a distinction between nature and reason, the "emotional side" is contrasted with "common sense." This tension, as Craig describes it, further reveals the importance of biological and social reproduction as a cultural mechanism for binding together sexual partners.

Similar expressions of possession, containment, and unity are present in the following comments from an HIV positive man:

For me, it's wanting the two of us to be inside each other, and not just the penis, but totally, conceptually. If I could crawl up totally inside him, I would. It's not the concept of a peak of sexual activities as such, but just getting completely enveloped by someone I really care about. It's hard to do that when there are barriers. I don't mean that in the sense that a condom is a barrier, but physically, emotionally, and conceptually. Escaping into each other. (Richard)
Interviewer: What do you mean by "escaping into each other"?
It's all the pressures and the hassles of day-to-day living. I suppose it is like a sanctuary. It's like a pure pleasure and feeling safe. (Richard)

The absence of a capacity for progeny from the union of two men reveals that even in the context of heterosexual sex, sexual union is not always, and in some cases never, about procreation. This is a further challenge to consider that gay men's desires are not necessarily radically different from normative heterosexual desires. The child, the product of sexual union, is the heterosexual couple's symbol of unity, and the condom is as much a barrier for procreation for them as it is for Richard. Escaping into the other is a desire for unity that receives material expression through sex without barriers. Such desire is perceived by Richard as far from risky. Instead, he says it is "pure," "pleasurable," and "safe." The notion that such intimacy is emotionally safe presents a potential challenge to the notion of "safe sex" as sex with condoms. Unprotected sex between Richard and an HIV-positive partner does not present a transmission risk, but it seems unlikely that the desires expressed here are predicated on, or indeed have anything to do with, a partner's serostatus.

Sex is not the only arena in which love is symbolized through the exchange of substance. Other forms of intimacy in which substances are implicated are salient in our culture. Sharing a bathroom, for example, is commonly regarded as intimate, something that many couples are shy about in the early stages of relationships. The sharing of personal hygiene tools is significant for the following informant in a relationship with an HIV-positive man, a relationship in which he became infected with HIV. Here he is reflecting on his thinking at the beginning of the relationship:

> Yeah, it was a hassle. It got in the way. The man I was in love with, and I couldn't use his toothbrush, his razor. I remember one day I stayed over at his house and I didn't have my toothbrush and Cameron was putting a toothbrush under hot water and I thought: "If I get into a relationship with him and I want to use his toothbrush, I'm not going to sit there sterilizing it and boiling toothbrushes." Like, we shared the same razor, the whole lot. (Justin)

"The whole lot" works much the same way as semen did for men discussed earlier, as substance symbolizing the other. It refers to both razors and toothbrushes but also, in the context of the interview, alludes to HIV itself. It is not that Justin seeks to encounter blood or saliva, but the tools are intimately connected with and imply these things—their significance rests upon this association. These bodily substances, while different in important respects from each other and semen, are nevertheless symbolically similar, in this context, insofar as they relate to the self, intimacy, and desire. Thus, in a slightly different way to the previously discussed men, Justin sees HIV as an unwelcomed barrier to bodily intimacy, which is both symbolized and materialized by the sharing of razors and toothbrushes. Indeed, the sharing of these implements represented a sort of refusal to allow HIV to function as the preeminent symbol of difference between them, the thing that keeps them apart, preventing unity.

The previous quotes have focused on meaning in the context of regular relationships. What, then, of casual sex, which features in the accounts of gay men who are in or not in regular relationships? Gay men in these studies did speak about the meaning of unprotected sex and intimacy in the context of casual sex. While love is not very common in such narratives, intimacy, or the desire for it, is relatively common. It suggests that although casual sex is often culturally understood to be in opposition to committed relationships such as marriage, certain ideas about intimacy pervade both casual sex and committed relationships. By looking at casual sex, we see some of the ways in which attempts to reserve love to regular relationships and to separate sex from love run counter to powerful cultural norms that insist on a bond between the two. The following man talks about the confusion he experienced in seeking intimacy in a casual, anonymous setting. Such confusion led to unprotected sex for him on a number of occasions:

> I was walking around the Den [a sex club in Sydney]. It was midweek. I went out looking for sex. I felt emotionally starved. Like there was this hole inside me that was so undernourished. I just wasn't getting any love, any intimacy, any passion. I just started to cry. It was always clear I was going there for sex, but I would never give myself parameters. (Mark)

Mark first combines and then tries to separate love and sex. At the outset, he says that he saw sex as a solution to feeling emotionally starved, which in turn is described as a kind of emptiness. Sex clubs are probably not the best environments in which to confuse love and sex, but at the same time their success turns, to some extent, on the fact that they are liminal (that is, culturally ambiguous) spaces where one cannot help mixing a range of emotions and behaviors in order to signify various kinds of sexual interests. Sex is rarely ever purely "mechanical" and less so in such venues where ambiguity is often prized. As with the other men quoted above, emotion is implicitly contrasted with reason. Mark attempts to demarcate the two by recognizing that he had failed to give himself "parameters" that allowed him to distinguish between his sexual and emotional desires. He believes that sex can be, and sometimes should be, mechanical, so as to protect himself from emotional distress and the risk of HIV.

Schneider (1968) emphasizes that biology is believed to explain kinship in the West. Kinship practices are regarded as natural rather than cultural. Many of the men in these studies use naturalness as a metaphor for sex without condoms, which are regarded as technical interruptions. If indeed safer sex is enabled by technology, and by implication reason, while sex without condoms is seen as natural, emotionally fulfilling, and perhaps irrational, then the depth of the cultural tensions that these gay men negotiate in their sexual relationships begins to be apparent.

In the case of Mark, the liminality of the sex club mirrors the indeterminacy he feels about his own desire. The distress he feels as a result of the mixing of emotions, which he understands at a cultural level to be inappropriate in this context, reveals a certain awareness of his own confusion over the meaning of sex and perhaps even love. He wants sex to symbolize love, but in the context of a sex club this meaning is refused. It is easy to see how sex and love without "parameters" become intertwined or even confused in ways that may lead to HIV infection. In this, casual sex resonates with aspects of regular or relationship-based sex.

The following informant, Adam, presents a variation to the theoretical framing of love as the keystone of sexual meaning. Indeed, at some level he seems successful at separating sex and love. He talks directly about semen as a symbolic substance but does so with a different emphasis. He became infected with HIV outside his regular relationship by a sexual partner he met on the Internet. He talks about having had a "fascination with barebacking," both on the Internet and in pornography, but he believed at the time, for various reasons, that the sexual partner who infected him was HIV negative, or at least believed himself to have been HIV negative. Adam says he was not looking for emotional fulfillment outside of his relationship, but rather a certain kind of sexual experience:

> Interviewer: Can you try and unpack what that was about? That "fascination with barebacking"?
> Um. I suppose it was just that, well, just the whole sexual act, or the exchange of fluids, I suppose. (Adam)
> Interviewer: What is it, do you think, about exchanging fluids?
> It's the exchange of taking someone else's, like being there, that whole mentality of being the passive, being dominated, and being there just for someone to deposit something. Maybe it's my female side coming through? With the boyfriends that I've had or the boyfriends that I've been with in the long term, we've had a very good sex life, but in sex the aim has always been to ejaculate inside. With my partner, I suppose that's where I felt safest in the past, is with partners who've done that. It's only really in the last few years that I've started to do things outside a relationship which has, of course, resulted in HIV. (Adam)
> Interviewer: With your partner, what is the kind of sex that you have with him?

I love him dearly, and I couldn't imagine not being with him, but the sex is not as intense as I would probably like or as, um, wild. I wouldn't say that he is . . . I mean, I'm very good at separating sex from love, like I know I love him to death, and I couldn't imagine being with anyone else. But I fear that because the sex is not [as intense as I would like] . . . I fear that that will be the end of us, but I don't want it to be. I think that's probably why I explore other areas, or have. Because at the moment, because of the diagnosis, . . . he's not really that good. Yeah, he's not, in some ways, I think he's more a bottom than a top. (Adam)

Interviewer: Right, and that's not entirely the right combo?

Yeah, but I know he likes being a top, but I think in reality, if really given a chance he would be more of a bottom. So it's quite frustrating [with] two bottoms being together. (Adam)

Adam makes a distinction between his regular relationship, which is based on love, and casual sex outside the relationship, which is based entirely on sex. This is a relatively common distinction made by people in sexually open relationships and is usually designed to protect the domestic sphere from the perceived threat of external emotional involvement.

Semen has been a symbol of love for Adam in the context of relationships, but it has a different meaning in the context of casual sex. As with Josh, some of the metaphors he uses to describe his fascination with unprotected sex are economic ones: the "exchange" of fluids and a "deposit" of semen. This recalls other examples of semen transactions, most notably among Sambia male adolescents and bachelors, suggesting that semen, for Adam, is a symbol of male potency (Herdt 1984). For Adam, to be dominated implies sexual satisfaction and fulfillment reaching a glorified status in ejaculation and the "exchange" of semen from his sexual partner into himself. This is not about the transfer of masculine potency to him in such a way that it enhances his masculinity (as with the Sambia of New Guinea). He understands this experience through a heteronormative framework in which he identifies with a female gender and sex role, since he equates sexual passivity with his "female side." This is fixed as an aspect of his self, rather than a stage through which he might pass, for instance, if he was participating in a ritual.

Superficially, this seems to support Schneider's view that the complementary opposition of female and male is the most salient opposition in

Western kinship. While Adam borrows this metaphor, his practice similarly undoes it. The figure of "opposites" is widespread in the context of Western sexual relations: "opposites attract." To recapitulate, sexual opposition is not necessarily grounded in gender, and for gay men it cannot be grounded in biological sexual difference. Tops and bottoms are not simply equivalent to men and women (understood as gender—a social category), much less biological males and females.

This helps to make sense of the tension Adam feels in relation to his regular partner, whom he characterizes as "really a bottom," like him. This is not a comment about the content of their sexual practice, or their sexual organs, but rather about his partner's disposition, his self-hood. Adam, in seeking sex beyond the relationship, explicitly sought opposition in the form of a person who is a dominant top to his being a passive bottom. For Adam, his regular relationship is described without ambivalence as loving but also as safe and mundane: love that goes on "to death." Adam's pursuit of the erotic leads to a partial displacement of sex from the domestic sphere to a more exciting but nonetheless romantic space positioned as wild and dangerous. Adam expressly wonders whether this will be "the end" of his relationship, indeed whether a loving partnership can be sustained in the light of what he regards as sexual incompatibility, thus revealing that sex and love for him are not—and, perhaps, never—separated in a definitive way.

Both Adam's and Craig's narratives raise the challenging question of whether the concept of substance should be extended to include HIV itself. It is worth considering that most men in these studies who were HIV positive did not make a link between the biogenetic substance of the virus itself inside their bodies and its substance inside the sexual partner who infected them. They did not understand the virus inside them as having any particular genetic identity, as persons do. Rather, it was generic. Relationships that did involve sharing bodily substances such as semen were commonly characterized by love or intimacy. For Adam, once he became infected, he e-mailed the casual sexual partner to inform him of his serostatus, but had no further contact with him. HIV was not a known feature of that sexual relationship in the first instance. He believed his sexual partner was HIV negative. He made sense of this by saying:

The AIDS epidemic existed basically all my adult life, because when it started I was fifteen. So I suppose, I just was getting slack. And I suppose I regret that now, but that's the decision I made and it's a risk

I took and that's why I don't . . . really, have any feelings towards the guy that gave it to me, or I don't have any anger towards him because I really accept the risk I took.

This statement reflects a common tendency of HIV-positive men in these studies to hold themselves individually responsible for what had happened to them. The discourse of risk that Adam draws on is tightly woven with a confident belief in the extent of his knowledge about HIV and the means to prevent it. Such knowledge implies choice for him, and the consequences of such a choice suggest individual responsibility. By virtue of it being infectious and its general salience, HIV infection is a symbolic possibility in most sexual relationships for most Western gay men. Despite the fact that HIV is transmitted sexually, these men experience it individually. By and large, they blame themselves. For Adam, as for many others, both no one is to blame, in the sense that it was bad luck, and only he is to blame, in the sense that he is responsible for the risk he took.

Craig's case is different insofar as he suggests that HIV does symbolize "substance." He talks about all of his friends having HIV. By drawing attention to this dimension of his social world he reveals that, for him, HIV is a kind of identity, which he imagines himself as able to occupy. This social space works to allow the possibility that getting HIV from his partner can be an expression of love *and* the entry into a certain social identity, that of the devoted partner who has changed himself at a fundamental biological level for the sake of love. His explicit comparison with pregnancy is thus culturally apt.

The narratives described in this chapter suggest that the practice of unprotected sex between gay men is commensurate with dominant cultural forms and ways of understanding intimacy. While the exchange of "substance" as a symbol of intimacy is consistent with and intelligible through Western kinship forms, HIV poses a particular problem that makes such literal practice potentially dangerous. It is doubtful that "blood" or "substance" will ever lack symbolic power. However, it is worth engaging a number of strategies that question their hegemonic position as the "natural order." By questioning what is regarded as natural opens up the possibility that "nature's way" may become less compelling and other forms of sexual practice, perhaps hitherto regarded as "unnatural," may become pleasurable and meaningful. Many of the men in this study implicitly regard condoms as "unnatural," leading to HIV exposure for some. Other "unnatural" acts that do not involve semen exchange might include kissing, sucking, and fisting (hand insertion into the anus). Just as assisted reproductive technologies are revealing that the relationship between kinship and nature is not entirely obvious or necessary, normative forms of love, romance, and kinship, or for that matter HIV, need not govern gay men's sexual practice.

Gay men deploy heteronormative forms of language and practice as a way to make sense of their desires and their lives in social and cultural settings where they are offered few alternatives. That they engage with and understand themselves through often conservative, gendered kinship systems is therefore not surprising. The material presented here reveals a particularly pernicious effect of such engagement. This lends greater impetus to the ongoing struggle to create more open and diverse possibilities for all intimate human relations.

Acknowledgments

Versions of this chapter were presented in 2003 at the HIV Center in Clinical and Behavioral Studies at the New York Psychiatric Institute and Columbia University, and the 102nd meeting of the American Anthropological Association. We warmly thank the audiences at both forums for their insightful and generous questions. Thanks in particular to Gary Dowsett for his extensive comments and Liam Leonard for his critical engagement. Data presented in this paper derive from two projects. The first, "A Study of Risk Factors Associated with HIV Infection," is a collaborative project of the National Centre in HIV Social Research, the National Centre in HIV Epidemiology and Clinical Research, University of New South Wales, and the Australian Research Centre in Sex Health and Society, La Trobe University. It is funded by the Commonwealth Department of Health and Ageing and the Department of Human Services, Victoria. The second, the "Sex Culture Project," was a study by the National Centre in HIV Social Research, University of New South Wales, funded by the Commonwealth Department of Health and Ageing.

Notes

1. For an extensive discussion of the complexities of substance, including Strathern's use of the term, see Carsten (2004).

2. All interviews were audiotape recorded, transcribed, and de-identified.

3. For the purposes of this discussion of Australian gay men, we accept Schneider's description of American kinship as also applying to Western culture more broadly.

4. While we agree with Schneider's view on this issue as expressed in 1997 that much gay and lesbian kinship practice does display an orientation to hegemonic cultural discourse, we differ insofar as we do not regard this as simply inevitable. Indeed, as Strathern (1997b) writes in the same issue of *Cultural Anthropology*, whether one stresses the power of the dominant cultural forms in shaping individual lives or the vitality of practice in creating new forms, it is a political choice. We choose the latter while remaining interested in the descriptive possibilities offered by the former.

5. This notion of opposites is a key element of Schneider's theoretical formalism. It is one that he uses to explain what he regards as the cultural fulcrum of Western kinship, the heterosexual couple. This is articulation between the orders of "blood" and law. Schneider later suggested that this dyad is mirrored in the opposition of "homosexual" and heterosexual (1997). While we again dispute this theoretical point on the grounds that it obscures the complexities of practice, we nonetheless find it a suggestive metaphor for understanding the meaning that many Western people bring to some forms of desire.

6. Martin's (1991) groundbreaking critique of the gendered cultural values inherent in the science of human reproduction is a different but equally apt approach to this question.

7. This echoes the small but interesting body of work that has concentrated on the meaning of semen in the context of assisted reproduction. See Kirkman (2004) and Tober (2001).

References

Bersani, Leo. 1995. *Homos*. Cambridge, Mass.: Harvard University Press.

Borneman, John, and Laurie Kain Hart. 2004. An elastic institution. *Washington Post*, April 14.

Butler, Judith. 1990. *Gender Trouble: Feminism and the Subversion of Identity*. New York: Routledge.

———. 1997. *The Psychic Life of Power: Theories in Subjection*. Stanford, Calif.: Stanford University Press.

Calzavara, L., A. N. Burchell, C. Major, R. S. Remis, P. Corey, T. Myers, P. Millson, and E. Wallace. 2002. Increases in HIV incidence among men who have sex with men undergoing repeat diagnostic HIV testing in Ontario, Canada. *AIDS* 16: 1655–661.

Carsten, Janet. 2004. *After Kinship*. Cambridge: Cambridge University Press.

Douglas, Mary. 1966. *Purity and Danger: An Analysis of the Concepts of Pollution and Taboo*. London: Routledge and Kegan Paul.

Dukers, N., J. Spaargaren, R. B. Geskus, J. Beijnen, R. A. Coutinho, and H. S. A. Fennema. 2002. HIV incidence on the increase among homosexual men attending an Amsterdam sexually transmitted disease clinic: Using a novel approach for detecting recent infections. *AIDS* 16: F19–24.

Elford, J., G. Bolding, and L. Sherr. 2002. High-risk sexual behaviour increases among London gay men between 1998 and 2001: What is the role of HIV optimism? *AIDS* 16: 1537–544.

Gendin, Stephen. 1997. Riding bareback. *Poz Magazine*, June.

Gold, Ron S., and Michael J. Skinner. 1992. Situational factors and thought processes associated with unprotected intercourse in young gay men. *AIDS* 6: 1021–30.

Gutiérrez, Ramon A. 1997. Response to Schneider's "The Power of Culture." *Cultural Anthropology* 12(2): 278–81.

Halperin, David M. 1995. *Saint Foucault: Towards a Gay Hagiography*. New York: Oxford University Press.

Haraway, Donna. 1991. *Simians, Cyborgs and Women: The Reinvention of Nature*. London: Free Association.

Herdt, Gilbert H. 1984. Semen transactions in Sambia culture. In *Ritualized Homosexuality in Melanesia*, ed. G. H. Herdt, 167–210. Berkeley: University of California Press.

Hull, P., P. Van de Ven, G. Prestage, P. Rawstorne, A. Grulich, J. Crawford, S. Kippax, D. Madeddu, D. McGuigan, and A. Nicholas. 2003. *Gay Community Periodic Survey: Sydney 1996–2002*. Sydney: National Centre in HIV Social Research, University of New South Wales.

Kalichman, S. C. 1999. Psychological and social correlates of high-risk sexual behaviour among men and women living with HIV/AIDS. *AIDS Care* 11(4): 415–28.

Kalichman, S. C., D. Cain, A. Zweben, and G. Swain. 2003. Sensation seeking, alcohol use and sexual risk behaviors among men receiving services at a clinic for sexually transmitted infections. *Journal of Studies on Alcohol* 64(4): 564–69.

Katz, M. H., S. K. Schwarcz, T. A. Kellogg, J. D. Klausner, J. W. Dilley, S. Gibson, and W. McFarland. 2002. Impact of highly active antiretroviral treatment on HIV seroincidence among men who have sex with men: San Francisco. *American Journal of Public Health* 92(3): 388–94.

Kirkman, Maggie. 2004. Saviours and satyrs: Ambivalence in narrative meanings of sperm provision. *Culture, Health and Sexuality* 6(4): 319–34.

Martin, Emily. 1991. The egg and the sperm: How science has constructed a romance based on stereotypical male-female roles. *Signs* 16(3): 485–501.

National Centre in HIV Social Research (NCHSR). 2003. *HIV/AIDS, Hepatitis C and Related Diseases in Australia: Annual Report of Behaviour*. Sydney: University of New South Wales.

Schneider, David Murray. 1968 [1980]. *American Kinship: A Cultural Account*. Englewood Cliffs, N.J.: Prentice-Hall.

———. 1997. The Power of culture: Notes on some aspects of gay and lesbian kinship in America today. *Cultural Anthropology* 12(2): 270–74.

Sedgwick, Eve Kosofsky. 1994. *Epistemology of the Closet*. London: Penguin, 1994.

Strathern, Marilyn. 1992. *After Nature: English Kinship in the Late Twentieth Century*. Cambridge: Cambridge University Press.

———. 1997a. Children of choice: Freedom and the new reproduction technologies. *Journal of the Royal Anthropological Institute* 3(2): 409–10.

———. 1997b. Dear David. *Cultural Anthropology* 12(2): 281–82.

Tober, Diane M. 2001. Semen as gift, semen as goods: Reproductive workers and the market in altruism. *Body and Society* 7(2–3): 137–60.

Wakeling, Louise Katherine, and Margaret Bradstock. 1995. *Beyond Blood: Writings on the Lesbian and Gay Family*. Sydney: Blackwattle Press.

Weeks, Jeffrey, Brian Heaphy, and Catherine Donovan. 2001. *Same Sex Intimacies: Families of Choice and Other Life Experiments*. London: Routledge.

Weston, Kath. 1991. *Families We Choose: Lesbians, Gays, Kinship*. New York: Columbia University Press.

Yanagisako, Sylvia Junko. 1978. Variance in American kinship: Implications for cultural analysis. *American Ethnologist* 5(1): 15–29.

Yanagisako, Sylvia Junko, and Carol Lowery Delaney. 1995. Naturalizing power. In *Naturalizing Power*, ed. S. J. Yanagisako and C .L. Delaney, 1–24. New York: Routledge.

13

The Movement That Was Not?

Gay Men and AIDS in Urban Greece, 1950–1993

BRIAN RIEDEL

On March 19, 2003, around 180 activists and other individuals interested in the rights of sexual minorities gathered in an auditorium of the Polytechnic University in Athens, Greece. It was the third in a series of meetings initiated in response to a police raid on a gay bar earlier that February.[1] While such raids were by no means rare, the names of those arrested had appeared in the press, causing one of them to commit suicide while in jail. Also among the activists at the March 19 meeting were members of several AIDS organizations, notably the Greek chapter of ACT UP (AIDS Coalition to Unleash Power) and a group called Synthesis. As the meeting wound to a close and conversations drifted into the corridors, a member of ACT UP was overheard to say: "We're not a gay organization, really."

It was a striking comment, and raises questions about just what the dividing lines might be between organizations, whether drawn through mission statements, historical tendencies in their activities, or through casual comments in corridors. Why was the distinction meaningful? Why would a member of ACT UP want to distinguish the group as not being a gay group? What might it indicate about what counts as a "gay group" for Greek activists? Further, what does it say about modes of cooperation available between organizations whose interests from time to time will intersect over the rights of sexual minorities, regardless of their mission statements? Beyond organizational politics, what might this distinction say about the relationships between gay men and AIDS in Greek culture?

From the outset, AIDS was linked to gay men. Recall the "gay cancer," Gay Related Immune Deficiency (or GRID), and the "four H's": homosexuals, hemophiliacs, Haitians, and heroin users. However, with the global spread of various HIV strains and our increasing medical understanding of the routes of its transmission, those initial links to gay men soon became insufficient to describe the demographic distribution of the viruses. Despite this shift, the power of the initial linkage persists.

Importantly, Greece is no exception to this pattern. According to official statistics from the Center for the Control of Special Diseases (KEEL), the Greek counterpart to the U.S. Centers for Disease Control and Prevention (CDC), in 1998 the category "men who have sex with men" was superseded for the first time (worryingly, by "cases of unknown origin") as the largest fraction of cumulative HIV-positive cases in Greece (KEEL 2002).

It is tempting, then, to interpret the comment "We're not a gay organization, really" in light of this changed atmosphere since the initial days of AIDS. AIDS is clearly everybody's business now, the argument goes, and thus there is a political and demographic point to be made by saying that ACT UP, while not denying that it does have something to do with some gay men, is not "really" (solely? merely? essentially?) a "gay group." That interpretation falls short, however, by leaving uninvestigated the history and texture of AIDS and gay rights organizations in Greece. Specifically, it fails to account for the fact that while gay men have often participated in AIDS service organizations in Greece and continue to do so, the involvement of gay rights activists in AIDS activism is the exception rather than the rule (by the activists' own accounts), even though gay rights activism predates the official appearance of HIV in Greece by six years. In short, while places such as the United States saw organizations like the Gay Men's Health Crisis form in the early days of the disease, Greece never saw the development of a similar organization. Where gay activists took the lead elsewhere, the response to AIDS in Greece came primarily from doctors and women's social work organizations.[2] Why?

Rather than cast this difference as a lack, as merely a form of disorganization among Greek activists, or as a sign of backwardness, this chapter aims to sketch the roots of this difference by presenting certain aspects of the history of AIDS activism and gay rights activism in Greece, and the relationships between them. Through archival work and interviews with current activists in Athens,[3] this chapter argues that the adaptation of activist strategies and arguments regarding AIDS was shaped by a range of partially articulated cultural assumptions about same-sex sexuality. This chapter suggests that those cultural assumptions, rather than fostering institutional connections between gay rights activism and AIDS activism, encouraged a structural divide between various activist endeavors.

The remainder of the chapter thus takes a historical turn, designed to illuminate a specific moment, and is organized chronologically, primarily on the basis of dates significant to gay rights activism and the history of AIDS in Greece. In keeping with the way that so many participants not only temporally frame their stories but also expose their feelings about that time, this chapter presents that chronology in the context of national party politics. Given the sheer size of the Greek state, even if that state is theorized only as an employer widely assumed to be invested in patron-client relations regardless of the politics of the moment (see Spanou 1998), political winds are a significant factor in the conditions of activism, if only because they are perceived to be so.

1950–1977: Visions of Sex Between Men

Throughout the history of the modern Greek state, same-sex acts have been subject to some form of legal control. Up until 1951, same-sex sexuality itself was specified as a criminal offense. However, after the formal end of the Greek Civil War in 1949, the country undertook a broad restructuring. As a result, a new penal code was written in 1950 in which, among other things, same-sex sexuality itself was no longer specifically criminalized (see Doko-umetzidis 1997). Instead, lawmakers appear to have been more interested in specifying under which conditions same-sex acts warranted legal control. Those conditions are listed in Article 347, located in a section of the code that broadly regulates public morals.

Specifically, Article 347 criminalizes any form of sex for pay between men (whether a one-time event or practiced repetitively) and any abuse of a relationship of dependence (economic or otherwise). It also places the age of consent for sex between males at seventeen, while for heterosexual sex the age of consent is fifteen. This article has survived intact to the present day, despite numerous revisions to the penal code as a whole. Further, only male same-sex acts were apparently deemed worthy of control; sex between females receives no mention in the penal code.

While Greece is thus technically among the first states to decriminalize same-sex sexuality per se, this shift ought not to be seen as a sign of any broad social acceptance of same-sex sexuality.[4] Rather, the shift appears to be more about the impact of then contemporary medical theories of sexuality, that same-sex sexuality was more properly a sickness and thus subject to medical, rather than legal, control (see Koukoutsaki 2002). Further, the decriminalization was not undertaken as a separate project, indicating the requisite political will, but occurred within a broad framework of legal and social reform focused primarily on healing a country exhausted from almost a decade of external and internal warfare.

Beyond legal and medical discourses, however, it is important to note that socially and culturally, sexual contact between men was not necessarily seen as indicative of any particular sexual identity inhering to one individual or another. James Faubion's analysis clearly captures the cultural absence of a socially available "sexual identity." As he writes, *omofilofilía*, the word for same-sex sexuality, "had no currency" in everyday spoken Greek prior to the 1980s. He continues, "it seems to have had no actual referent, either" (Faubion 1993: 217). Rather, any instance of sex between men during that time ought to be read through the lens of how the men engaging in this behavior do or do not retain their status as properly masculine. "Behavioral effeminacy has its specifically sexual counterpart in the 'passive' homosexual posture" (Faubion 1993: 222). On the one hand, the relationship of effeminate gender behavior to sexual practices is one of suggestion. The socially observed gender behavior points to the possibility, but not the necessity, of passive, nonmasculine sexual practices. On the other hand, sexual passivity of one man to another is in itself effeminizing. This is not to say that the effeminate man was simply a contemporary gloss for what we might call a "homosexual," however. As Faubion is careful to note, "The effeminate man in Greece, traditionally and still today, is among the most scorned of social subversives. He is not always, and of course should not be, confused with the 'homosexual'" (Faubion 1993: 222).

Thus, Faubion presents us a system where social disgrace or humiliation falls not on a sexual identity, but rather on those men who do not live up to the standards of their gender. The notion of an identity called "the homosexual" does not precisely fit this system. What does circulate socially in this system is gender identity. Among the many ways one might fail to perform the proper standards of manhood is engagement in passive sexual positions. In this way, any male could have sex with another male and not be judged for it, so long as his sexual actions are all "aggressive" or "active." His manhood does not come into question so long as he does not willingly "give up" his masculinity to another by taking a passive part. This emphasis on the centrality of how masculinity is figured runs throughout the ethnographic literature on Greece.[5]

This understanding of male-to-male sex in Greece indicates something of the social structuring of it as well. It suggests that social connections between men were not bound by the idea that sexual contact between them was illicit in and of itself. Further, though we can suppose that there were men whose sexual lives revolved exclusively around other men, we can be certain that exclusivity was by no means a prerequisite for participation in that sexual economy. The only prerequisite was that the workings of that sexual economy, pervasive though they might be, must remain in the realm of the unarticulated common secret. Sex between men was not for social identities, but for private enjoyment. The outlines of this sexual economy can be easily discerned in the autobiographical writings of the celebrated Greek author Kostas Taktsis, especially in his recollections of the years during and just after the fall of the military dictatorship in 1974 (see Taktsis 1989).

1977–1981: The Foundation of a Movement

The euphoric years after the fall of the junta gave an unprecedented mandate to Konstantinos Karamanlis and his governing political party, the center-right New Democracy (ND). By 1977, however, a regression into dictatorship was looking less and less likely, and ND was beginning to lose some of its luster. Although elections were not to be held until 1978, Karamanlis chose to call them a year early, lest electoral sentiment slide even further toward PASOK, the Panhellenic Socialist Movement of Andreas Papandreou. In the year leading up to that 1977 election, the ND government floated a draft law regarding "the prevention of venereal diseases." Reaction to that draft resulted in the founding of the first same-sex movement in Greece.

There are several different versions of the story, but the agreed upon features can be summed up as follows: the draft law sought to control sexually transmitted diseases by giving the police the right to arrest anyone loitering in a public space if the police deemed that they were loitering with the intent to seduce men. Further, the only evidence to be required by the law was a written deposition. In theory, anyone would be able to write a letter to the police, and whomever was charged would be duly arrested. The law was thus seen as a direct threat both to men cruising for sex and to *travestí* (transgendered persons).[6] Some also saw it as a blatant bid for the votes of the petite bourgeoisie.[7] A group of recent university graduates, many of whom had been studying in Italy and France during the junta and who had also witnessed there the workings of gay rights movements, saw the draft law as the perfect moment to begin organizing a gay rights movement in Greece.

That movement was to be called the Greek Homosexual Liberatory Movement, or AKOE by its Greek acronym. The former students attempted to marshal every resource they could, including foreign contacts, the Greek *travestí*, and intellectuals like Loukas Theodorokopoulos and Kostas Taktsis. Regardless of which version of the story you follow from there, the draft law was eventually withdrawn from the Greek parliament, partially as a result of the international pressure that AKOE had been able to muster on the issue. By the spring of 1978, the group had begun publishing a seasonal magazine, *AMFI*, in which it chronicled its achievements. By the early 1980s, the movement would gain enough members to sustain an additional small monthly newspaper, *Lamda*.[8]

Despite the broad support it eventually achieved, the beginnings of AKOE were not entirely smooth. Certain details reveal tensions between the cultural assumptions of "gay liberation" brought by those who were abroad during the junta, and the assumptions at work in the Greek male-to-male sexual economy discussed earlier.

One of those tensions is evident in the way that Taktsis originally responded to the invitation to help start AKOE. He was approached by Andreas Velissaropoulos, who had studied theater direction in Paris. The two had met previously in 1972, at which point they had a discussion of sexuality that Taktsis later wrote about:

> Velissaropoulos insisted that anyone who went to bed with someone of his same sex be called a homophile [*filomófilos*]. If one accepts that, however, and given the social stigma suffered by homophilia [*filomofilía*], it was like denying the right of the majority of men to sleep now and then with another man without necessarily considering themselves a homophile, with all of the negative connotations that word has even for homophiles themselves. (Taktsis 1989: 292)

Taktsis's evaluation of that first meeting with Velissaropoulos thus clearly reflects the sexual economy described by Faubion. Taktsis's personal participation in that economy also clearly played a role in his response to the invitation to help found AKOE. Velissaropoulos's proposal to Taktsis was to transplant the ideas of the French same-sex movement, organizing a joint demonstration with the *travestí* to protest the draft law. Taktsis wrote later of his refusal:

> At that moment, I knew the police would see the protest as a provocation, therefore it shouldn't happen, and I told that to Velissaro-

poulos. Even if those insane girls [*aftes oi treles*] insist on exposing themselves, I told him, I advise you to avoid getting involved at all. Founding AKOE under the skirts of some prostituted *travestí* would be the same as founding the women's movement with the whores on Sokratous street. (Tsarouchas 1995: 227)

It appears Taktsis judged that the seriousness of the movement could not be established if AKOE were founded in concert with the very people who flouted society's rules of gender so brazenly, despite the fact that Taktsis had already for some time been dressing as a woman and working the streets much like the *travestí* he had just disparaged. As argued by Kostas Tsarouchas, a respected figure in the old school of investigative journalism in Greece, these sexual practices were for Taktsis a private fetish, a personal kink, and not an identity as practiced by the *travestí*. Regardless of Tsarouchas's interpretation, Taktsis clearly saw a conflict between, on the one hand, the imported French model of same-sex activism exemplified perhaps by Velissaropoulos's insistence on identifying people as homophiles, and, on the other hand, the cultural assumptions of the Greek sexual and gender economy to which Taktsis, among many others, had so grown accustomed.

Another indication of the tensions at play in the founding of AKOE can be seen in the pages of *AMFI*. When the magazine first came out in 1978, the subtitle read *gia tin apelefthérosi ton omofilófilon* (for the liberation of same-sex persons). Liberation, it would seem, was to be for a class of people, an identity, a specifiable subgroup of people, now no longer homophiles, but "homosexuals." Several issues later, in the summer of 1979, however, the subtitle changed to read *gia tin apelefthérosi tis omofilófilis epithimías* (for the liberation of same-sex desire). Now the object to be liberated was no longer a person or even a type of person, but a desire that could be resident in anyone. The argument remained cogent for some time to come. As late as 1987, the editor at the time, Ghrighoris Vallianatos, saw fit to remind the readers of *AMFI* of the original argument behind the change in subtitle, that the magazine "is interested in every instance of homosexual desire, not only regarding particular people, but for all who might have homosexual desires alongside their heterosexual identity" (Vallianatos 1987: 5).

This early shift in stance—toward the desire itself and away from the specification of the desiring subject—points to a debate between the demand for sexual liberation and the power of the cultural assumptions of the sexual economy that preceded AKOE. The resolution toward "homosexual desire" also points to a platform of radical social reform, from a clearly leftist position, that resonated well at the turn of the 1980s in Greece: everyone has the right to autonomy and self-determination, including what they do with their bodies. That leftist foundation would prove double-edged over the following years.

1981–1983: An Epidemic of Information

In 1981, PASOK turned its 1977 electoral gains into a solid victory, and the government of Andreas Papandreou initially enjoyed enormous power, arguably even more so than ND had enjoyed after the dictatorship. Papandreou used that power to engage in a raft of governmental and social reforms, addressing many of the inequalities around which people had begun to organize in the years of the ND government. The mood politically was of the redress of grievances. Even the Communist Party of Greece was supportive of the changes PASOK was championing. This vibrant sense of political change had some unexpected side effects, one of which was that the government's successes rather abruptly took the momentum away from the social movements of the Left, including AKOE. Indeed, the fast pace of AKOE's initial years began to falter, a shift visible both in the complete lapse in 1981 of the monthly newspaper *Lamda*, and in the ever-lengthening gaps between issues of *AMFI*, which fell from three issues published in 1980 to just one in 1983. As a leftist philosophy floating in a sea of leftist politics, the force of AKOE's message was diluted, and its membership began to wane.

At the same time, another sea change was brewing on the other side of the Atlantic. A mysterious "gay cancer" was beginning to make headlines in the gay press of New York City, and soon across the world. By the end of 1981, the CDC in Atlanta classified the disease as an epidemic called Kaposi's sarcoma and opportunistic infections (KSOI), and some in the medical community began calling it Gay Related Immune Deficiency (GRID). By August 1982, they were promulgating a new name for it—AIDS (Feldman 2006). That same year, Nathan Fain, Larry Kramer, Larry Mass, Paul Popham, Paul Rapoport, and Edmund White officially founded the Gay Men's Health Crisis in New York City.

As these momentous changes swept through the world of gay men in the United States and elsewhere, the events were also reported in Greece. As yet, however, there were no official cases of people with HIV/AIDS in Greece. This lag in time between a media-fueled awareness of the disease and the arrival of the virus has been a foundational point in the social analysis of AIDS in Greece, particularly in the work of Demosthenes Agrafiotis, a sociologist at the Greek National School of Public Health in Athens, and his colleagues. As they write, "information about the disease arrived before the virus itself, and the AIDS epidemic began as an epidemic of information" (Agrafiotis et al. 1999). They document how Greek mass media of the time referred not only to the disease but also to the identification of the disease with so-called high-risk groups, particularly with same-sex men, persons with hemophilia, and injecting drug users.

The argument of the epidemic of information holds not only for the high-circulation mass media of which Agrafiotis and his colleagues write, but also for more specialized outlets like *AMFI*. Despite the ebb in activity in AKOE, the magazine maintained a regular stream of news from abroad, some of which was supplied by Ilias Diakos, corresponding from New York City. In the winter of 1982, his column titled "Kaposi's Sarcoma: 'Our' Cancer, or Their Bullshit?" detailed the discovery that Kaposi's sarcoma had also been found in a number of young Haitian men who identified as straight and who did not report using poppers (inhalant drugs common then among gay men) (see Diakos 1982). Clearly, and certainly through more channels than Diakos alone, AKOE was aware of AIDS significantly before HIV reached Greece.

The significance of the argument of the epidemic of information is that it accounts for how social perceptions of AIDS in Greece found a window of opportunity in which to crystallize and become fairly widespread. Two related arguments could be made for any other locale that experiences the time lag between awareness and arrival of the virus: in any information-saturated society, social panics can occur even before a "disease agent" becomes physically present. At the same time, realistic humanitarian responses can be crafted before the problem becomes serious. This dual potential, opened by knowing about a disease before it strikes, points to the limits of the epidemic of information as an argument. Although it helps us understand how certain categories enter into a list of *potential* associations to AIDS in any given place, it cannot in itself explain why specific attitudes toward AIDS become dominant, among all of the attitudes possible.

Exceptionally, perhaps the one perception in Greece for which the epidemic of information may account, at least initially, is that AIDS is essentially a foreign disease. It was literally happening only elsewhere. That perception gained a foothold during the two-year window from the first signs of AIDS in the United States to the diagnosis of the first official case in Greece. This perception was subsequently bolstered by the details of that first case, a twenty-five-year-old student from Zambia who had arrived in Greece in early 1983. His first symptoms appeared that July, and by November of the same year he had died. His foreignness was the key issue for the media.[9] As the marker of the official entrance of the epidemic into Greece, his story retained immense symbolic value and was recycled in the media for some years thereafter, further reinforcing the foreignness of the disease. Since the student was from Africa, the Greek public was able to maintain the belief that AIDS was something foreign, that Greeks themselves were not at risk. His death also coincided with the first reports of large outbreaks of AIDS in central Africa. Also, at the time his symptoms first appeared, he had only recently arrived in Greece, fostering the perception that he could not have possibly contracted the disease while in Greece.[10] Unavoidably, however, with the Zambian student's death, the epidemic in Greece had suddenly ceased to be one of information alone.

1983–1993: Who Are They? And Who Will Help Them?

Thus, by 1983 AIDS had substantially cohered for many Greeks into a disease primarily of foreigners, and then more specifically of same-sex men, persons with hemophilia, and injecting drug users. Once AIDS had ceased to be exclusively foreign, there was a rush to determine to what degree the country was exposed to any one of the "high-risk group" populations. One exponent of this argument is the journalist Giannis Tzimourtas, who concludes the following in his 1985 exposé on AIDS in Greece: "As is well known, AIDS to a large extent threatens specific groups of people, such as homosexuals, drug addicts and people who need frequent transfusions. In Greece, however, where the number of homosexuals and drug addicts is small, in relation to other countries, the problem is seen most often in transfusions" (Tzimourtas 1985: 30).[11]

It is worth noting here that in 1984, the Greek government had already instituted mandatory reporting of AIDS cases; hence, government data ought to have been available in some form to Tzimourtas and others who were in a position to mold public opinion. However, his story does not accord with those statistics. Official (although retrospective) data from KEEL for 1985 show the largest fraction of cumulative HIV cases to be among men who have sex with men (KEEL 2002). According to the same report, cumulative to 2002, the only route of transmission in Greece recorded less often than blood transfusion was intrauterine transmission from mother to child.

Tzimourtas's assertions would not last, however. Less than ten months later, on May 16, 1985, the following alarmist headline ran in one of the newspapers of record, *Eleftherotypía*: "AIDS Found in 10% of Homosexuals." The text of the article clarifies that the 10 percent figure does not represent actual AIDS cases; rather, it represents the 26 self-identified gay men who tested positive for HIV out of 243 who participated voluntarily in a study by Giorgos Papaevangelou, one of the more respected authorities on AIDS at the time (see Papaevangelou 1988). Significantly, the *Eleftherotypía* article maintained the association of HIV as not Greek, specifically noting that the research revealed that of the 26 who tested positive, 61.5 percent had sexual encounters while abroad, and none of the 26 reported injecting drugs. While the article did not claim that the study was able to establish that the infections had been acquired outside of Greece, the implication was allowed. The same article also reported on another study of injecting drug users. In that study, only 6 out of the 288 users studied tested positive. Transfusions received no mention at all in the article.

Comparing the *Eleftherotypía* article with Tzimourtas's claims points to a tremendous spread of opinions and beliefs about who is susceptible to AIDS, and the extent to which those people are imagined to be present in Greece. In this media-fueled context of vacillating perceptions of danger and exposure, organized responses to AIDS gradually began to occur in Greece, following a pattern seen in many locales—grassroots organizers respond first, followed by the apparatus of the state.

The first recorded grassroots response came with the founding in 1985 of the organization Prostasía, a collective of doctors responding to the disease in the context of their own practices. Government statistics then put the cumulative number of HIV/AIDS cases at 18. Prostasía was followed in 1987 (123 cases) by AIDS Sensitization and in 1989 (370 cases) by Elpída. Both AIDS Sensitization and Elpída were initiated and staffed largely by women. Then the Center for Inspirational Living was founded in 1990 (589 cases), offering a holistic approach to providing support services for HIV-positive individuals. While the center's initial and subsequent staffs have included gay men, the organization specifically distances itself from being for gay men alone. It serves the needs of all people living with HIV/AIDS.

In 1992 (1,154 cases), the Greek chapter of ACT UP was founded by a group of doctors and others frustrated with the lack of response from the government. ACT UP Greece has remained significantly tied to the medical profession to this day. The current president and secretary are both doctors from the Syngrou hospital, one of the major centers for HIV/AIDS services in Athens. Finally, in 1993, a decade after the first case, nine years after reporting of AIDS cases was made mandatory, and in the same year of a change of government from ND to PASOK, KEEL was established as a permanent government body within the Ministry of Health to monitor and manage AIDS and other infectious diseases. By that time, there were 1,454 recorded cases of HIV/AIDS in Greece.[12]

In all of these organizational efforts, there is a startling consistency. None of these organizations defines itself as a "gay group" or even as "a gay group about AIDS." The initiatives for their founding came not from activists within the same-sex movement but from doctors and from women engaged in social work. Although gay men helped and volunteered in these organizations, the first decade of AIDS in Greece saw no organization started by gay activists specifically to address HIV/AIDS.

So what were the gay activists doing after the entrance of AIDS into Greece? As an organization, AKOE certainly provided a more or less constant stream of HIV/AIDS information in *AMFI*. Beyond their magazine, however, the activists themselves seem to have maintained a distance from the disease, a tendency confirmed through interviews with several former AKOE members. This tendency also appears to have held for the organization's public events, judging by a 1984 publication containing the speeches read at a weeklong exhibition of liberation and alternative movements, including AKOE. The exhibition ran from November 28 to December 5, 1983, just days after the death of the Zambian student made headlines and over a year after initial reports of "gay cancer" were published in *AMFI*. Yet there is no mention of AIDS in any of the AKOE texts published from the exhibition (Gryponisiotis 1984: 57–70).

This is not to say that individual members may not have acted independently. Several former members noted in their interviews that some members were "better connected with the government." One person in particular was at a loss to specify what AKOE did as an organization about AIDS, but asserted "surely some of them were writing letters, or something like that." Recall, however, that the shift of government in 1981 had taken the wind from AKOE's sails: attendance at meetings dropped significantly, *AMFI* came out less frequently, and the newspaper stopped altogether. By 1987, AKOE was having a number of organizational and financial problems due at least in part to the drop in numbers. Moreover, there were legal problems that had to be resolved if publication of *AMFI* were to continue. At the time, mass action on AIDS may have been of secondary importance to the future of AKOE as an organization.

By the spring of 1987, AKOE had in effect collapsed. For a transitional period, Vallianatos personally took on the publication of *AMFI*, explaining somewhat evasively in the editorial of the first issue he produced that "*AMFI* is not subsidized by anyone, but it has ceased to be 'published through contributions from the membership of AKOE.'" After several issues under Vallianatos, the publication was taken over in 1988 by a new organization created by former members of AKOE. That new organization was called the Greek Homosexual Community, or EOK by the Greek acronym. EOK took the legal form of a corporation, a structure more suited to its significantly smaller membership. It would come to be led by Vangelis Giannelos, who remained its president until his death in 2006. Irene Petropoulou would initially serve as editor of *AMFI*.[13]

All this to say that, at least for AKOE, internal organizational pressures could have distracted it from approaching AIDS in any effective way beyond the pages of *AMFI*. One might also assert that with only six years of experience behind it, the same-sex movement of Greece was in no position to take on AIDS as well. While both of these arguments have some merit, they are incomplete without a third argument, one that would connect the cultural assumptions at work within AKOE about same-sex sexuality and AIDS.

By the time Ghrighoris Vallianatos became editor of *AMFI* in 1987, the periodical was emphasizing that there were not "high risk groups," but only "high risk practices," the core of the prevention message that was then being broadcast around the world under the label of "safer sex." Concurrently, as Vallianatos later noted, "it was necessary from the beginning to separate the disease from homosexuality."[14] This tactic was deemed necessary in part because the damage worked by AIDS included the further stigmatization of those seen as susceptible to it, and despite AKOE's initial successes, gay men hardly enjoyed broad social acceptance in Greece by the time AIDS appeared on the scene. Consider also a report released by the Greek National Center for Social Research in 1983, the same year that the Zambian student died. Based on a survey of attitudes toward the legal system completed in 1977 of over 2,000 individuals in a demographically diverse sample,[15] the report found that 79.9 percent of those surveyed stated that same-sex relations between men should be a criminal offense, even though thirty years had passed since same-sex sexuality per se was decriminalized (Daskalakis et al. 1983: 258).

Thus, the responses to AIDS by gay movement activists were dominated by an attempt to fit together three necessary positions: the safer sex message, the need to separate same-sex sexuality from the disease, and the sexual

244 / B. Riedel

philosophy of the liberation of same-sex desire, begun in AKOE and subsequently continued in EOK through both the magazine *AMFI* and the fact that many members of EOK had also been members of AKOE.

When the activists' articulated and unarticulated assumptions are seen together in this way, it appears that the arrival of AIDS brought out at least two unforeseeable consequences of a sexual philosophy that had its roots in a sexual economy based on a hierarchy of gendered roles rather than sexual identities that inhere in the individual. In the context of a movement based not on sexual identities but instead on a politics focused on a desire that anyone might have, safer sex was a "natural" fit. A response to AIDS that focuses on the modification of specific behaviors dovetails easily both with the practice-oriented sexual economy of gendered roles into which AKOE emerged and with the philosophy of a universally available desire that AKOE formed in response to that economy. Indeed, safer sex messages are present early on in the pages of *AMFI*. It was almost as if the Greek same-sex movement had been prefabricated to accept the safer sex message.

The second unforeseeable consequence of adopting a sexual philosophy based on desire is that by not operating on the assumption of sexual identities, the interpretation of how one goes about "separating the disease from homosexuality" becomes more complicated than saying that not all gay men are necessarily HIV positive. If a sexual philosophy based on desire and not on desiring subjects is to be retained, "separating the disease from homosexuality" requires a somewhat more extended formulation, like the following: just because a man would follow his desire to have sex with other men does not mean that he is HIV positive, and just because a man is HIV positive does not mean he has a desire to have sex with other men. From the beginning, the members of AKOE had embraced a sexual philosophy that encouraged them to imagine the target population in need of outreach to be far larger than just those who identify as "homosexual."

In practical terms, this second consequence leads to a specific strategy regarding AIDS. Given the liberation of same-sex desire as the ultimate goal, and since that desire can exist alongside any socially available sexual identity, it would not make sense to organize a movement exclusively around any particular sexual identity. Analogically: the same-sex movement could not address itself to an identity-based class of people; nor could it imagine a response to AIDS that way. In other words, beyond any organizational difficulties AKOE may have faced as AIDS began to spread through Greece, the activists also had a number of cultural assumptions about sexuality—some articulated (the sexual philosophy) and some not (the sexual economy)—that made the option of a GMHC-like organization both unthinkable and undesirable. Not only would such an organization have deleteriously worked in the Greek context to reinforce the connection of AIDS with gay men, it would have run counter to the sexual philosophy on which the movement was predicated.

Following much the same path that AKOE had established, EOK continued to keep a minimal relationship with AIDS activism, even into the 1990s. As observed by Panagiotis Damaskos, currently director of the Office of Psychosocial Support at KEEL and former member of EOK, EOK "never engaged in activism around AIDS because it did not want to add any more weight to the idea that homosexuality was the same thing as AIDS."[16] To be fair, EOK's involvement in AIDS issues is not nonexistent. In December 1990, EOK organized a public demonstration "with a bullhorn, four speakers, and a group of 20 people" (EOK 2004). Since then, it has participated several times in World AIDS Day marches and in a number of colloquia on the topic. Giannelos himself argued that, with the presence of several AIDS organizations, there was less need for EOK to engage the subject.[17]

By the time EOK was founded, however, the historical moment of the sexual philosophy articulated through AKOE was already beginning to fade. As if signaling a turn toward a new direction, EOK hosted the European convention of the International Lesbian and Gay Association in 1989. With the suspension of *AMFI* in 1990, EOK seemed to leave the articulation of that philosophy entirely in the past. As argued both by Faubion (1993) and Giannakopoulos (1998), a new perception of sexual identities was beginning to take root in Greece in the 1970s—at least among those urbanites who might identify as "homosexuals"—a new perception that could coexist and compete with the sexual economy of the years before AKOE. Faubion refers to this new perception in his discussion of Vallianatos's displeasure with the term "homosexual" and his preference for the term "gay" (Faubion 1993: 237).[18] For his part, Giannakopoulos describes the new perception as a recognizable and visible "gay homosexuality" (gay *omofilofilía*) in contradistinction to a "masculine homosexuality" (*arrenopí omofilofilía*), which designates "sexual practices which do not entail a homosexual identity" (Giannakopoulos 1998: 82).

All the same, at the moment when AIDS arrived in Greece, that new perception had not yet taken hold. Whether we call it "masculine homosexuality," a sexual economy, or a sexual philosophy of desire, the articulated and unarticulated cultural assumptions of sexuality at the time shaped the way that activists in the same-sex movement in Greece responded to AIDS. Years later, as visible gay social identities increasingly percolate through the sexual economy of Greece, it seems that the liberation legacy of AKOE is remembered, cursed, and forgotten, all in the same comment: "We're not a gay organization, really."

Acknowledgments

The fieldwork from which this chapter is drawn was supported in part by the Research Institute for the Study of Man and the Rice University Center for the Study of Institutions and Values. I am in especial debt to Anna Mihopoulou and the Delfys Archives of Women's History in Athens. My deep thanks go to Thodoris Andonopoulos, Anna Apostolidou, James Faubion, Andrea Gilbert, Bowie Hinger, and Aimee Placas for reading, conversations, and commentary.

Notes

1. These meetings would later become known as the "Polychromo Forum." From their inception in a gay bar, they evolved into a monthly open meeting of activists and interested individuals, with the responsibilities of coordinator and moderator rotating among the different recognized activist groups.

2. By no means do I want to imply that the initial response to AIDS in the United States was entirely from gay organizations, nor do I mean to oversimplify the composition of those organizations that responded to AIDS in general in the United States. Rather, I am pointing to a qualitative difference in the response in Greece. For analyses of the texture and social composition of early responses to AIDS in the United States, see Altman (1986), D'Emilio (1992, 2002), Kayal (1993), and Stoller (1998).

3. The archival work and interviews took place as part of a larger ethnography of LGBT rights activism in Greece conducted over twenty-seven months from May 2001 through July 2004.

4. See Dokoumetzidis (1997: 123) for a note about the extent to which the law might actually reflect social perceptions at the time.

5. To name a core group of studies germane to the connections of gender with sexuality, see specifically and Apostolidou (2005), Boukli and Kappas (2003), Giannakopoulos (1998), Herzfeld (1985), Karagiannis and Tolis (1998), Loizos and Papataxiarchis (1991), Phellas (2002), and Vasilikou (1998).

6. *Travestí* is a self-descriptive term used by Greek men who dress and behave as women, some of whom also engage in sex work. Although they may have taken hormones or undertaken breast construction surgery, they have retained their male geni-

talia. While there are significant parallels to *travestí* discussed by Kulick (1998), there are significant differences, too, which are further complicated by the shifting fortunes of *travestí* as a social category in Greece over the last three decades. I did not hear of silicone injections, for example, during the time that I was in Greece. Further, within the organization SATTE (Greek Organization of Support for *Travestí* and Transsexuals), there is considerable discussion as to whether they are "still" gay, or whether being gay men was a stage they passed through on their way to becoming women, or whether they are something else entirely.

7. As noted by the *travestí* Betty (1979: 159).

8. The breadth of that support was evidenced repeatedly during my fieldwork; when interviewing people in their midforties and older, it was rare that they had not at some point at least passed through one AKOE function or another, even if they no longer wanted to be involved in activism of any sort.

9. As far as my archival research has been able to determine, his sexuality was never discussed in the media reports, nor was drug use mentioned. Future research may determine otherwise in both cases.

10. Valantis Papathanasiou notes that the foreignness of AIDS continues to be marked by the retention of the English "AIDS" in popular discourse, rather than the proper Greek acronym SEAA, which circulates almost exclusively in medical and social science discourse (Papathanasiou and Agrafiotis 2003). Another mode of marking the foreignness of AIDS occurs in medical exams required for the residence permit. At my exam, I was ordered by the panel of doctors to take an HIV test, even though Greek law specifies only that foreign nationals be tested for tuberculosis at a Greek hospital (diagnoses from foreign doctors are not admissible). The trope of AIDS as foreign to Greece is discussed further in Chliaoutakis et al. (1993), Giannakopoulos (1998) and Tsalicoglou (1995).

11. This evasion of AIDS as a sexually transmitted disease is also documented over a decade later (see Giannakopoulos 1998: 77).

12. Not to speak of cases that were never recorded, a phenomenon that Giannakopoulos (1998) and members of ACT UP and Synthesis suggest is far more widespread than is officially recognized by KEEL.

13. It is worth noting that AKOE still exists, but in a very different form. The lawyer Manthos Peponas took on the admittedly reduced responsibilities of the organization in 1988 and still carries them out as of this writing. Interestingly, after EOK abandoned *AMFI* in 1990 as an economic impossibility, Peponas attempted to revive it, producing two volumes in 1994 and 1996. He still talks of reestablishing it.

14. Personal interview, November 2003.

15. The research results thus reflect attitudes that significantly predate both AKOE and AIDS in Greece (see Daskalakis et al. 1983: 139–40).

16. Personal interview, October 2003.

17. Personal interview, April 2004.

18. Intriguingly, after he stepped down as editor of *AMFI*, Vallianatos began publication of a magazine titled *GAY*.

References Cited

Agrafiotis, Demosthenis, E. Ioannidi, and P. Manti. 1999. HIV prevention in Europe: Policy and practice. The Greek case. Department of Sociology, National School of Public Health, *Research Monograph* 18.

Altman, Dennis. 1986. *AIDS in the Mind of America*. Garden City, N.Y.: Doubleday.

Apostolidou, Anna. 2005. Kaleidoskopiká sómata: Diaseksoualikótita kai i kataskeví enallaktikís thulikótitas sti súnchroni Elláda (Kaleidoscopic bodies: Transsexuality and the construction of alternative femininities in modern Greece). In *The Production of the Social Body*, ed. M. Michailidou and A. Halkias, 175-201. Athens: Katárti Publications and Diní Feminist Journal.

Betty [Periklis Vakalidis]. 1979. *Betty*. Athens: Exándas Press.

Boukli, Evi, and Panagiotis Kappas. 2004. Ypóthesi Spices (The Spices case). Study for the seminar Social Representation of Crime in the Mass Media, taught by Afroditi Koukoutsaki. Department of Sociology, Pánteion University, Athens.

Chliaoutakis, Joannes, Fotini Socrati, Christina Darviri, Nikos Gousgounis, and Deanne Trakas. 1993. Knowledge and attitudes about AIDS of residents of Greater Athens. *Social Science and Medicine* 37(1): 77-83.

Daskalakis, Ilias, Angeliki Avdritou, Panagiota Papadopoulou, Petros Pappas, Ioanna Perandzaki, and Dimitra Tsabarli. 1983. *Apomoní tis Poinikís Dikaiosúnis stin Elláda* (Expectations of the Criminal Justice System in Greece). Athens: National Center for Social Research.

D'Emilio, John. 1992. *Making Trouble: Essays on Gay History, Politics, and the University*. New York: Routledge.

———. 2002. The *World Turned: Essays on Gay History, Politics, and Culture*. Durham, N.C.: Duke University Press.

Diakos, Ilias. 1982. Sarkóma Kapósi: Karkínos mas i blakíes tous? (Kaposi's sarcoma: "Our" cancer, or their bullshit?) *AMFI* (Winter, 2nd period, 12-13): 83-84.

Dokoumetzidis, Giorgos. 1997. *Provlímata Prostasías ton Dikaiomáton tou Anthrópou* (Problems in the Protection of Human Rights). Athens: Kastaniótis Press.

EOK. 2004. 17 Chrónia EOK (17 years of EOK). Informational flyer produced by EOK. Copies available at the Delfys Archives of Women's History in Athens.

Faubion, James. 1993. *Modern Greek Lessons: A Primer in Historical Constructivism*. Princeton, N.J.: Princeton University Press.

Feldman, Douglas A. 2006. Personal communication.

Giannakopoulos, Kostas. 1998. Politikés seksoualikótitas kai igeías tin epohí tou AIDS (The politics of sexuality and health in the age of AIDS). *Súchrona Thémata* 66: 76-86.

Gryponisiotis, Andreas, ed. 1984. *7 Méres Amfisbítisis: Eptaímero Enallaktikón Apeleftherotikón Kiníseon* (7 Days of Questioning: Seven-day Event of Alternative and Liberation Movements). Athens: Kínisi.

Herzfeld, Michael. 1985. *The Poetics of Manhood: Contest and Identity in a Cretan Mountain Village*. Princeton, N.J.: Princeton University Press.

Karagiannis, Evthimia, and Pantelis Tolis. 1998. Omofilofilía kai koinonikí pragmatikóti-ta (Homosexuality and social reality). Thesis, SEYP School, Irakleio.

Kayal, Philip. 1993. *Bearing Witness: Gay Men's Health Crisis and the Politics of AIDS*. Boulder, Colo.: Westview Press.

KEEL. 2002. *HIV/AIDS Surveillance in Greece*. Issue 16, December.

Koukoutsaki, Afroditi. 2002. *Chrísi Narkotikón, Omofilofilía: Simberiforés mi Simórfosis Metaxí Poinikoú kai Iatrikoú Elénchou* (Drug Use, Homosexuality: Non-Conforming Behaviors Between Criminal and Medical Control). Athens: Kritiki.

Kulick, Don. 1998. *Travestí: Sex, Gender, and Culture among Brazilian Transgendered Prostitutes*. Chicago: University of Chicago Press.

Loizos, Peter, and Evthymios Papataxiarchis. 1991. Gender, sexuality, and the person in Greek culture. In *Contested Identities: Gender and Kinship in Modern Greece*, ed. Peter Loizos and Evthymios Papataxiarchis, 221–34. Princeton, N.J.: Princeton University Press.

Papaevangelou, Giorgos. 1988. *AIDS*. Thessaloniki: Paratiritís.

Papathanasiou, Chrysobalantis, and D. Agrafiotis. 2003. AIDS in the workplace: Attitudes and social representations of employers concerning HIV infected persons. *Greek Archives of AIDS* 11(3): 149–60.

Phellas, Constantinos N. 2002. *The Construction of Sexual and Cultural Identities: Greek-Cypriot Men in Britain*. Aldershot: Ashgate.

Spanou, Calliope. 1998. European integration in administrative terms: A framework for analysis and the Greek case. *Journal of European Public Policy* 5(3): 467–84.

Stoller, Nancy. 1998. *Lessons from the Damned: Queers, Whores, and Junkies Respond to AIDS*. New York: Routledge.

Taktsis, Kostas. 1989. *To Foberó Víma* (The Amazing Step). Athens: Exándas.

Tsalicoglou, Fotini. 1995. A new disease in Greek society: AIDS and the representation of "otherness." *Journal of Modern Greek Studies* 13: 83–97.

Tsarouhas, Kostas. 1995. *Alkistís: To Skotádi Kai to Fos Sto Erotikó Énstikto* (Alkistis: Shadow and Light in the Erotic Impulse). Athens: Elliniki Grammata.

Tzimourtas, Giannis. 1985. AIDS. *ENA* 33 (August 15): 30.

Vallianatos, Ghrighoris. 1987. Ekdidoména. *AMFI* (May) (3rd period, issue 1): 5.

Vasilikou, Katerina. 1998. Tautótita fílou, epikindinótita, kai AIDS: Néoi ándres omofiló-filoi kai diahírisi tou kindínou ékthesis ston ió tou AIDS (Gender identity, risk, and AIDS: Young men and the management of the danger of exposure to the AIDS virus). Thesis, National School of Public Health, Athens.

14

Gay Men, Sex, and HIV/AIDS in Belgium

JOHN VINCKE, RALPH BOLTON, AND RUDI BLEYS

Gay life in Belgium is vibrant and dynamic. Major cities throughout the country offer a rich diversity of venues for public socializing. Although not as renowned in gay tourist circles as Amsterdam in the Netherlands, Brussels, a highly cosmopolitan city with a large foreign population of European civil servants, and Antwerp, the largest city in Flanders (northern Belgium), with an international reputation not only as a diamond center but also as a magnet for men into leather sex, possess a large array of bars, discos, clubs, saunas, cafés and restaurants that cater to gay men. According to the *Spartacus International Gay Guide 2005/2006*, both Brussels and Antwerp each boast nineteen gay bars (Bedford 2005). From leather bars to drag bars, from hustler hangouts to dance clubs, there is a place for every taste or inclination. While bars may tend to come and go, some of them have existed for decades (see Gmünder and Stamford 1988). The same is true of bathhouses, which exist not only in Brussels and Antwerp but also in some smaller cities such as Ghent and Ostend and which have continued to operate even throughout the AIDS era (Bolton et al. 1992, 1994). In addition to bars and baths, there are many cafés and restaurants popular among gays and lesbians in Brussels, Antwerp, Ghent, and other cities.

Not all gay men in Belgium participate in the public gay scene, of course. Many partnered men as well as closeted married men live their lives largely outside a gay context. There are no gay ghettoes in Belgium comparable to those found in some American cities—for example, West Hollywood (Los Angeles), the Castro (San Francisco), and Montrose (Houston). Similarly, while some gay social, political, and sports organizations exist on a small scale in the country, this aspect of a gay subculture is not highly elaborated in Belgium.

However, by any standard Belgium is one of the world's most progressive, tolerant, and accepting societies in relation to same-sex sexuality. While generally tolerant, European attitudes toward gays and lesbians exhibit con-

Table 14.1. Comparative data on European attitudes toward gays and lesbians: "Gays and lesbians are free to live as they wish."

	Strongly agree	Agree	Neither agree nor disagree	Disagree	Disagree strongly
Denmark	45.2	44.2	4.8	3.8	2.0
Netherlands	42.7	45.6	7.2	2.9	1.7
Austria	39.1	33.3	13.8	7.9	5.8
Belgium	37.7	42.7	10.7	5.0	4.0
Finland	34.4	27.3	14.7	11.6	12.0
Spain	34.1	36.1	20.7	6.7	2.4
Italy	28.2	45.3	14.4	8.3	3.7
Sweden	27.5	54.3	11.4	4.3	2.5
Germany	27.1	47.6	12.4	8.8	4.1
Czech Republic	25.9	31.9	23.8	9.6	8.8
Ireland	23.6	58.9	12.0	4.5	1.0
Portugal	23.6	47.2	19.3	7.2	2.7
Norway	22.4	53.8	12.5	8.3	2.9
United Kingdom	17.7	57.5	12.9	8.3	3.6
Greece	17.2	33.5	21.1	15.6	12.5
Hungary	15.9	32.2	22.3	16.6	13.0
Poland	9.4	36.7	23.6	18.7	11.6

Source: European Social Values Studies 2002–2003.
Note: The above order is not necessarily a true ranking of countries since it is based on the order of those who "strongly agreed." Combining those who agreed, however strongly, on the one hand, and those who disagreed, on the other hand, would yield a different order. Norway, for example, would be seen as more accepting, while Finland would be seen as lower in acceptance.

siderable variation. The position of Belgium within Europe is at the positive end of the spectrum. Table 14.1 demonstrates that Belgium scores very high compared to other countries in the European Union regarding attitudes on same-sex sexuality (European Social Values Studies 2002–2003). Almost 90 percent of the people in Denmark and the Netherlands agree with the statement that "gays and lesbians are free to live as they wish." Belgians rank third, with 80.4 percent agreeing. Countries with the lowest levels of favorable attitudes tend to be those from the former Communist Eastern Europe. Poland, still predominantly Catholic and less secularized, manifests the least tolerance and acceptance of same-sex sexuality in Europe.

In recent years, the legal rights of gays and lesbians have been significantly advanced in Belgium. The Belgian federal government granted gays and lesbians civil marriage in 2003 (Waaldijk 2003–2004). As a result, Belgium became the second of four countries to grant marriage rights to gays and lesbians, following the Netherlands (2001), but earlier than Canada and Spain (2005). In 2003 and 2004, 3,535 gay marriages took place in Flanders. Although the Flemish population is about 58 percent of the total population, gay marriages in Flanders accounted for 75 percent of all gay marriages in Belgium. There were also more gay male marriages (56 percent) than lesbian marriages. In April 2006, the gay adoption bill was also accepted within the nation's parliament. Therefore, gays and lesbians now have civil marriage rights equal to heterosexuals.

In February 2003, a more inclusive antidiscrimination law came into effect in Belgium. Prior to the implementation of this law, discrimination on the basis of race could be prosecuted, but discrimination on other grounds was not prohibited. Discrimination based on sexual orientation, however, is now illegal and provides grounds for prosecution. During a ten-month period since the new law went into effect, 267 nonracial discrimination complaints were lodged with the Center for Equal Opportunities in Belgium. Of these complaints, 35 (13 percent) dealt with discrimination on the grounds of sexual orientation. More than half of these complaints have to do with homophobic statements in publications, on the Internet, or on television. Other complaints have to do with social exclusion from schools, restaurants, and dance studios. Given the population of Belgium (approximately ten million inhabitants), these figures are not alarming. However, they should be interpreted very cautiously. Not everybody is fully aware that there is now a legal basis to protect against discrimination on sexual orientation grounds. Only after a certain period of implementation of the law will it be possible to know if it will be followed with appropriate judicial decision making and become truly effective.

Among gays and lesbians, youth are a vulnerable subpopulation (the age of consent in Belgium is sixteen). As in other countries, there has been a lot of discussion of the suicidal behavior and ideation of young gays and lesbians. A matched case control study conducted in Belgium provided strong evidence that young gays and lesbians run a higher risk for committing suicide. Young gay males were about two and one-half times more likely to have suicidal ideas than young heterosexual males. Young lesbians had over a six times' higher chance of having experienced a suicidal attempt than heterosexual girls in the same age bracket (Van Heeringen and Vincke 2000).

In Flanders, the Dutch-speaking part of Belgium, a rather extensive network of gay youth groups exists. These groups are associated with Wel Jong, Niet Hetero (Young, But Not Straight), the coordinating organization. Their target group consists of youth between fifteen and twenty-six years of age.

They organize social activities and distribute information to these youth. They also perform a very important sensitization function directed to non-gay youth organizations, schools, and the government. Their work appears to be quite successful. They help to construct a positive image of young gays and lesbians in the media. They also seem to attract a lot of young people requesting information on being gay or lesbian, or on gay subcultures. For example, in May 2004 their Web site counted 72,645 unique visitors, a number that corresponds to approximately 10 percent of the population between fifteen and twenty-six years of age. This informational activity gives us some idea of the importance and role of this youth organization.

In sum, while Belgium is more or less accepting of same-sex sexuality, some problems still persist. Cases of discrimination on the basis of sexual orientation have been documented, and notwithstanding the existence of a legal framework for combating discrimination, it is not known at this time how judges will interpret and apply the law. Young people still encounter difficulties when coming out (Vincke, Bolton, et al. 1993). They show higher rates of suicide ideation and attempts than do their heterosexual counterparts. Nonetheless, the situation of gays and lesbians has improved substantially in the past couple of years, thereby potentially opening up opportunities for enhanced HIV prevention directed to gay men.

HIV Prevention in Flanders

The history of AIDS prevention in Flanders reflects a process of structural integration of formerly independent nongovernmental organizations (NGOs) whose main aim was to develop prevention campaigns for specific target groups or to deliver care for people with AIDS. The AIDS NGOs (for example, The AIDS Team, an AIDS prevention organization for gay men) emerged in the mid-1980s. Although they had some connections with the gay subculture, these entities functioned independently of, and sometimes in opposition to, gay organizations.

Given the absence of a culture or tradition of private funding of health-related activities in Belgium, these NGOs almost immediately attempted to obtain financial support from the Flemish government. As a result of their appeal for funds, the government was more or less forced to develop initiatives that could be called an "AIDS policy."

The first integration initiative began in 1988. The newly formed NGOs were brought together for discussions and the development of a plan of coordination with a loose structure. Funding was relatively small. Organizations as such were not funded, but they could get funding for projects that they submitted for financial support. In effect, the NGOs did not get structural support for their work. Rather, continued financial aid depended on positive approval from the Flemish government on an annual basis. As a result, their existence could never be taken for granted. Each year there was the possibility of a lack of funding and the resulting disintegration of the organizations. One could say that the ideology and culture of the welfare state resulted in reducing almost all private initiative regarding donations, making NGOs very government dependent.

In 1991, a next step in organizational growth occurred. The network of AIDS organizations became part of a more inclusive organization dealing with health promotion in general. Although funding was still rather small, the existing organizations managed to run their operations well. The AIDS Team, targeting gay men, developed several prevention campaigns. New infections declined, and it seemed as if the epidemic was under control.

In 2001, integration and centralization "fever" struck again. AIDS organizations became part of one new large organization, SENSOA (Vlaams Service en Expertisecentrum voor Seksuele Gezondheid en HIV; Flemish Service and Expertise Center for Sexual Health and HIV). This organization does not specialize in HIV/AIDS. Its central tasks are related to sexual relations, sexual health, and sexually transmitted infections (STIs) in general. Older organizations, such as The AIDS Team, have now disappeared completely from public view. This development has important implications for prevention targeting gay men. The AIDS Team had cultivated close connections with the gay movement and the gay subculture. Gay men were the "owners" of the prevention targeted at their group. This gave The AIDS Team a high level of credibility. For purposes of social-marketing, The AIDS Team was very well positioned. It was regarded as a trustworthy, competent organization run by gay men, owned by gay men, and focusing on gay men.

The new organization, SENSOA, is not positioned as an AIDS prevention organization and is not seen as a product of Flemish gay life. Although there still are prevention campaigns aimed at gay men, their positioning within social-marketing space has changed dramatically. As of 2005, there is no longer any "gay-owned" AIDS prevention taking place in Flanders. The impact of this demise of gay-controlled HIV/AIDS organizations on the credibility of AIDS prevention for gay men is difficult to assess. It is even more difficult to estimate its impact on the evolution of the ongoing epidemic.

Not only did AIDS prevention targeting gay men disappear as a visible and identifiable initiative, but so did AIDS prevention research among gay men. The first AIDS-related research on gay men in Flanders began in 1989. It was the result of a close collaboration between a sociologist and an anthropologist (first and second authors, respectively, of this chapter) and a medical doctor. Together, they organized the first empirical study ever on gay life in Flanders (N = 389). This study came to be known as the Gay Service Research Project (Mak, Vincke, and Bolton 1990). By 1991, the first national AIDS Research Program was initiated. Part of this program involved studying the sexual lives and risk behaviors of gay men, with Vincke and Bolton chosen to conduct this part of that larger project (Bolton and Vincke 1996; Mak, Bolton, et al. 1990; Vincke and Bolton 1992, 1997a; Vincke, Mak, et al. 1993; Vincke et al. 2001).

Seen in an international context, this was a modest research endeavor. Its budget made it possible to hire one full-time investigator for four years and to collect data on 553 men who have sex with men (MSM). Building further on the previous initiative, it was clear that this study should also address various aspects of the life situation of Flemish gay men. The philosophy and hypothesis were that risk behaviors by gay men are an integral part of their life organization resulting from an adaptation to a sometimes hostile environment (Vincke and Bolton 1993, 1994, 1996; Vincke et al. 1999). This research program lasted for one year; thereafter, no coordinated research initiatives on HIV/AIDS were carried out in Flanders.

However, the broad scope of the research carried out by Vincke and Bolton attracted interest not only from gay prevention organizations but also within the gay movement. This research tradition could be extended by developing studies on gay identity and on mental health issues and suicide among gay youth.

During the 1990s, the political landscape in Flanders changed considerably. For more than forty years, the Christian Popular Party (CVP) dominated the political scene, together with the Old Left socialist (materialist) movement. In the 1990s, this socialist party became transformed more and more into a New Left party, Socialistische Partij. Anders (SP.A), embracing postmaterial values. This transformation coincided with a significant change in the party's base from the industrial working class to the middle class. Sexuality, social welfare, and diversity became new political issues. As a result, in 1997 the Flemish government ordered research aimed at describing as statistically accurately as possible the living conditions of gay men and lesbians. Through this initiative, the know-how and expertise developed in the area of gay research could be preserved, and at present the government has commissioned follow-up research. Thus, a small institutional base capable of conducting research without large amounts of grant money was developed.

The report that follows is based on data on gay men and their risk behaviors gathered as part of a project entitled "Vital Questions." The principal aim of the project, which was completed in 2001, was to describe the sexual behavior of Flemish gay men more than fifteen years after the first cases of HIV/AIDS were detected in Flanders.

Methods

Sample

The study sample consists of 633 men whose mean age is 33.5 years (standard deviation: 10.3). Sixty percent of the men are between the ages of 25 and 45 years. As in most research on gay men, older men are undoubtedly underrepresented. In this sample, only 11 percent of respondents are older than 45 years. Almost half of the sample had some higher education or training (university or nonuniversity). Three out of four men have a steady job. In sum, our sample consists primarily of rather young, well-educated, employed men.

Respondents were recruited through gay organizations (26.5 percent) and in cruising areas such as parks and "tearooms" (public restrooms where sex occurs) (21 percent). Others were recruited in bathhouses, in gay bars, and through networks of friends. The majority of men identify as gay, are open regarding their sexual orientation, and only have sex with men. A small minority (6.3 percent) report having sex with both men and women. Finally, 70 percent of the men did not use any kind of drugs, including recreational or soft drugs (poppers, Ecstasy, marijuana) when having sex during the previous three months.

Definitions

In this study, we define unsafe sex as unprotected (condomless) anal sex involving known or presumptively known serodiscordant partners (where one is HIV positive and the other is HIV negative). Partners can be steady partners or casual (nonsteady) partners such as "fuck buddies," sex workers, or anonymous contacts in "dark rooms" (sometimes called "backrooms," where anonymous sex between or among men occurs), bathhouses, and cruising areas. This definition of unsafe sex is not perfect. We are aware that incidental infections can result from condom failure and at least hypothetically during oral sex, or during "fisting" (insertion of the hand into the partner's anus). Yet epidemiologic research consistently shows that the overwhelming majority of new infections result from unprotected anal penetrative sex between serodiscordant partners. One implication of our definition is that when gay men consciously have anal penetrative sex without a condom because they know that they have the same serostatus (either both HIV positive or both HIV negative), then, for purposes of this study, we do not consider this to be unsafe sex. In the remainder of this chapter, we discuss some statistics on these strategies of seroselection. These strategies can be designated as either negotiated safety or negotiated risk. In the prevention literature, there is discussion on the extent to which these strategies are effective (e.g., Kippax et al. 1997).

To obtain data on the sexual behavior of the men in our sample, we used a two-step procedure. First, we asked if the men had a partner in anal penetrative sex during the preceding three months. The results were as follows: 41.6 percent (N = 263) had not engaged in anal penetrative sex; 41.2 percent (N = 261) had engaged in anal penetrative sex with only one partner; and 17.2 percent (N = 109) had engaged in anal penetrative sex with multiple partners.

Men who practice penetrative anal sex follow a typical northern European and North American pattern. Most men who had engaged in anal penetrative sex reported being "versatile," that is, engaging in both insertive and receptive anal sex (55.4 percent; N = 205). And contradicting the common stereotype in some gay communities of a preponderance of exclusive "bottoms," in this sample exclusive "tops" (26.8 percent, N = 99) outnumbered exclusive "bottoms" (17.8 percent, N = 66). There is no association between respondents' educational level and sex role. However, there is a small association between sex role and age, with older men more likely than younger men to report being an exclusively top (chi square = 8.07, 4 df, p < 0.08).

Results

Penetrative Anal Sex: No Partner or One Partner

When the gay men in this sample have only one penetrative anal sex partner, that partner is their significant other or a steady partner in two out of three cases. In the other case it is a "fuck buddy" with whom one does not have an intimate relationship. We first focus our attention on the group of men with a steady partner. By "steady" or "regular" partner, we refer to a partner with whom one has the intention to have ongoing sexual relations—that is, a partner with whom one has had sex more than once and where second and subsequent sexual encounters were not accidental and with whom one intends to continue having sex in the near future (Davies et al. 1993). Only 24.7 percent of men with a steady partner (N = 145) have a penetrative anal sex partner who is not their steady partner. More than four out of ten men in steady relationships engaged in no penetrative anal sex at all (44.8 percent, N = 263). And about three out of ten (30.5 percent, N = 179) practiced penetrative anal sex only with their steady partner.

We have the impression, however, that when asking these questions, we were touching upon a sensitive aspect of the sexual lives of the men in our study. Of men with a steady partner, forty-six (7.3 percent) did not answer the above question about the steady partner being the penetrative anal sex partner. Even more men declined to answer our follow-up question dealing with condom use. Responses by men with one penetrative anal sex partner to the question about condom use were as follows: 69 men (26.4 percent) did not use condoms or used them inconsistently with steady partners, 84 men (32.2 percent) consistently used condoms with steady partners, and 108 men (41.4 percent) did not answer this question. Thus, it appears that approximately one-third confirmed that they are practicing safer sex within their steady relationships. But of those who answered the question, most (54.9 percent) say that they are practicing safer sex within their steady relationships

There is an important difference regarding condom use whether or not the penetration partner is a steady partner. Condom use is less frequent with steady partners than with "fuck buddies" (57 percent of the men with steady penetration partner versus 21 percent without). This is not surprising because trust becomes more important when the sex partner is also a partner with whom one has a close emotional relationship.

Penetrative Anal Sex with Multiple Partners

Inconsistent condom use among men with multiple partners (17.2 percent of the sample) is even more problematic compared with men who had a single partner. Slightly more than half of the men with multiple partners consistently use a condom (53 percent), whereas 47 percent of these men do not use condoms consistently. We asked to what extent "dipping" or "nudging" (anal sex with ejaculation outside the body) was used as a strategy by the men in our sample. Among those who are tops in anal sex, 20.4 percent use this strategy to reduce the risk of HIV infection. Among bottoms, 18 percent report that they employ this risk reduction method.

Knowledge of Serostatus

One out of three men with one penetrative anal sex partner has knowledge of the serostatus of his partner, while 29 percent do not know their partner's serostatus. Again, we find that probing for details about sexual encounters involving anal sex yielded resistance on the part of respondents: 37.5 percent of the men with one penetrative partner did not answer this question.

It is not surprising that knowledge of the serostatus of one's partners among men with multiple partners is even more problematic. Most of these contacts involve anonymous episodes without information exchange. Only 10 percent reported knowing the serostatus of each of their partners. While 33 percent of these men know the status of some of their partners, 57 percent do not know the serostatus of any of their partners. Only 46.8 percent of men with multiple partners consistently use condoms.

Attitudes and Perceptions

Elford and colleagues (2001), Hickson and colleagues (1998), Murphy and colleagues (1998), Ostrow and colleagues (1998), and Vandeven and colleagues (1999) speculate about whether the increasing frequency of unsafe sexual behavior could be attributed to changing attitudes regarding safer sex. More specifically, they investigate to what degree knowledge of the new HIV treatment therapies, available since 1996, have changed the perception of AIDS. It is known that these new therapies have a tremendous impact on prolonging the life expectancy of people infected with HIV. Knowledge of these therapies could result in less stringent norms regarding safer sex. With the AIDS epidemic in its third decade, both increased fatalism and complacency could occur. A more optimistic perception regarding treatment of HIV infection could contribute to a form of AIDS complacency. In this research, we included questions related to the above-mentioned problems. We asked respondents if and to what extent they agreed with the following statements:

Practicing safe sex is getting more and more difficult.
I find it more bothersome now than in the past to discuss safe sex with
    my sex partners.

I still manage to keep my sex life as safe as in the past.

Currently, I deviate more from the safe sex rules compared with the
past.

I'm still as enthusiastic as ever about safe sex.

These five items were combined into a Safer Sex Easiness Scale. We calculated the mean score of this scale ranging from 1 ("safe sex" is a burden) to
5 ("safe sex" is easy). It should be noted that the term "safe sex," rather than
"safer sex," was actually used in the study, even though it is acknowledged
that "safer sex" would be a more precise term. The mean score on the scale is
3.97. This implies that for most men in our sample, "safe sex" is not considered a serious burden. Some age differences are found, however. Men older
than forty-five years perceive safer sex to be less burdensome than do men
age twenty-five to forty-five (ANOVA $p < 0.01$; Scheffé test for differences,
$p < 0.02$). Other age-grouping comparisons do not show significant differences. There is also no association between educational level and the Safer
Sex Easiness Scale.

Is there a relationship between the availability of new therapies and risk
taking? More than half of the men (53.1 percent) think that gay men are
taking more risks because therapy is available. The majority of the men (82
percent) are convinced that more risks are being taken now than was true in
the past. We do find some age differences regarding this perception. Older
men are more convinced than younger men that sex is less safe compared
with the past. This has probably to do with the fact that older men can
make comparisons over a longer time span than can the younger men in
our sample.

We investigated the perceived effects of the availability of new therapies.
Most men (82 percent) were aware of the existence of new treatments for
AIDS. Men who are optimistic to very optimistic about the possibilities offered by these new therapies comprise 30.5 percent of the sample. Otherwise
stated, we can say that slightly less than one out of three men is optimistic.
The reverse, however, is that two out of three men are not at all, or not very,
optimistic about the possible effects of the new therapies. Therefore, we can
conclude that "AIDS optimism" in this group is not the prevailing sentiment.

We also asked to what extent the availability of new therapies changed
the perception of AIDS. To measure that perception, we constructed an
AIDS optimism scale. Table 14.2 shows the different items together with
the factor loadings. The factor loadings give an indication of the relative

Table 14.2. AIDS optimism and the new HIV/AIDS therapies

Item	Factor Loading
The new treatments make safe sex less important	0.84
The new medications lower the viral load in infected persons so that safe sex is not that important anymore	0.82
I have less safe sex now that there are new treatments	0.76
AIDS is a less important threat than in the past	0.66
AIDS can be almost completely cured	0.62
Being infected with HIV is not as threatening anymore because there are better treatments	0.54
Safe sex is as important as it used to be	0.54
If AIDS could be cured then I would stop having safe sex even if treatment would be intensive and tough	0.54

Note: (Expl.Var.): 3.66; (Prp.Totl.): 0.46.

importance of each item. The higher the factor loading, the more that item contributes to the total scale value.

We calculated the mean score on this scale, which ranges from 1 (high optimism) to 5 (low optimism). Respondents show little optimism (mean = 4.44). However, we did find significant differences among subgroups. People with lower educational levels are more optimistic compared with men with higher levels of education. Older men with a low education level are particularly likely to express a higher level of AIDS optimism (mean = 3.71).

Is It Getting Better or Is It Getting Worse?

Considering all of the available evidence, we believe that three out of five men are being safe, and two out of five are not. In 1995, the Bravo!-Campaign was launched in Flanders to act as a positive reinforcement for behavior change among gay men. It was a campaign intended to support safer sex by emphasizing that three out of four Flemish gay men were practicing safer sex. Apparently, seven years later the situation became less favorable, with only 64 percent consistently engaging in safer sex. To be more specific: 42 percent do not practice penetrative anal sex; 13 percent have only one penetration partner and always use a condom; 9 percent have several penetration partners with whom they always use condoms. The other 36 percent of the men in our sample do not have safer sex consistently: some of them have only one penetration partner but do not use condoms, even if they do not know the partner's serostatus. A second group has anal sex with several nonsteady partners without the use of condoms. Others do not use condoms consistently. The absence of information about one's partners' serostatus can result in new infections if this occurs within a context of unsafe penetrative sex. Knowledge of serostatus is far from perfect, which is understandable in a culture emphasizing anonymity. To be sure, given the window period between becoming infected and testing positive and the heightened infectivity that often characterizes this period, even "knowing" a partner's probable serostatus as determined by a recent test is problematic and carries some risk of becoming infected with HIV.

New campaigns should target this problem. Prevention workers should develop strategies to handle negotiated safety as a way of harm reduction in a culture still built in part on anonymity and the absence of exchange of information between sexual partners. Inconsistent and improper use of condoms coupled with a far from perfect knowledge about one's own and one's partner's serostatus can lead to a new wave of infections. This will especially be the case now that other STIs such as syphilis and gonorrhea appear to be regaining a footing in the Flemish gay male population.

As in parts of the United States as well as in other countries in Europe, syphilis has resurfaced in Belgium after a period in which there were hopes that it could be eradicated in Western countries. Since 2001, the incidence of syphilis in Belgium has increased dramatically. In 2001, 2002, and 2003 there were 271, 204, and 300 cases registered, respectively, with still more cases reported in 2004. Previously, in the mid to late 1990s, syphilis cases in Belgium numbered from 14 to 30 annually. In this new outbreak, most cases were registered in the province of Antwerp, but a significant increase in cases has also occurred in Brussels, as well as in other cities. Of the new infections among men, 79.9 percent were detected among MSM (Sasse et al. 2004). It is important to note that a majority of cases among MSM (58.6 percent) involve men who are coinfected with HIV (most of whom knew their HIV status before their syphilis diagnosis). Together with the rise in incidence of other STIs, this resurgence of syphilis suggests a lower level of condom use by gay men than in the past, perhaps notably by and between MSM who are HIV positive.

In recent months, there has been a rise in cases of lymphogranuloma venereum (LGV). LGV is an STI resulting from a variant of the chlamydia bacteria. Typically, this infection occurs only in tropical areas. Infections were registered in the Netherlands and Belgium among gay men from the leather, "fisting," and fetish scenes. Normally, a case of LGV is found in Belgium once every ten years, usually among people who traveled in tropical countries. Finding more than ten infections in a very short time interval recently is alarming, especially since it is quite likely that there are other individuals infected with LGV whose infections have not yet been detected and reported.

HIV Incidence among MSM in Belgium

Comparing our statistics regarding unsafe sex with the incidence of HIV infection among MSM, we see that the increase of unsafe sex runs parallel with a higher incidence of new HIV infections among MSM. It is difficult to decide if we really have a new trend because we only have an augmentation of new infections for the last five years. However, year after year from 1985 through 1998, the number of new infections between MSM diminished steadily (see table 14.3). In 1985, when HIV infections were first registered in Belgium, there were 167 cases. By 1998, that figure had been more than halved, reaching a low point of 73 new HIV infections among MSM. In 2003, 129 new cases were detected. Thus, the incidence is clearly on the rise. Are there specific subgroups among MSM that can be singled out to account for this increase in new HIV infections?

Problem Groups?

Are there specific groups within the population of MSM that are more prone to engaging in behaviors leading to an increased risk of HIV infection? For example, are young men taking more risks than older men? Are men in steady relationships, because of their closer emotional bonding, more open for unprotected sex compared to men in nonsteady relationships? Or should we look at social class, ethnic status, or an emerging subculture of "barebackers" (Bolton 2000)?

We did find some differences regarding age. Young men have rather romantic expectations regarding their relationships. Because of this, they may become very intimate early with new partners and willing to take higher risks and omit condoms when having anal sex. The small differences that we found, however, are suggestive only since they were statistically weak (see Vincke and Bolton 1997b). Older men could experience higher levels of condom fatigue. This could be a problem when older seropositive men remain healthy because of taking new AIDS medication if they do not use condoms consistently and if they have sex with seronegative partners. However, our data do not give us any indication that older men are taking more risks. The only age difference that we found was in combination with a lower educational level. Older men with lower levels of education showed more

Table 14.3 Data on HIV incidence among men in Belgium, 1985–2003

Year	HIV+ Nonresident males N	HIV+ Nonresident males MSM transmission percent	HIV+ Nonresident males MSM transmission N	HIV+ Belgian males N	HIV+ Belgian males MSM transmission percent	HIV+ Belgian males MSM transmission N
1985	262	9.2	24	259	64.5	167
1986	208	13.9	29	248	61.8	153
1987	222	19.4	43	305	54.8	167
1988	194	13.4	26	240	52.9	127
1989	283	13	37	265	49.5	131
1990	305	12.2	37	257	50.1	129
1991	285	12.3	35	242	57.0	138
1992	407	9.3	38	204	56.4	115
1993	380	8.9	34	193	47.7	92
1994	347	9.3	32	199	48.2	96
1995	260	9.6	25	192	52.6	101
1996	223	13.9	31	159	56.0	89
1997	203	5.9	12	164	51.2	84
1998	256	8.9	23	139	52.5	73
1999	263	9.5	25	149	50.3	75
2000	375	10.6	40	218	50.4	110
2001	396	12.4	49	174	54.6	95
2002	447	12.3	55	184	57.0	105
2003	457	13.1	60	238	54.2	129

Note: Nonresident male: a man who has resided in Belgium less than five years; Belgian male: Belgian man who is a citizen or long-term resident (five years or more).

AIDS optimism because of the new treatments. Thus, this may constitute a subgroup deserving specific prevention efforts.

Although we do not have adequate data on cultural or ethnic identity, there are some indications that ethnicity could be important in engaging in behaviors leading to an increased risk of HIV infection. While in absolute numbers new infections are still low, we know that since 1997, the number of such infections among non-Belgian MSM is on the rise. In 2003, sixty new infections were found in that category. This reflects a five-fold increase over 1997, the low point of infections in this group. We are not able to determine the exact ethnic origin of these non-Belgian men. However, we suspect that the increase since 1997 is due to more immigration from eastern Europe and Russia. Although exact statistical data are not available, it is known that gay sex work is characterized during recent years by a substantial increase in young men from eastern Europe. Given that most of them are in Belgium illegally, we surmise that the problem is much larger than what the official statistics show. Registration as an HIV-infected person necessarily implies that one has contact with health-care practitioners. Such contact is often problematic for illegal immigrants in general and male sex workers in particular.

Conclusion

In this chapter, we have discussed several aspects of gay life in Belgium, with special attention to Flanders. Our key objective was to describe current trends in risk behavior and HIV infection. The situation in Flanders is not dramatic, but HIV infections are on the rise. This is also true for other STIs such as syphilis and LGV. We are aware that we are dealing with short-term change. Therefore, we must be cautious in making generalizations and even more cautious in attempting to explain this change. It was not our intention to provide a "causal" explanation for this evolution. Instead, we have outlined some changes in the Flemish social and political landscape that can serve as an interpretive frame. The major changes that we noted deal, on the one hand, with the changing nature of HIV infection, and, on the other hand, with the changing political context in Belgium.

It cannot be said yet that HIV infection is a chronic disease. Time elapsed since the introduction of the new therapies is too short to allow for that conclusion. However, notwithstanding the tremendous burden of therapy compliance (Vincke and Bolton 2002), we can say that HIV-infected individuals can live with the disease and have a completely new perspective on the future of living with HIV. Although we did not find hard evidence that this affects the perception of AIDS, this could lead to AIDS optimism. Our respondents, we should point out, did not mention that they themselves were more optimistic about HIV infection. The dominant perception, however, was that risk behavior was more prevalent now compared with the past.

The low level of HIV prevalence in the Flemish gay population also reduces the visibility of AIDS. HIV infection is not a part of the daily reality of gay men in Flanders. Together with more optimism regarding treatment successes, this could lead to higher levels of complacency.

Attitudes toward gays in Belgium are tolerant. Gays and lesbians recently obtained the same marriage rights as heterosexuals. The extension of the antidiscrimination law now to include nonracial forms of discrimination creates a legal framework to combat discrimination based on sexual orientation. The social context of sexual diversity has changed positively over these past several years.

In contrast with the United States, there is not really a counterforce trying to undo the positive achievements of gays and lesbians as a minority. Although the public still frowns when gay culture becomes explicitly visible, an antigay countermovement is not really present. One possible threat could come from continuous growth of the political power of the Vlaams Blok, an extremist right-wing party known for its antigay stance. Governments in Flanders and the rest of Belgium are always coalitions among several parties. Therefore, it is doubtful that Vlaams Blok could reverse the positive changes of recent years.

The liberal and accepting Flemish environment makes a defensive strategy for the gay movement unnecessary. The movement works from inside with its representatives on the various committees of the Flemish government dealing with topics of relevance for gays and lesbians specifically. The government, in essence, embraces the gay movement. This positive atmosphere does make it difficult to mobilize gays and lesbians politically. Although some problems persist, gays and lesbians do not see themselves as a threatened minority that should close ranks and act in a united manner. Combating AIDS here cannot be positioned as a political act. AIDS has no political connotations in the Belgian context. This results in low rates of volunteering and low levels of activism with respect to HIV/AIDS prevention. It also contributes to the gradually diminishing visibility of AIDS organizations targeting gay men.

It is not possible to state that the growing AIDS complacency, the lack of political alertness, and the invisibility of AIDS organizations targeting gay men are causally connected to the rise in new HIV infections. However, together these phenomena do constitute the context within which this increase has taken place. That context may have contributed to an absence of vigilance for the imminent threat that HIV infection was, and still is.

References

Bedford, Briand, ed. 2005. *Spartacus International Gay Guide 2005/2006*. 34th ed. Berlin: Bruno Gmünder Verlag GMBH.

Bolton, Ralph. 2000. Barebacking: The emergence of a gay counterculture. Paper presented at the annual meeting of the American Anthropological Association, San Francisco, November 15–19.

Bolton, Ralph, and John Vincke. 1996. Risky sex and sexual cognition: The cartography of eros among Flemish gay men. *Journal of Quantitative Anthropology* 6(3): 171–208.

Bolton, Ralph, John Vincke, and Rudolf Mak. 1992. Gay saunas: Venues of HIV transmission or AIDS prevention? *National AIDS Bulletin* 6(8): 22–26.

———. 1994. Gay baths revisited: An empirical analysis. *GLQ: A Journal of Gay and Lesbian Studies* 1(3): 255–73.

Davies, Peter, Ford C. I. Hickson, Peter Weatherburn, and Andrew J. Hunt. 1993. *Sex, Gay Men and AIDS*. London: Francis and Taylor.

Elford, Jonathan, Bolding Graham, and Lorraine Sherr. 2001. HIV optimism: Fact or fiction? *Focus: A Guide to AIDS Research and Counseling* 16(8): 1–4.

European Social Values Studies. 2002–2003. ESVS at Tilburg University 2000, 2001, 2002, 2003.

Gmünder, Bruno, and John D. Stamford, eds. 1988. *Spartacus International Gay Guide '88*. 17th ed. Berlin: Bruno Gmünder Verlag.

Hickson, Ford, David S. Reid, Laurie A. Henderson, Peter Weatherburn, and Peter G. Keogh. 1998. Treatment advances, risk taking and HIV testing history among gay men in the UK. Paper No. 14159 presented at the Twelfth International AIDS Conference, Geneva.

Kippax, Susan, Jason Noble, Garrett Prestage, June Crawford, Danielle Campbell, Don Baxter, and David Cooper. 1997. Sexual negotiation in the AIDS era: Negotiated safety revisited. *AIDS* 11: 191–97.

Mak, Ruud, Ralph Bolton, John Vincke, J. Plum, and L. Van Renterghem. 1990. Prevalence of HIV and other STD infections and risky sexual behavior among gay men in Belgium. *Archives of Public Health* 48: 87–98.

Mak, Ruud, John Vincke, and Ralph Bolton. 1990. *Gay Services Research Project: Een Multidisciplinair Onderzoek, Eerste Rapport*. Ghent: Rijksuniversiteit Gent.

Murphy, Sheila T., Lynn C. Miller, Paul R. Appleby, Gary Marks, and Gordon Mansergh. 1998. Antiretroviral drugs and sexual risk behaviour in gay and bisexual men: When optimism enhances risk. Paper No. 14137 presented at the Twelfth International AIDS Conference, Geneva.

Ostrow, David G., David McKirnan, Paul Vanable, and B. Hope. 1998. The impact of new combination HIV therapies on knowledge, attitudes and behaviors among Chicago gay men. Paper No. 43260 presented at the Twelfth International AIDS Conference, Geneva.

Sasse, A., A. Defraye, and G. Ducoffre. 2004. Recent syphilis trends in Belgium and enhancement of STI surveillance systems. *Eurosurveillance Monthly* 9(12): 5-6.

Vandeven, Paul, Susan Kippax, Stephanie Knox, Garrett Prestage, and June Crawford. 1999. HIV treatment optimism and sexual behavior among gay men in Sydney and Melbourne. *AIDS* 13: 2295–298.

Van Heeringen, Cees, and John Vincke. 2000. Suicidality in homosexual or bisexual young people: A study of prevalence and risk factors. *Social Psychiatry and Social Epidemiology* 35: 494–99.

Vincke, John, and Ralph Bolton. 1992. Sexual behavior changes among gay men in Flanders, Belgium, 1989–1993. *Archives of Public Health* 53: 537–48.

———. 1993. Social stress and risky sex among gay men: An additional explanation for the maintenance of unsafe sex. In *Culture and Sexual Risk*, ed. Han ten Brummelhuis and Gilbert Herdt, 183–203. New York: Gordon and Breach.

———. 1994. Social support, depression, and self-acceptance among gay men. *Human Relations* 47(9): 1049–62.

———. 1996. The social support of Flemish gay men: An exploratory study. *Journal of Homosexuality* 31(4): 107–21.

———. 1997a. Beyond the sexual monad: Combining complementary cognitions to explain and predict unsafe sex among gay men. *Human Organization* 56(1): 38–46.

———. 1997b. Younger versus older gay men: Risks, pleasures and dangers of anal sex. *AIDS Care* 9(2): 217–25.

———. 2002. Therapy adherence and highly active antiretroviral therapy: Comparison of three sources of information. *AIDS Patient Care and STDS* 16(10): 487–95.

Vincke, John, Ralph Bolton, and Peter De Vleesschouwer. 2001. Cognitive structure of the domain of safe and unsafe gay sexual behavior. *AIDS Care* 13(1): 57–70.

Vincke, John, Ralph Bolton, Rudolf Mak, and Susan Blank. 1993. Coming out and AIDS-related high-risk sexual behavior. *Archives of Sexual Behavior* 22(6): 559–86.

Vincke, John, Lieven De Rycke, and Ralph Bolton. 1999. Gay identity and the experience of gay social stress. *Journal of Applied Social Psychology* 29(6): 1316–331.

Vincke, John, Rudolf Mak, Ralph Bolton, and Paul Jurica. 1993. Factors affecting AIDS-related sexual behavior change among Flemish gay men. *Human Organization* 53(3): 260–68.

Waaldijk, Kees. 2003–2004. Others may follow: The introduction of marriage, quasi-marriage, and semi-marriage for same-sex couples in European countries. *New England Law Review* 38(3): 569–90.

15

Postscript

DOUGLAS A. FELDMAN

So, where do we go from here?

By the late 1980s and early 1990s, in the United States, most sexually active men who have sex with men (MSM) involved in relationships outside their regular partner were routinely practicing safer sex most of the time. Gay men had learned to use condoms correctly, had reduced their number of partners, and were engaging in less risky sexual practices. Many had participated in HIV risk reduction workshops targeting the gay community. Others were serving as "buddies" to assist gay men with AIDS through their local AIDS community-based organizations.

Today, things have changed. Most of the buddy programs have disappeared. There are remarkably fewer HIV risk reduction workshops being offered. And while many gay men are still using condoms, continue to reduce their number of partners, and continue to engage in less risky sexual practices, "barebacking" (anal sex without condoms) has increasingly become acceptable behavior.

In 2008, the Centers for Disease Control and Prevention (CDC) reevaluated their data and concluded that the number of new HIV cases annually was not 40,000 as estimated, but rather was closer to 56,300, and it had been at that level for several years. More crucially, most of this difference was due to increasing risk among MSM. In particular, black MSM and—quite surprisingly—white men in their thirties and forties show the highest increased risk. Among MSM overall, there were more new HIV infections in young black MSM (in their teens and twenties) than any other MSM group. Also, white MSM accounted for 46 percent of HIV incidence in 2006, with most new infections occurring among white MSM in their thirties, followed by those in their forties. Hispanic/Latino MSM also had elevated levels of risk (CDC 2008a).

A variety of factors could be driving this increased HIV risk. "Stigma, lack of access to effective HIV prevention services, underestimation of personal risk, not having personally experienced the severity of the early AIDS epidemic, and partnering with older black men (among whom HIV prevalence is high)" are all factors that probably play a role in making young black MSM the highest category of those with a new increased HIV risk in the United States (CDC 2008a: 2).

There has been an assumption that young white MSM are also at an elevated HIV risk, but the data show that it is older (thirty-to-forty-nine-year-old) white MSM who are truly at greatest risk today. Factors that contribute to continued transmission in these age groups include homophobia, substance use, higher HIV prevalence within this group, and the difficulty of consistently maintaining safer-sex behaviors for decades (CDC 2008a).

Since the beginning of the epidemic, over 300,000 MSM have died in the United States, accounting for 68 percent of all male adults and adolescents with AIDS who had died (CDC 2008b). By sheer numbers alone, the profound social and cultural impact on the gay community in the United States has been enormous.

But it is not just the United States and other developed nations where the impact of HIV/AIDS on MSM has been severely felt. An analysis of thirty-nine low-income and middle-income nations from all regions found that the HIV prevalence rate among MSM is—on average—12.8 times the rate among the entire adult population (IFRC 2008: 56). The rate is high in both high-incidence and low-incidence countries: in Kenya, the rate among MSM is 6.9 times the rate among all adults; in Mexico, it is 109 times the rate among all adults (IFRC 2008).

Clearly, the gay and bisexual male population of the entire world is in dire peril. Stigma, discrimination, and often isolation are all key factors that perpetuate the AIDS crisis among MSM worldwide. Seventy-nine nations still have laws that criminalize sex between men, and even where it is legal, it is in too many nations considered taboo.

Applied medical anthropologists are in a unique position to understand the dynamics of HIV risk among MSM throughout the world and to contribute to the amelioration of this health crisis. We need to take our leadership position in order to achieve this critically important task.

References

Centers for Disease Control and Prevention (CDC). 2008a. *MMWR* Analysis Provides New Details on HIV Incidence in U.S. Populations. Factsheets. www.cdc.gov/hiv/topics/surveillance/resources/factsheets/printMMWR-incidence.html.

———. 2008b. HIV/AIDS Among Men Who Have Sex With Men. Factsheets. www.cdc. gov/hiv/topics/msm/resources/factsheets/print/msm.htm.

International Federation of Red Cross and Red Crescent Societies (IFRC). 2008. The disaster of HIV. In *World Disasters Report 2008*. www.ifrc.org/publicat/wdr2008/ summaries.asp.

Contributors

About the Editor

Douglas A. Feldman, Ph.D., is professor of anthropology at The College at Brockport, State University of New York, near Rochester, New York, where he has previously served as chair of the Department of Anthropology. He has conducted research on social, behavioral, and epidemiologic aspects of HIV/AIDS in Zambia, Rwanda, Uganda, Senegal, and the United States. He is one of the first anthropologists to conduct research on AIDS in the United States (among gay men in 1982) and the first anthropologist to conduct research on AIDS in Africa (Rwanda, 1985). He has edited five volumes: *The Social Dimensions of AIDS: Method and Theory* (1986), *Culture and AIDS* (1990), *Global AIDS Policy* (1994), *The AIDS Crisis: A Documentary History* (1998), and *AIDS, Culture, and Africa* (2008). Previously, he has served on the faculties of the University of Miami School of Medicine and Nova Southeastern University, and was the founding executive director of the AIDS Center of Queens County in New York City. He was awarded the Kimball Award for Public and Applied Anthropology in 1996, and the AIDS and Anthropology Research Group Distinguished Service Award in 2008. He was a visiting professor at the University of Debrecen in Hungary during the spring semester 2009.

About the Contributors

Fernanda Bianchi, Ph.D. is senior research scientist of the Psychology Department at George Washington University. She has served as project director and coinvestigator in several National Institutes of Health projects in the area of HIV/AIDS among Latino men who have sex with men. She is an advocate in the Latino community and interested in immigrant health.

Rudi Bleys, Ph.D., studied at the Katholieke Universiteit Leuven, Belgium, and Boston University. He is the author of *The Geography of Perversion*

(1996) and *Images of Ambiente* (2000). He currently is head of the Research and Programs Department of Sensoa, the Flemish Centre of Services and Expertise on Sexual Health.

Frederick R. Bloom has worked for the STD Division (DSTDP) of the National Center for HIV, Hepatitis, STD, and TB Prevention (NCHHSTP) at the Centers for Disease Control and Prevention since 1998. His research areas include marginalized populations in the United States, health-care access, structural interventions, and rapid ethnographic assessment methods. He is currently the deputy associate director of science for the DSTDP at the NCHHSTP and leads the NCHHSTP Public Health Ethics Team.

Ralph Bolton is professor of anthropology at Pomona College in California. He has published numerous articles on HIV/AIDS prevention. Bolton edited *The AIDS Pandemic* (1989) and coedited *Rethinking AIDS Prevention: Cultural Approaches* (1992) and *The AIDS Bibliography: Studies in Anthropology and Related Fields* (1992). He chaired the AIDS and Anthropology Research Group and served as cochair of the Society of Lesbian and Gay Anthropologists. He was a member of the American Anthropological Association's commissions on AIDS and on LGBT issues. He teaches courses on human sexuality, gay rights, and lesbian and gay ethnography.

Scott Clair's research has focused on the application of social network models to risk behavior; examining risky behavior, particularly the HIV risk behaviors of drug users; the effects of oral HIV testing on HIV transmission beliefs; and the dissemination of effective interventions.

Charles Collins, Ph.D., is the section chief for the Science Application Team in the Capacity Building Branch of the Division of HIV/AIDS Prevention at the Centers for Disease Control and Prevention. His team of behavioral scientists is responsible for the national diffusion/dissemination of evidence-based behavioral interventions into HIV prevention public health practice.

Samuel Colón is a doctoral candidate in anthropology at American University. His dissertation examines how indigenous peasant producers in the remote highlands of Oaxaca, Mexico, organize to participate in fair trade coffee networks. He is currently living and working in Oaxaca.

Carlos U. Decena teaches in the Departments of Women's and Gender Studies and Latino and Hispanic Caribbean Studies at Rutgers University. His articles have been published in the *Journal of Urban Health*, *Sexualities*, and *GLQ*.

Jeanne Ellard is a research officer at the National Centre in HIV Social Research, University of New South Wales, Sydney. There she conducts research with gay men who have recently acquired HIV infection. She has also worked extensively on issues of masculinity and kinship in relation to Australian family law and is soon to complete her Ph.D. dissertation on heritage and space in the context of inner-city gentrification.

Carolyn A. Guenther-Grey holds a M.A. in communications research. She joined the U.S. Centers for Disease Control and Prevention in 1993, where she has worked as a behavioral scientist in the Division of HIV/AIDS Prevention (DHAP). She is currently the deputy branch chief for the Prevention Research Branch, DHAP.

Camilla Harshbarger is currently working on a project to diffuse behavioral interventions for HIV prevention to community- based organizations and health departments across the United States. She is a behavioral scientist in the Division of HIV/AIDS Prevention, National Center for HIV, STD and TB Prevention, at the Centers for Disease Control and Prevention. Previously, she consulted in international development throughout sub-Saharan Africa, Central America, and the United States. She received her Ph.D. in anthropology in 1995 from the University of Florida.

Jeffrey H. Herbst holds a Ph.D. in psychology. He is a former psychologist at the National Institute on Aging, National Institutes of Health, in Baltimore. He joined the U.S. Centers for Disease Control and Prevention in 2002, where he has worked as a behavioral scientist in the Division of HIV/AIDS Prevention.

William L. Leap is professor of anthropology at American University (AU), where he coordinates the annual AU Conference on Lavender Languages and Linguistics. His papers on language and AIDS have appeared in several venues, including *Word's Out: Gay Men's English* (1996). His recent work examines the "new" and not-so-new languages of sexuality emerging in response to globalization and other forms of neoliberal processes.

Jami S. Leichliter is a behavioral scientist in the Division of STD Prevention at the Centers for Disease Control and Prevention. Her research interests include high-risk or marginalized populations such as persons repeatedly infected with STDs and impoverished communities in the United States and South Africa. Additionally, she analyzes data from national surveys focusing on sexual behavior. She has a Ph.D. in applied experimental psychology.

Thomas Lyons is a medical anthropologist whose research focuses on substance abuse and HIV among gay and bisexual men, and on substance use disorders in the criminal justice system. He is a research fellow at the University of Illinois at Chicago and at TASC, a case management agency for persons with drug problems in the criminal justice system. He is currently developing an intervention for gay and bisexual stimulant-using men that is focused on healthy sexuality. He has a Ph.D. from the University of Chicago and was a NIDA postdoctoral fellow at George Washington University.

Janet W. McGrath is associate professor of anthropology at Case Western Reserve University. She is principal investigator and codirector of the National Institutes of Health–funded Center for Social Science Research on AIDS. Her research interests include HIV risk, HIV prevention, women's health, clinical and vaccine trials, microbicides, and access to HIV treatment.

Miguel Muñoz-Laboy is an associate research scientist in the Center for Gender, Sexuality and Health and the Department of Sociomedical Sciences at the Mailman School of Public Health at Columbia University. He is the coordinator of the Masters in Public Health track in Health Promotion and Disease Prevention. He specializes in issues of masculinity, sexuality, culture, HIV/AIDS, and social-community mobilization among Latino communities in the United States.

Mary Spink Neumann holds a Ph.D. in anthropology. She is a former academic specialist for USAID and Senior Fulbright Scholar in Honduras. After joining the Centers for Disease Control and Prevention in 1987, she worked in public health programs for three years. She is currently a behavioral scientist in the Division of HIV/AIDS Prevention.

Richard Parker, Ph.D., is professor and chair of the Department of Sociomedical Sciences and director of the Center for Gender, Sexuality and Health in the Mailman School of Public Health at Columbia University and president of the Brazilian Interdisciplinary AIDS Association in Rio de Janeiro. Among his many publications are *Bodies, Pleasures and Passions: Sexual Culture in Contemporary Brazil* (1991), *Sexuality, Politics and AIDS in Brazil* (1993), and *Framing the Sexual Subject: The Politics of Gender, Sexuality and Power* (2000).

Marcelo Montes Penha has a bachelor's degree in law and jurisprudence (University Santa Úrsula, Rio de Janeiro, 1988), has a master's degree in cultural anthropology (Hunter College and Graduate School-CUNY, 1996), and is a Ph.D. candidate at the American Studies Program (Department of Social and Cultural Analysis) at New York University. His research interests include race relations and racial representation, media and popular culture, and gender and sexuality.

Paul J. Poppen, Ph.D., is chair of the Psychology Department at George Washington University and the Thelma Hunt Professor of Psychology. He received his Ph.D. from Cornell University. His research interests concern risk-taking behavior, with a special focus on HIV and sexual risk among Latino men who have sex with men.

Carol A. Reisen, Ph.D., is lead research scientist of the Department of Psychology at George Washington University. She is coinvestigator of several major national and international National Institutes of Health–funded projects to study HIV/AIDS and sexual risk among Latino men who have sex with men.

Brian Riedel is the projects coordinator for the Center for the Study of Women, Gender and Sexuality at Rice University. He is currently working on a book-length ethnographic history of the Montrose neighborhood of Houston, Texas.

Michele G. Shedlin, Ph.D., is professor at the New York University College of Nursing and a medical anthropologist with extensive experience in reproductive health, substance abuse, and HIV/AIDS research in Latin America and the United States. She has designed and implemented behavioral studies and qualitative research training at the community, regional, and national levels to inform and evaluate prevention and care. She is currently involved in National Institutes of Health–funded research on HIV risk for Colombian refugees in Ecuador, ARV adherence among U.S.-Mexico border populations, acculturation, and HIV risk for men who have sex with men populations.

Merrill Singer, Ph.D., a cultural and medical anthropologist, holds a dual appointment as a senior research scientist at the Center for Health, Intervention and Prevention and professor of anthropology at the University of Connecticut. He has published twenty books and more than 200 articles and book chapters on health and social issues.

Sean Slavin is a research fellow at the Australian Research Centre in Sex, Health and Society, La Trobe University, Melbourne. After earning his Ph.D. in 1998 looking at contemporary pilgrimage practice in Spain, he has worked primarily in HIV and gay male research. Through his ethnographic work, he seeks to explore key social theoretical concerns in ways that challenge behaviorist paradigms and to better explain the social and cultural meanings that gay men give to their lives.

Laura D. Stanley received her Ph.D. in cultural anthropology from the University of California, San Diego (UCSD) in 2002. Her dissertation fieldwork examines how the stigma associated with AIDS affects the treatment, adherence, and health-care decisions of persons living with HIV. It additionally explores their strategies to overcome this stigma through transfiguring and redeploying spiritual tropes. Since finishing her dissertation, she has been employed by the UCSD Civic Collaborative researching and publishing on the psychosocial underpinnings of the digital divide.

John Vincke was professor of sociology and chair of the Department of Sociology at Ghent University in Belgium. His research focused on AIDS risk behavior, the mental well-being of gay men, and identity theory. He was a past president of The AIDS Team, an HIV prevention organization in Flanders. Since 1989, Vincke and Bolton had collaborated on a major Belgian research project on the lives of gay men in Belgium. Their work reflects a blend of sociological and anthropology insights and approaches.

David K. Whittier is a research behavioral scientist in the Division of HIV Prevention, Centers for Disease Control and Prevention (CDC). His main duties in this position are to provide technical assistance and guidance on HIV prevention within the CDC and to CDC's various partners. His general interests include integrating social theory and science into public health prevention practice and especially that related to sex and gender into HIV prevention. He received his Ph.D. in sociology at Stony Brook University, New York.

Maria Cecilia Zea is a professor of psychology at George Washington University. She conducts research on disclosure of HIV status and on sexual risk of Latino men in the United States who have sex with men and on HIV prevalence and sexual risk among men in Bogotá, Colombia, who have sex with men.

Index